D0146229

# Charlotte Smith

## Twayne's English Authors Series

Herbert Sussman, Editor

*Northeastern University*

TEAS 528

PORTRAIT OF CHARLOTTE SMITH, BY GEORGE ROMNEY.
*Courtesy of National Portrait Gallery*

# Charlotte Smith

Carrol L. Fry

*Northwest Missouri State University*

Twayne Publishers
An Imprint of Simon & Schuster Macmillan
New York

Prentice Hall International
London • Mexico City • New Delhi • Singapore • Sydney • Toronto

*Twayne's English Authors Series No. 528*

*Charlotte Smith*
Carrol L. Fry

Copyright © 1996 by Twayne Publishers

Twayne Publishers
An Imprint of Simon & Schuster Macmillan
1633 Broadway
New York, NY 10019-6785

Library of Congress Cataloging-in-Publication Data

Fry, Carrol Lee.
    Charlotte Smith / Carrol L. Fry.
        p.      cm. — (Twayne's English authors series : TEAS 528)
    Includes bibliographical references (p.    ) and index.
    ISBN 0-8057-7046-1 (cloth)
    1. Smith, Charlotte Turner, 1749–1806—Criticism and interpretation.
    2. Literature and society—England—History—18th century.   3. Women and
    literature—England—History—18th century.   I. Title   II. Series.
PR3688.S4Z64    1996
823'.6—dc20                                                                96-20000
                                                                                    CIP
The paper used in this publication meets the minimum requirements of American
National Standard for Information Sciences—Permanence of Paper for Printed Library
Materials, ANSI Z39.48-1984. ∞ ™

10 9 8 7 6 5 4 3 2 1

Printed in the United States of America

Citations of and quotations from several of Charlotte Smith's letters are used with permission of The Huntington Library, San Marino, California; with permission of the Princeton University Libraries; and with permission of the Beinecke Rare Book and Manuscript Library, Yale University.

# Contents

# Preface

After nearly two hundred years of obscurity, the poetry and fiction of Charlotte Turner Smith (1749–1807) has gradually come to be recognized as some of the most important literature of the late 18th century. Smith was one of the most popular and prolific writers of her day. But her radical political views resulted in her works' being consigned to the lumber room of literary history. The British reaction against revolutionary thought after the excesses in Paris during the 1790s and the years of warfare with France almost certainly eroded her popularity.

Charlotte Smith's life mirrors the worst fears of women of her time. Her family arranged for a marriage before her sixteenth birthday to Benjamin Smith, the son of a wealthy London merchant with holdings in the West Indies. Young Smith proved a total failure as a husband and father. After his own father's death, he so mismanaged the estate and angered other legatees that a legal battle ensued; it was finally settled in the year of Charlotte Smith's death.

After years of abuse by a feckless and philandering husband, Smith took an unusual step for a woman of her day: She established a separation. But by that time, she had borne 10 children. So for the remainder of her life, she wrote fiction and poetry to support her family, a total of 11 novels, three books of poetry, six books for children, and one translation.

More than those of any other author of the late 18th century, Smith's works reflect the sweeping political and cultural changes of her time. She enhanced the novel of sensibility with the romantic description of nature for which she became famous. She also brought the language of the Burkean sublime to fiction, using the sublime and the picturesque as part of the sentimental-gothic style that she first developed and Ann Radcliffe later imitated. It is in Smith's early novels—*Emmeline* (1788), *Ethelinde* (1789), and *Celestina* (1791)—that we first see the beautiful and vulnerable heroine of the sentimental novel against the backdrop of the sublimely ruined gothic castle.

Also, *Elegiac Sonnets* (1784), her first volume of poems, revitalized the sonnet form and earned Smith almost instant celebrity. She gradually added to the work, eventually expanding it to two volumes as she brought out nine editions and several reprints.

If Smith had written nothing more than the early novels and the first few editions of *Elegiac Sonnets*, she might justly be remembered as the innovator of an amusing but trivial subgenre of fiction and a poet with a feel for popular taste. Her later novels, however, are on the cutting edge of change at a critical moment in history. Works such as *Desmond* (1792), *The Old Manor House* (1793), *Marchmont* (1796), and *The Young Philosopher* (1798) reflect the idealism of British liberals in the early days of the French Revolution, contemporary republican views on issues that would be part of the British reform movement for the next hundred years, and criticism of abuses of the law possible for those with wealth and power. Also, an implicit theme throughout her later novels is the "wrongs of woman," the powerlessness of women in the patriarchal society of the late 18th century.

Moreover, Smith's later poetry demonstrates both the skill of a mature lyric poet and romantic themes and style that Wordsworth and his contemporaries had not yet made popular. Her genuine passion for nature, her sympathy for the common man and woman, and the social concerns that dominate her poetry after 1797 place her in the forefront of the romantic movement. Poems from the final editions of *Elegiac Sonnets*, *The Emigrants* (1793), and the posthumously published *Beachy Head, with Other Poems* (1807) demonstrate that Smith deserves to be remembered as a worthy contemporary of the male British romantic poets.

This study brings to modern readers an awareness of Charlotte Smith's importance as one of the most significant writers of the late 18th and early 19th centuries. No writer's works more clearly present the cultural and political changes of this pivotal moment in history, a time when democratic revolutions swept aside ancient privilege and created a new social order, women writers began the feminist critique, and romanticism was aborning. *Charlotte Smith* is unique in that it is the only full-length study of this important author's works to appear in the past 50 years. It presents Smith's life and times as seen both from the perspective of her poetry and fiction and from letters held in archives. The book will bring a new respect for Smith's works and a fresh insight into the importance of this powerful woman writer in the canon of romanticism.

Carrol L. Fry

# Acknowledgments

I am grateful to Herb Sussman for helping me make it better, and to Doni Fry and Craig Goad for their encouragement and suggestions.

I also express my gratitude to the Huntington Library, San Marino, California; the Beinecke Rare Book and Manuscript Library, Yale University, New Haven, Connecticut; and the Princeton University Libraries, for granting permission to quote from Charlotte Smith's manuscript letters.

# Chronology

<table>
<tr><td>1749</td><td>Birth of Charlotte Turner, eldest daughter of Nicholas Turner, a well-to-do country gentleman with eminent family connections.</td></tr>
<tr><td>1765</td><td>Marriage to Benjamin Smith.</td></tr>
<tr><td>1776</td><td>Death of author's father-in-law, Richard Smith. Troubles with Richard Smith's will begin financial ruin for Benjamin Smith.</td></tr>
<tr><td>1783</td><td>Residence in debtor's prison with husband for seven months.</td></tr>
<tr><td>1784</td><td>First edition of Elegiac Sonnets. Eight more would follow by 1800. Lives in Normandy with Richard Smith when he flees debts.</td></tr>
<tr><td>1785</td><td>Translation of Prévost's Manon Lescaut withdrawn from publication by Smith after criticism of the work's morality. Book sold by publisher without author's name.</td></tr>
<tr><td></td><td>Smith establishes separation from Benjamin Smith.</td></tr>
<tr><td>1786</td><td>The Romance of Real Life, a translation of Les Causes Célèbres.</td></tr>
<tr><td>1788</td><td>Emmeline, or the Orphan of the Castle, a novel.</td></tr>
<tr><td>1789</td><td>Ethelinde, or the Recluse of the Lake.</td></tr>
<tr><td>1791</td><td>Celestina, a novel.</td></tr>
<tr><td>1792</td><td>Desmond, a novel.</td></tr>
<tr><td>1793</td><td>The Emigrants, a poem; in two books.</td></tr>
<tr><td></td><td>The Old Manor House, a novel.</td></tr>
<tr><td>1794</td><td>The Wanderings of Warwick.</td></tr>
<tr><td></td><td>The Banished Man.</td></tr>
<tr><td></td><td>Marriage of Augusta, Smith's favorite daughter, to a French émigré, the Chevalier de Faville.</td></tr>
<tr><td>1795</td><td>Rural Walks: in dialogues intended for the use of young persons.</td></tr>
<tr><td></td><td>Montalbert, a novel.</td></tr>
</table>

1795   Death of Augusta de Faville after a lingering illness.

1796   *Rambles Farther: a continuation of Rural Walks: in dialogues intended for the use of young persons.*

      *A Narrative of the loss of the Catherine, Venus and Piedmont Transports and the Thomas, Golden Grove and Aeolus Merchant ships near Weymuth.*

      *Marchmont, a novel.*

1798   *Minor Morals, interspersed with sketches of natural history, historical anecdotes, and original stories.*

      *The Young Philosopher, a novel.*

1799   *What Is She? a comedy, in five acts, as performed at the Theatre Royal, Covent-Garden.* Uncertain attribution.

1800   *Letters of a Solitary Wanderer, containing narratives of various descriptions.* First two volumes published in 1799. Three additional volumes added for publication in 1800.

1804   *Conversations, Introducing Poetry; chiefly on subjects of natural history for the use of children and young persons.*

1806   Death of Benjamin Smith. Agreement on settlement of Richard Smith estate established.

      Death of Charlotte Smith, October 25.

      *History of England, from the earliest records, to the peace of Amiens, in a series of letters to a young lady at school.*

1807   Posthumous publication of *Beachy Head, with other poems* and *The Natural History of Birds, intended chiefly for young persons.*

# Chapter One
# A Woman of Her Time

The last quarter of the 18th century was a time of change that saw the collision of opposing political, economic, artistic, and social movements. The long first sentence of Dickens's *A Tale of Two Cities,* which describes Europe in "the year of Our Lord one thousand seven hundred and seventy-five"[1] as "the best of times" and "the worst of times," distills the contrarieties of the period, as ideologies struggled for supremacy, economic changes transformed the nature of work and sent thousands streaming to indusstrial cities for employment, and new approaches to art and literature reshaped tastes. But as critiques of the existing order grew, so did resistance to change.

The balance of geopolitical power was in flux. After a victory in the Seven Years' War in 1763, Great Britain was firmly on the road to empire, having won India and Canada. But those gains created yet other currents of change. The war left a large public debt in Great Britain, and when the government levied taxes on the American colonies to help retire it, the result was the first of the century's democratic revolutions and a new nation with a political system that became the envy of reformers throughout Europe.

On the continent and in England, change was in the air. In France, the works of Jean-Jacques Rousseau, François-Marie Arouet de Voltaire, and the Encyclopedists stimulated discussion both in the salons of the aristocracy and, perhaps more importantly, among the educated middle class of France. The nation remained a monarchy in which, as Dickens writes in *A Tale of Two Cities,* "a king with a large jaw and a queen with a fair face" ruled by divine right, while in Britain, "a king with a large jaw and a queen with a plain face"[2] were constrained by that legal tradition which the British call a constitution. But a revolution in France ended aristocratic privilege, and a heated dialogue in Great Britain called even that nation's relatively enlightened system of aristocracy into question during the 1790s. In Britain, however, the nascent fervor for reform was quickly stifled by public reaction to the excesses of the Parisian mob.

A technological revolution fundamentally altered the British economic base from agriculture to industry and brought massive population shifts. The efficiencies of steam power drove cottagers to the cities and gradually created a huge and, in the perception of many, dangerous urban proletariat. At the same time that this quiet revolution created a new working class, it established a commercial aristocracy that vied with the landed gentry and aristocrats for status and political power. Mercantile capitalism, as it unfolded in the 19th century, was beginning to develop.

Change—and resistance to change—was not limited to technological, political, and economic arenas. New artistic tastes were evolving. The Age of Reason became the age of feeling, and readers of Rousseau's *Julie, ou La Nouvelle Héloïse,* might well have nodded in agreement when Madame d'Orbe writes in one of her letters to Saint-Preux, "While teaching us to think, you have learned from us to feel, and whatever your English philosopher may say, this education is truly as good as the other. If it is reason which constitutes the man, it is sentiment which guides him."[3] Poets, dramatists, and novelists adapted the taste for sentiment during the second half of the century, producing poetry that emphasizes the feelings aroused by nature's beauties and horrors, as well as plays and novels featuring characters with melting sensibilities and gothic settings that inspire the sublime shiver.

Yet the impact of the "cult of sensibility" transcends literary fashion. Literature of the period began to teach readers to feel not just for fictional characters' distress but for victims of real social abuses. By the end of the 18th century, writers made the novel a sounding board for discussion of social issues, appealing to the readers' feelings by making the characters' distress the result of identifiable social problems. The cult of sensibility became an important element in a critique of British society.

No writer's works more clearly chart the shifts in British culture and the flow of ideas in politics and art during this time of change than do those of Charlotte Turner Smith. She was one of the most popular writers of the final two decades of the 18th century and among the most prolific. Her first three novels established the conventions that dominated the sentimental and gothic novel of the 1790s. Her early poetry, like her first novels, reflects 18th-century tastes, but her later poems place her in the forefront of the romantic movement.

In her later work, Smith used her fiction and poetry as vehicles for the presentation of political ideas. Both her life and her art epitomize the "wrongs of woman" in the 18th century. Aware that her audience was largely female and that young women received little education, she sought to inform her readers on the important issues of her day. Brilliant and well-read, she had both the sensitivity to feel the injustices done to her sex and the talent to portray women's issues in her fiction. In yet other novels and poems she attacks abuses of the law and economic privilege. Smith was one of the most talented and prolific writers of her day, and her works offer fascinating insights into the political and cultural movements of her time and the historical events that changed Great Britain and Europe at the close of the 18th century. By the end of her life, Charlotte Smith had developed not only into one of the finest poets of her day and a novelist who expanded the horizons of fiction but also into a writer whose works epitomize the romantic sensibility of the early 19th century.

Few writers have presented themselves in their works so fully as did Charlotte Smith. She established herself as the persona in her sonnets and told her story over and over again in her novels through autobiographical characters, often older women who serve as mentors to the heroines. She was, moreover, quite forthright in the prefaces to her novels and books of poetry in describing her own unhappy life. Also, few authors have written more of their day-to-day problems to correspondents than did Charlotte Smith. In addition, a number of biographical accounts of the author appeared shortly after her death.[4]

Charlotte Turner was born in 1749, the eldest daughter of Nicholas Turner, a country gentleman of distinguished lineage with estates in Sussex and Surrey, the South Downs region whose natural beauty the future author would describe in her poetry and use as the setting for scenes in her novels. Her mother died when Charlotte was four, and her father left most of the child's upbringing to her aunt. Turner apparently took great pride in his precocious daughter, arranging lessons in art, dancing, and other feminine accomplishments. She was an omnivorous reader and, according to one of her contemporary biographers, "seized with undiscriminating avidity, all that she could meet with; by this means acquiring a superficial acquaintance with various subjects of knowledge, that . . . led, in subsequent periods to more complete information."[5]

From all accounts, Charlotte was beautiful and talented. When not in school, she lived in the Turner home near Stoke, in Sussex, where she developed the love of nature and of this region that distinguishes her poetry and fiction. After his wife's death, however, Nicholas Turner enjoyed the social scene in London and on the continent and lived beyond his means. When Charlotte was 12, he brought her to London,

where he engaged music and drawing masters for her and introduced
her to the society.

Turner, whose extravagant lifestyle had led to financial distress,
remarried in 1764, choosing a young wife with a £20,000 dowry and,
from all accounts, a most assertive disposition.[6] The aunt who raised
Charlotte feared that her niece, who had been indulged in all her wishes,
would be made miserable by a stepmother of uneven temper. She and
Turner therefore decided to find a suitable husband for the young
woman, who was 15 by this time, an early age for marriage in England
even by 18th-century standards.

Thus, Charlotte Turner was introduced to Benjamin Smith, the son of
Richard Smith, a wealthy merchant with estates in the West Indies. The
young people (he was 21) were attracted to one another, and they were
married in February 1765. In her letters and the autobiographical passages of her novels and poetry, the author indicates that her later troubles date from this occasion.

Charlotte Smith found herself in a world quite foreign to a woman of
the country gentry. Richard Smith, her father-in-law, in whose home the
young couple lived when first married, seems to have fit the definition of
the "cit" ridiculed in novels and plays of the period, a man whose life
was, as Smith wrote in one of her poems, focused on ". . . drawbacks,
bottomry, insurance,/With samples drawn, and tare and tret."[7] He and
his wife (the latter died soon after the author's marriage) disapproved of
their daughter-in-law's lack of practical skills in homemaking and economy, and the senior Smith regarded the young woman's love for literature as "so many sources of expenses, and as encroachments on time,
which he thought should be exclusively dedicated to domestic occupa-
tions."[8] Charlotte, in turn, missed the countryside in which she had
grown up and found it difficult to adjust to crowded, soot-filled London.

In many respects, Charlotte Smith's life after her marriage is a cameo
of the lot of women in the 18th century. She gave birth to her first child
when she was 17. This child died within a day of the birth of her second,
little more than a year later.[9] For the first 15 years of her marriage, she
would be either pregnant or recovering from childbirth, and 4 of her 10
children would die before her. Benjamin Smith, moreover, proved to be
the sort of husband that every woman must have feared she would get: a
ne'er-do-well, gifted in begetting but deficient in providing.

Richard Smith eventually became fond of his daughter-in-law;
and after his wife's death, he depended on her both as a companion and
as a writer. According to Catherine Anne Dorset, Charlotte's sister, the

young woman wrote a tract that "vindicated his character from some illiberal attack," and he stated that she "could expedite more business in an hour from his dictation, than any one of his clerks could perform in a day."[10] Apparently, the elder Smith recognized his son's inability to operate the family business because he offered Charlotte a "considerable annual allowance" if she would assist with his enterprises. Dorset reveals her class prejudice when she concludes that "obvious reasons prevented her acceptance of this proposal."[11] The Turner sisters were of the gentry, and both gender and class assumptions made such an offer so clearly unacceptable that no explanation seemed necessary.

Smith's growing family responsibility (by 1774 she had seven living children) and the grubby environment of Tottenham, at that time a working-class suburb of London, made her long for the countryside. She therefore persuaded Richard Smith to buy her husband a country estate, Lys Farm, in 1774, thinking that Benjamin, who had demonstrated his extravagance and poor judgment, might be more successful in agriculture. But the countryside produced no change in his behavior.

Then in 1776, Richard Smith died, and Dorset writes, "From his death may be dated the long course of calamities which marked her subsequent life."[12] The elder Smith had foreseen that things might go badly for his son's family after his death and was most anxious to protect his grandchildren from Benjamin Smith's folly. He thus wrote his own will, hoping to make his wishes clear, but ironically his effort had the reverse effect. The language of the will was so hopelessly muddled that the document engendered an entanglement rivaling Dickens's *Jarndyce vs. Jarndyce*.[13]

Richard Smith had married Charlotte's aunt (the woman who had raised her) after the death of his first wife. The will lists the second Mrs. Richard Smith and Charlotte as joint executors of the estate with Benjamin Smith. Apparently the elder Smith judged his son incapable of the task without some restraint on his authority. But Dorset states that the two women were unable to control Benjamin in his administration of the will, and ill feelings from others named in the document as well as genuine bemusement as to just what the decedent had intended brought about the legal battle that continued for 30 years.

Troubles soon began for Smith and her children. During the years at Lys Farm, Benjamin Smith procured what Dorset calls a "lucrative contract" with the government, presumably to furnish foodstuff for the war in America, and he was named sheriff of the county, an office that entailed considerable expense.[14] But he lost his contract with the peace of 1782. He had behaved irresponsibly enough as executor of the disputed will to cause other beneficiaries to take action against him. To compound matters, Smith had run up large debts, having squandered the profits from his contract. Thus, he was committed to King's Bench prison as a debtor for seven months in 1783–1784.[15]

Family life was possible in prisons during the 18th century for those with the means; and Charlotte Smith, who by this time had borne three more children, stayed with her husband for much of his incarceration. Dorset quotes a passage from a letter Smith wrote to a friend, describing her sensations during an attempt by inmates to "procure their liberation by blowing up the walls of the house."[16] As with so many incidents of her life, her prison experience became grist for the writer's mill. Smith describes scenes set in debtors' prisons in two of her novels. The heroine of *Ethelinde, or the Recluse of the Lake,* visits her brother when he is incarcerated for debt. Smith wrote a more extensive description of prison life in *Marchmont.* The heroine, Althea, lives with her husband, the title character, during his imprisonment; and the author sets scenes like those she had described in the letter to Dorset.

For many years, Smith had written poetry, especially favoring the sonnet form. Desperate for funds, she decided to seek publication. James Dodsley, a prominent publisher, declined her proposed book. Smith describes the scene to the printer-publisher Joseph Johnson in a letter. The author teases Johnson about his lack of enthusiasm for her work and his tendency to see "ladies' literature a little like the late James Dodsley, who when I offered him my sonnets in 1793 said: 'I suppose now this is all loving stuff about shepherds and shepherdesses; & little lambs and all that,' " which, he told her, was a drug on the market (July 12, 1806, Beinecke).[17] Another publisher rejected her before she persuaded William Hayley, a well-known literary figure, to permit a dedication of the work to him. Smith then brought out *Elegiac Sonnets* at her own expense through Dodsley in 1784. The little book proved quite popular and over the next 16 years went through nine editions as she expanded it to two volumes. Two more editions appeared after her death, in 1811 and 1851.

After his release from King's Bench in 1784, Benjamin Smith fled to Normandy, taking his wife and children. There they lived in a drafty old manor house with little fuel or other supplies. Smith bore her twelfth child during this time, and in a letter she describes a group of priests entering her home a few days after the birth, forcibly taking the baby to the local church for baptism during bitterly cold weather, and returning him unharmed.[18]

The Normandy experience brought about Smith's translation of the French novel *Manon Lescaut* by the Abbé Prévost, which she read while in France. The book was published in 1785 after her return to England. But the passionate and illicit love affair that this novel portrays was out of step with British morality; and George Steevens, whom Florence Hilbish identifies as a "celebrated English critic" and to whom Smith had sent her translation hoping for a favorable review, roundly condemned it. He told her he would gladly promote her works when "Mrs. Smith can be prevailed on to employ her admirable talents on subjects more worthy of her than Werters and Manons."[19] When a magazine attacked her for plagiarism, on the grounds that another translation had recently appeared, she withdrew the book from publication, but it was sold without her name by the publisher. Smith continued her work as a translator, however, publishing *The Romance of Real Life* in 1786. The book is a translation of *Les Causes Célèbres,* stories about famous court trials in France.

In 1785 Charlotte Smith took an unusual step for a woman of her time: She legally separated from her husband. They never lived together again, although she continued to try to untangle the snarl of Richard Smith's will. Unfortunately, she failed to establish legal protection from Benjamin Smith's rights to her income. Dorset writes that friends thought she had erred in not insisting on "previous legal arrangements, and secured to herself the enjoyment of her own fortune."[20] But in the 18th century, a woman's husband owned her "fortune," unless the marriage contract specified otherwise. Getting control of her funds would have been quite difficult, and Smith seems to have been ready to get out of the marriage on any terms possible.

The author's letters indicate that her father had left £7,000 in her name, which should have realized over £300 per year in interest,[21] but she actually got little of that income. She did have an arrangement with her husband that he would give her £100 per year, keeping the rest for himself. She mentions in a letter from 1804 to William Davies, her publisher, that her husband had "taken everything else from me but £100 per year,"[22] but in other letters she notes that he did not always remit even that small sum.

Smith's biographer, Florence M. A. Hilbish, notes that although no formal financial settlement was reached between Benjamin and Charlotte Smith, "their relationship remained friendly."[23] The author's letters paint quite another picture. In letter after letter, she portrays Benjamin Smith as abusive and rapaciously selfish. On January 14, 1788, for instance, she writes to Thomas Cadell, begging him to deposit whatever funds were owed her with another party in order to hide them from her husband, who had declared he would demand them. He had written her, "saying he had *taken* his passage to Barbados and beg'd to see his children before he went." But when he arrived at her house in Godalming, Surrey, Smith writes, he "took possession of it, and treated me with more than his usual brutality—threatening to sell the furniture, the books and [everything?] which I have saved from the rapacity of his creditors." He is connected, she continues, with those in London "who are engaged in the desperation of gaming houses and I know not what—and from such a man so acquainted I and my family have everything to fear." She concludes that she is "firmly resolved never again on any pretense whatever to see him" and that she has "no longer the least wish to keep terms with him" (Princeton). And much later in her life (apparently February 1804, although the year is not cited), she writes to her friend Sarah Rose, "I have laboured for the children of one who lived only to disgrace them & insult me, while he rendered those labours abortive & made me every day & every hour ashamed, that I had ever been sold the victim of a being, human only in form" (Huntington).

For the remainder of her life, Smith moved her family from place to place, although she most often lived in the South Downs area. Brighton, then called Brighthelmstone, was a favorite dwelling spot, but as she later wrote of one of her autobiographical characters, Mrs. Denzil in *The Banished Man,* "Every place where the oppressed heart has received the additional load of sorrow, becomes hateful to the unhappy sufferer: and change of situation seems for a while to afford relief."[24] She repeatedly mentions in her letters her distaste for London and refers to the Bignor area, near her family home, as "the beautiful and beloved spot" (to Davies, August 28, 1799, Beinecke).

Although *Elegiac Sonnets* established Smith as a writer, she earned very little from the work. Novels paid much better, and she was desperate for money to support her family. Therefore she ventured into fiction with *Emmeline, or the Orphan of the Castle,* in 1788, and the work sold well. The next 12 years saw an extraordinary burst of productivity. Between 1788 and 1800, Smith published 11 novels. She also wrote *The Emigrants,* a long blank-verse poem, published five new editions of *Elegiac Sonnets* (with regular additions that expanded the work to two volumes), and produced three children's books. She achieved this productivity while caring for her large family and constantly struggling to settle her children's estate.[25]

The years after Charlotte Smith's separation from her husband were difficult ones, although she may have thought they were better than those that preceded it. In 1793 her son Charles Dyer Smith, an officer in the British expeditionary force in France, lost a leg below the knee in battle and returned home in her charge. Smith had sole responsibility for supporting a large family, which increased as grandchildren were born. Her health was precarious, and she describes in her letters the pain she suffered from writing, apparently due to crippling arthritis (Dorset calls it an "imperfect gout") in her hands. She was involved in constant legal embroilments that arose from Richard Smith's will, and as she became more and more bitter against the trustees who controlled the Smith estate, she spoke out sharply against them in print.

Smith tells her sad story over and over in her novels. Like the author, Mrs. Denzil in *The Banished Man* is involved in an unending legal battle over a will. She writes to support her family and has the same hardships that Smith describes in her letters and prefaces: dunning merchants, eviction from a home, and publishers who demand work that has been paid for. Smith no doubt had her own condition in mind in the following passage:

> Thus harassed by pecuniary difficulties, driven about the world without any certain home, she [Mrs. Denzil] experienced, from day to day, the truth of the adage, "That the ruin of the poor, is their poverty"; for she was thus made liable to much greater expenses, than would have happened in a settled establishment; perplexed by creditors, and sickening from the sad conviction that her power of supporting her family by her literary exertions must every year decline, while her friends became more and more weary of her long continued sorrows; the health and fortitude of Mrs. Denzil, such together—To one born in affluence, and long accustomed to its conveniences, it is hard to be content at once with sickness and indigence; yet the bitterest ingredients of the cup she was thus compelled to drink, were the cruel reflections that were ever present to her mind on the future fate of her children, when her own troubles should be at an end. (II, 198)

Like Smith, Mrs. Denzil speaks out against her persecutors: "I shall endeavour," she writes in a long letter to d'Alonville, the hero, "to shew what they are to a world who is already but little disposed to think well of them" (I, 274).

The most painful blow of Charlotte Smith's life was the death of her daughter Augusta. In 1793 the young woman had married the Chevalier de Faville, a refugee from the political upheaval in France following the fall of the Bastille. Augusta became ill in 1794, after the birth of a child (who soon died). Smith's letters during the next year reveal her distraction. Augusta was her favorite, serving not only as a copyist for her work but as her companion. "Tho I have so many other Children," she writes in a letter to William Davies, "the dear child is the most precious" (July 22, 1794, Beinecke). Her letters for the next year are filled alternately with hope and despair, as Smith tried desperately to raise money for Augusta's treatment. On March 15, 1795, she writes to Davies begging an advance: "Even 5£ would be of use should you have no more. I am half distracted and know not what I write."[26] But her daughter died in the spring of 1795. Afterwards, she tells Davies in an undated letter, the trustees of the estate "refused me not only assistance for my daughter while she lived, but wherewithal to bury her" (Beinecke).

A continual vexation during these years was a shortage of money that extended, she suggests in her letters, to an inability to pay local tradespeople. Her correspondence with publishers is filled with pleas for loans on future work. On March 9, 1797, for instance, she begs for an advance of £5 from Davies because "I really had not a shilling" (Beinecke). Yet Smith earned a good deal of money in what she refers to as her "literary business."[27]

Smith's letters show that she normally earned £50 per volume for novels, although she sometimes took less in exchange for advances. She also normally received £10 per volume for new editions of her novels. She mentions her earnings in a letter to Davies in 1797: "I still have resources in my own endeavors which have already produced me near 300£ [presumably during the preceding year]."[28] Moreover, she usually received £100 per year from her fortune, occasional payments from the Smith estate, and after 1794, an allowance of £100 per year from her son William Towers Smith, by then an East India Company civil servant. Judith Stanton[29] estimates that the author was paid £4,190 during her 22-year writing career, which should have left her, counting her other income, an average of over £400 per year. Since £40 per year would provide subsistence for a family of five in the 1790s,[30] Smith's avowed poverty is at first blush hard to understand.

But as do so many aspects of Smith's life and work, the author's pecuniary distress mirrors the condition of women during the period. As she often mentions in her letters and prefaces, she was a gentlewoman and not trained in home economies. Also, although she understood that writing was a business, she was certainly a bad bargainer in selling her work. So far as her novels were concerned, financial distress drove her creativity. In letters, she consistently proposes novels to publishers with the proviso that she draw against the £50 per volume price immediately. And she knew full well that such a practice cost her in bargaining power. In negotiating for *The Young Philosopher,* she writes to Davies, "Mrs. [Elizabeth] Inchbald . . . hinted to me that she got more [than £50 per volume] for hers which are very small books," and says she has heard that Ann Radcliffe received £100 per volume for *The Mysteries of Udolpho* (June 24, 1797, Beinecke).

There may be an element of exaggeration in the author's complaints. A passage in *Marchmont,* for example, suggests that financial distress might have been relative to a gentlewoman of her day. Smith describes Mrs. Marchmont and her two daughters as living in grinding poverty. When Althea, the heroine, first visits them, however, a maid answers the door.

But Smith's letters reveal her generosity to her children and the great expense of establishing them in life. At one point, she had nine minor children in her charge, ranging in age from 2 to 17, and as each came of age, some provision had to be made for her or him. She bought commissions for her sons Lionel and George Augustus, paid off outfitting debts for both, and apparently paid for some of Lionel's promotions, including at least part of his colonelcy. When her daughter Lucy eloped with William Newhouse, who proved as feckless and abusive as Benjamin Smith, her mother first supported the young woman and her husband and eventually paid for physicians' charges and burial when the man sickened and died. She also supported Augusta and the Chevalier de Faville during their brief marriage and paid as much of Augusta's physicians' fees as she could during the long illness as well as the burial costs.

Smith's last years were difficult, then, plagued with illness, financial distress, and Richard Smith's omnipresent will. Finally, an agreement was reached in 1806 that would eventually end the impasse over the will. For years, Smith had been aided by the Earl of Egremont, and in a letter in 1802,[31] she mentions that after Benjamin Smith had refused an offered compromise and insisted on money from the estate, Egremont advised a Chancery suit as a last resort, a process that, true to the literary representations of that court, took four years. Ironically, Benjamin Smith died in the spring of 1806, never, according to Edgerton Brydges, "to have conquered his habits of imprudence" because he died "in legal confinement."[32] On October 25 of the same year, Charlotte Smith died;[33] she was buried at Stoke, near her father's ancestral seat in the region whose natural beauty she describes so often in her poetry and fiction.

Charlotte Smith was a woman of her time, and both her class and gender biases show in her attitude toward her "literary business." "I am well aware," she writes in the preface to the sixth edition of *Elegiac Sonnets,* "that for a woman—'The Post of Honor is a Private Station' " (6). Her attitude toward fiction was ambivalent. In the Preface to *Marchmont,* for instance, she writes, "In the composition of what are called novels, I have been engaged (from necessity, and by no means from choice) for eight years."[34] In a letter to Joseph Cooper Walker (a friend and frequent correspondent), she mentions a novel that a young woman had asked her to correct, and she comments, "I own to you that ... I love Novels 'no more than a Grocer does figs' " (October 9, 1793, Huntington). The novel had not achieved the status of other literary genres, and Smith's comments reflect the general attitude of the day. Fiction was a livelihood for her, not a passion, and she rarely mentions her novels in the surviving correspondence except to propose projects and beg for advances from booksellers. She hated, as she wrote to Davies (September 8, 1805), appearing "in the character of a distressed author," and the "humiliating necessity, of accepting whatever price is offered" for her books (Beinecke). She also describes the rapacity of booksellers and the fickleness of the reading public through characters in her novels who try literature for a living in *Marchmont* (the title character), *The Old Manor House* and *The Wanderings of Warwick* (Captain Warwick), and *The Banished Man* (Mrs. Denzil). The passages suggest the pain of personal experience.

But she took pride in her success, especially in her poetry. In the September 8, 1805, letter to Davies cited above, she writes: "Though I am as little as may be infected by the vanity of an author ... yet I will not affect to say I am not conscious of being some degree above most of the lady writers of the day." It is worth noting that the words "most of" are penned in above the line, perhaps as an afterthought.

She was aware, moreover, that her literary success not only had supported her family but had advanced the careers of her sons. William Towers Smith achieved promotion in India after presenting a copy of *Emmeline* to his superior, and when she asked Davies in a letter to send a volume of the Seventh Edition of her sonnets to each of her sons, she notes that William "owes the greatest success he has had, and the best friend he has found in India, to the former book published by his mother, of which that mother is with reason proud" (May 18, 1797, Beinecke).

Smith could well take pride in her sons. William Towers Smith achieved considerable success in the Indian civil service, eventually becoming a judge. She was able to help Lionel Smith advance in rank, and he went on to become a baronet and a governor in the West Indies. Indeed, Lionel seems to have inherited his mother's hatred of tyranny, as he executed the order for the emancipation of slaves, despite the resistance of plantation owners in the Windward and Leeward islands and later in Jamaica. Charles, the son who was wounded in France, continued in the army and died of yellow fever during a trip to the West Indies to settle debts against the Smith estate. She helped George Augustus, the son born in the old Norman manor house in 1785, purchase a commission, and he served well under his brother Lionel until his death in 1806, just before his mother passed away. Another son, Nicholas Hankey Smith, served in the diplomatic service as minister in India and ambassador in Persia.

Information about Smith's daughters is sketchier. Three survived their mother. In a letter, Smith mentions Charlotte Mary, the eldest of the daughters, as representing her in negotiations with the trustees of the Smith estate, but her name rarely appears in surviving correspondence. In *Biographia Literaria* (1815), Sir Edgerton Brydges mentions that a member of Smith's family was preparing a collection of her letters for publication.[35] And Rufus Paul Turner cites a letter from William Hayley written to Joseph Cooper Walker shortly after the author's death that refers to his encouragement of Charlotte Mary to collaborate with Dorset in such an enterprise.[36] But the two women apparently abandoned the project. Charlotte Mary died in 1842, never having married. After a disastrous marriage, Lucy was widowed by 1801, but little more is known of her. Harriet married a Mr. Geary, apparently a stable though not wealthy gentleman. All of Smith's children who survived into adulthood seem to have inherited their mother's good qualities rather than their father's bad ones.

Born into the country gentry, Smith hated her role as "needy author." But she supported her family with energy and industry. In the process of caring for her children, she also developed into one of the finest poets of her day and a novelist who broke new ground for the genre. Her works reflect the currents of change in her time: the growth and final culmination of romanticism, the geopolitical and national issues of an age of revolution, and the problems with which women had to cope in a patriarchal society. Charlotte Smith was a woman of her times, but she was a truly exceptional one.

# Chapter Two

# Poetry

"Those paint sorrow best—who feel it most." These words, which Smith adapted from Alexander Pope's "Epistle from Eloisa to Abelard" for her first poem in *Elegiac Sonnets* ("Sonnet One," 13), established the tone for nearly all of the poetry she was to write in the ensuing 16 years. She was the poet of "the children of Despair and Woe" ("To the moon," 15), and she established a loyal audience among those responsive to the new sensibility, "Children of Sentiment and Knowledge born" ("Sonnet Nine," 18).

Although Smith was one of the more prolific writers of the 1780s and 1790s, she was unable to write poetry as rapidly as she did fiction. Her letters reflect a concern for composing only poems in which she could take pride. To William Davies she confides, "I assure you that poetry, such as one can endure to risk, will not always come when it is called, though sometimes it will come when it is *not* called."[1] Despite a relatively small output of poetry, the nine editions and various reprints of *Elegiac Sonnets,* as well as the testimony of contemporaries, demonstrate that she was one of the most popular poets of the day.

Smith began her writing career in a time of poetic transition, when neoclassicism was in decline and romantic tastes in all areas of the arts were on the ascendant. Fellow writers from both the late neoclassical tradition and those whom literary historians have credited as being the architects of romanticism admired her poetry. William Hayley and William Cowper were her mentors. But Wordsworth also liked her poems, writing in 1833 that she was a "a lady to whom English verse is under greater obligations than are likely to be either acknowledged or remembered. She wrote little, and that unambitiously, but with true feeling for rural Nature, at a time when Nature was not much regarded by English Poets."[2] Also, in his "Preface to the Sonnets," Coleridge credits Smith and William Lisle Bowles with making the sonnet "popular among the present English" and feels justified in "deducing its laws from *their* compositions."[3]

In the Preface to his edition of her poetry, Stuart Curran writes: "Charlotte Smith was the first poet in England whom in retrospect we would call Romantic."[4] Elsewhere, he finds the theme of "a disembodied sensibility at the mercy of an alien universe and without discernible exit from its condition"[5] to be central to romantic literature and a key element of Smith's poetry.

Curran makes a persuasive case. But establishing a writer as the first romantic requires a more precise definition of the term. A. O. Lovejoy demonstrated that there are many romanticisms.[6] Moreover, some distinctions between Smith's early and late poems must be made. Her later poems do indeed parallel the Wordsworthian model for romanticism. Her early poems, on the other hand, reflect the popular preromanticism of the period, which J. R. Foster defines as including an emphasis on feeling, a dawning appreciation of nature, a taste for the sublime and for gothic horrors, and a tone of melancholy.[7]

But her work gradually evolved to the sort of sympathetic identification with nature that characterizes Wordsworth's poetry, beginning with a perception of correspondences between nature and the poet's mood or experience and moving toward a realization of nature's permanence and healing power. Many of the later poems portray what Wordsworth called the "Low and rustic life" where "elementary feelings co-exist in a state of greater simplicity" and where "the passions of men are incorporated with the beautiful and permanent forms of nature."[8] Like Wordsworth, she contrasts this mode of life with British and European civilization, which corrupts it. In her later poetry, moreover, Smith achieves the simplicity and compression of language to which Wordsworth alludes when he mentions his attempt "to bring my language near to the language of men." Smith's last poems are nearly free of poetic diction. Also like Wordsworth, Smith uses her life as material for her poetry. To these elements of Wordsworthian romanticism, she adds a powerful sense of social injustice and the need for change. The post-Augustan fine feelings of the heart, enjoyed for their own sake, become in Smith's works a radical sensibility—a perception, through feeling, of the need to change an oppressive system of laws and government.

These elements are first fully in place in poems added to the Seventh Edition of *Elegiac Sonnets,* published in 1797. *Beachy Head, with other poems,* which appeared posthumously, shows the full flowering of Charlotte Smith as a romantic poet. Therefore, one must qualify any statements about her work as romantic with reference to its chronology.

# In Search of the "World Serene": *Elegiac Sonnets*

## THE GENESIS OF *ELEGIAC SONNETS*

If necessity is the mother of invention, then Benjamin Smith's financial disasters and subsequent imprisonment provided the spark that led to Charlotte Smith's career as a poet with the First Edition of *Elegiac Sonnets* in 1784. Despite the modest size of the work (only 26 pages and 20 poems), it was immediately successful, going within months to the nearly identical Second Edition. A reviewer for the *Critical Review* catches the spirit of the book's appeal. After quoting "To the moon," the writer notes that "almost all these pieces are of the plaintive kind and evidently the genuine effusions of the heart. Every reader of sensibility must be concerned to find, that the amiable writer has had any reason to shed a tear."[9]

The reviewer's comments echo the language of sensibility, which permeates the literature of the 1780s and 1790s.[10] By the second half of the century, a considerable body of poetry celebrates the capacity for feeling. The Epitaph of Thomas Gray's "Elegy Written in a Country Churchyard" catches the spirit of the day with its eulogy to a "Youth to Fortune and Fame unknown," whom "Melancholy . . . marked for her own."

> Large was his bounty, and his soul sincere,
>> Heav'n did a recompence as largely send:
> He gave to Mis'ry all he had, a tear,
>> He gain'd from Heav'n ('twas all he wish'd) a friend.[11]

*Elegiac Sonnets,* then, reflects the literary tastes of the "cult of sensibility." Both the poetry and fiction of this tradition celebrate the joys of melancholy, evoke empathetic response to the distress of others, show a reverence for simplicity and an appreciation for nature, and demonstrate a sense of alienation from "the world"—those who lack sensibility. In "To My Lyre," Smith speaks for all who prized sensibility when she describes her relationship with the Smith family after her marriage by writing, "I was of a different species" (310).

## THE SONNET FORM AND
## EARLY EDITIONS OF *ELEGIAC SONNETS*

In its origins, the sonnet is a love poem. But despite her awareness of the Petrarchan and Elizabethan tradition, Smith wrote no love poetry in her own voice, the melancholy persona of her poems. The reading audience of her day would surely have found a sequence of love sonnets inappropriate for a woman writer. The initial sentence in the Preface to the First Edition acknowledges this reality: "The lines[12] which are here called Sonnets have, I believe, no very just claim to that title: but they consist of fourteen lines, and appear to me no improper vehicle for a single sentiment." Smith knew that the "single sentiment" in conventional sonnet sequences was romantic obsession, a topic forbidden to her. Therefore, when she speaks in the voice of the persona of the sonnets, she substitutes her theme of hopeless melancholy, which in later editions she attributes to specific events in her life.

She does include a few sonnets on the traditional "single sentiment," but in an alternate voice. The First Edition offers three translations of love sonnets by Petrarch. Also, she writes three poems in the voice of Werther in the First Edition and adds two more in the Third. Goethe's novel *The Sorrows of Young Werther,* published in Europe 10 years before *Elegiac Sonnets,* tells the story of a young man who loves Lotte, a married woman, so deeply that he commits suicide in despair. The intensity of Werther's attachment makes him "Passion's helpless slave" and thus an appropriate voice to utter the "single sentiment" of the traditional sonnet—a complaint against the "cruel tyrant of the human breast," hopeless love ("Supposed to be Written by Werter," 26).

After the publication of *Elegiac Sonnets,* some reviewers questioned whether Smith's poems were sonnets at all. They assumed the Italian form as the correct style.[13] Smith, however, adopted the English, or Shakespearean, model. "To the moon"[14] exemplifies both the style and content of most of her sonnets.

> Queen of the silver bow!—by the pale beam,
>> Alone and pensive, I delight to stray,
> And watch thy shadow trembling in the stream,
>> Or mark the floating clouds that cross thy way.
> And while I gaze, thy mild and placid light
>> Sheds a soft calm upon my troubled breast;
> And oft I think—fair planet of the night,
>> That in thy orb, the wretched may have rest:
> The sufferers of the earth perhaps may go,
>> Released by death—to thy benignant sphere;

> And the sad children of Despair and Woe
>
> Forget, in thee, their cup of sorrow here.
>
> Oh! that I soon may reach thy world serene,
>
> Poor wearied pilgrim—in this toiling scene! (15)

The poem follows the form and organization of the English sonnet. It has the familiar 14-line iambic pentameter form,[15] with the abab, cdcd, efef, gg rhyme scheme. Smith organizes the poem into three recognizable quatrains, followed by a couplet that offers a summary statement of the preceding 12 lines.

Smith, then, uses the form she inherited from Shakespeare. But she changes the subject from obsessive love to the sort of melancholy rumination prized by the "cult of sensibility" and in the couplet applies the preceding quatrains to the sorrows of the poem's persona, Charlotte Smith.

Within a few years, specifics of her sorrows were well known. Smith's letters are quite explicit about the knavery of her husband, the rapacity of the trustees of Richard Smith's will, and the tragedies of her own life. Apparently gossip spread some of those details because in 1788, a reviewer of *Emmeline* follows high praise of the novel with the comment: "In one or two instances, she seems to have aimed at persons. . . . We hope that she has not looked at home, in the misfortune of Mrs. Stafford" (the autobiographical character in the work).[16] And if readers of her poetry had been in any doubt as to the source of the author's melancholy, the Preface to the Sixth Edition of *Elegiac Sonnets,* published in 1790, would have informed them, for Smith launches there a direct attack on the trustees of her children's estate.

The poems in the first two editions of *Elegiac Sonnets* are written in the idiom of late-18th-century neoclassicism. Smith's early poems too often begin with apostrophes to personifications. Titles, for instance, include "To hope," "To spring," "To sleep," and, in one of her Werther poems, "To solitude," as well as the mythic personification of the moon in the poem quoted above. She often relies on poetic clichés: the "wild-woods and untrodden glades" and the "cup of sorrow," for instance. Many poems focus on abstractions and include conventional apostrophes such as the predictable "Ah!" or "Oh!" Although Smith has mastered the form of the sonnet and created both a persona and an acceptable "single sentiment," the language and style of her verse remain rooted in the 18th century. Also, if musical qualities, vivid and original language, and striking imagery are the qualities of great lyric poetry,[17] then the author has not mastered her art at this stage of her career.

Yet some of her descriptions of nature presage the romanticism of her later works. Most poems that portray scenery, such as "To spring," fail to rise above generalities. But "To the South Downs" shows flashes of the romantic lyricism that would come in later editions, perhaps because she wrote of the "beautiful and beloved spot."

Indeed, it would be fair to describe Charlotte Smith as a regional poet. Over and over in her poetry, she celebrates the beauties of the South Downs, an area extending approximately 20 miles inland from Eastbourne or Brighton on the east to Southhampton on the west. Smith spent her early years at Bignor Park near Bignor, a village a few miles north and west of Arundel—a region of great natural beauty in the poet's day. The area also has many literary associations. Both Thomas Otway and William Collins, writers whom she honors repeatedly in her poems, were native to the Downs. Smith apparently felt both a regional and an emotional kinship with poets whom Janet Todd mentions as examples of "the melancholic, the unhappy solitary genius who is an innocent in a vicious world."[18]

Smith writes in a later edition of *Elegiac Sonnets,* "My early vows were paid to Nature's shrine."[19] "To the South Downs," written for the first edition, shows evidence of a lyrical voice and an appreciation of nature that transcends the generalities of her early work. Smith praises the natural beauty of the area, describing the happiness she had experienced as a child, then moves to the contrast with her present life. She apostrophizes the "hills belov'd" and recalls that she "wove your blue-bells into garlands wild,/And woke your echoes with my artless song." She also celebrates "Aruna," the river Arun, which flows south to the sea a few miles east of Bignor Park. But after establishing the beauty of the area, in rhetorical questions she asks whether the hills can "For one poor moment soothe the sense of Pain" and whether the Arun can bestow a "Lethan cup." She ends with a couplet in answer to her question, "Ah! no!—when all, e'en Hope's last ray is gone,/There's no oblivion—but in Death alone" (15–16).

The poem follows the pattern for Smith's "single sentiment," the sad musings of the persona. But she relies less on abstract language and neoclassical conventions such as personification than she does in most of the other sonnets in the First Edition. Moreover, "To the South Downs" demonstrates an approach to nature that would appear more frequently and in more sophisticated fashion in Smith's poetry as her art matured: an establishment of correspondence between nature and the experience or mood of the persona.

The Third and Fourth Editions, which both appeared in 1786 and, like the First and Second, are nearly identical, grew by 20 sonnets to 43 pages. The subjects changed somewhat, including homages to individuals: "To Hayley," "To Mrs. G.," "To the Earl of Egremont," and "To the Countess of A————,"[20] for instance, poems that Smith may have thought would be welcome after the success of her first efforts.

But only two new poems address personifications—"To Friendship" and "To Fortitude." A third, "To Melancholy," is subtitled "Written on the Banks of the Arun, October, 1785." Six of the additional 20 poems focus on the South Downs region, four of them on the Arun. Because of their more concrete language, these poems stand out as the best work of the volume.

Two sonnets bear the title "To the River Arun," and in each the author alludes to earlier poets from the South Downs region. The second of these poems, Sonnet 30, stresses the superiority of rural over urban scenes. "Be the proud Thames of trade the busy mart!/Arun! to thee will other praise belong." The Arun is a place for sensitive souls and poets, inspiring "Otway's plaintive strain" and the "deeper tone/Of Collins' powerful shell" (33). Smith ends the poem with an homage to William Hayley, whom she describes as the river's own. The diction is neoclassical in tone ("glittering fanes," "marble domes," and "Collins' powerful shell," for instance), but these and other poems in this edition show a greater emphasis on nature. The poet's ability to express her response to it, however, developed gradually.

In the Third Edition, she brings greater intensity to the "single sentiment" of the early sonnets. In Sonnet 27 (its title is simply XXVII), the speaker observes a "little troop at play,/By sorrow yet untouched," and goes on to comment on the "thorns that lurking lay" that will make them "rue the hour that gave them birth." The poem's theme resembles Thomas Gray's in his "Ode on a Distant Prospect of Eton College," but the final lines return to the poet's situation with her reference to "prosperous folly" that "treds on patient worth" and to "deaf Pride" to whom "Misfortune pleads in vain!" (30–31).

Smith's early poetry, then, shows flashes of the joy in nature that would intensify in her later works. Yet to call the poems of the first four editions truly romantic would be to stretch the limits of the word. Smith relies heavily on neoclassical conventions—apostrophe, personification, elaborate similes, and poetic diction. When she does describe nature, the poems' language tends toward abstraction, and such poems are often closer to the conventional pastoral, replete with nymphs, shepherds, and shepherdesses,[21] than felt response.

## THE FIFTH AND SIXTH EDITIONS
## OF *ELEGIAC SONNETS*

The Fifth Edition of the sonnets was a subscription publication, dated 1789.[22] William Wordsworth, then a student, appears on the subscription list published with the book. The Sixth Edition appeared the following year. The two editions increase the size of *Elegiac Sonnets* by 30 poems, although 12 of them had appeared in *Emmeline* and *Celestina*.[23]

The editions of 1789 and 1790 show some change in the author's range of subject and style. The poems written for her novels are an interesting innovation for fiction, one with which Smith became identified. By 1790 she had published *Emmeline* and *Ethelinde* and was apparently at work on *Celestina*. Poems from the novels give her a new opportunity for an alternate voice, sometimes that of a character who can speak the language of Eros typical of the Petrarchan tradition but unavailable to a woman of Smith's time. Godolphin, Emmeline's lover, is the speaker in Sonnet 38. In the octave, he describes dreams in which "Fancy then, dissolving human ties,/Gives me the wishes of my soul to see;/Tears of fond pity fill thy soften'd eyes:/In heavenly harmony—our hearts agree." But in the sestet, Godolphin laments that he can be with her only when "cruel Reason abdicates her throne" to sleep, and the lover awakens to pain (38). Smith also includes love sonnets, though properly restrained, in the voices of Celestina and Emmeline. And a passionate outburst in Sonnet 40 is credited to Adelina Trelawny, from *Emmeline,* a young woman who has gone mad after an illicit love affair and has a heart that "bleeds with vain remorse and unextinguish'd love" (39–40).

Nature figures more prominently in the new poems for these two editions, specifically in descriptions of the "beautiful and beloved spot," the South Downs region. Smith also continues to refer to other writers who had graced the area. In Sonnet 45, "On leaving a part of Sussex," she bids farewell to the Arun, once again honoring earlier poets. She resigns "Thy solitary beauties" where to "Fancy's ear . . . /The Enthusiast of the Lyre who wander'd here [Collins]" seems still present "to call forth Pity's tenderest tear,/Or wake wild phrenzy—from her hideous cell" (43).[24]

Of the 30 new poems, 10 focus directly on nature. As Smith wrote more poems with descriptions of natural scenery, she often drew correspondences between her persona's thoughts and the natural scenery that she describes. Nature mirrors the mood or parallels the situation of the persona. Yet the "single Sentiment" of her sonnets remains. In "Composed during a walk on the Downs, in November 1787," for instance, she sets a scene in winter, "the ruins of the year," before noting that the "propitious Spring" will repaint the landscape. But in the final lines, the persona contrasts her state with nature, finding that spring will bring neither the "Syren Hope" for her nor "chase the vulture Care—that feeds upon the heart" (40). Descriptions of natural scenery often correspond with the poet's joyless life.

In the Sixth Edition, Smith openly refers to her personal problems. Many readers knew of her situation as the cause of the persona's melancholy before 1790. The Fifth Edition subscription was generally understood to be a benefit for her and her children.[25] But the Preface to the Sixth Edition should have erased all doubt as to the source of the author's melancholy. Smith describes a dialogue with a friend who recommends a few poems in "a more cheerful style of composition." And she answers, "'Are grapes gathered from thorns, or figs from thistles? Or can the *effect* cease while the *cause* remains?'" She goes on to detail the cause of her unhappiness. "The time is indeed arrived," she writes, "when I have been promised by the 'honorable men' who *nine years ago,* undertook to see that my family obtained the provision their grandfather designed for them,— that 'all should be well, all should be settled.' But still I am condemned to feel the 'hope delayed that maketh the heart sick.'" She ends the preface with a threat: "*I shall be sorry,* if on some future occasion, I should feel myself compelled to detail its causes at more length" (5–6).

## A NOTE ON THE CONCEPT OF THE SUBLIME

The Fifth and Sixth Editions, published in 1789, see the first systematic adaptation of the concepts of the sublime and the picturesque in Smith's poetry, although in *Emmeline,* a year earlier, she describes sublimely ruined castles and landscapes that inspire delicate horror. A taste for the great and rugged in nature had gradually developed in the earlier part of the century, as evidenced in essays by Joseph Addison, William Temple, and others. But it remained to Edmund Burke to establish a language for describing the sublime with *A Philosophical Enquiry into the Origin of Our Ideas of the Sublime and the Beautiful* in 1756. Burke linked sublimity to powerful emotions, especially fear, and contrasted it with "the beautiful," which inspires tranquility. Later in the century, Uvedale Price, William Gilpin, and others brought the word "picturesque" into popular parlance, establishing it as an intermediate quality between the sublime and the beautiful.[26]

A taste for the sublime developed gradually during the 18th century; and while the word "sublime" may not appear in the poem, the appeal to vicarious horrors is apparent in poems such as Robert Blair's "The Grave" or William Collins's "Ode to Fear." However, only one of Smith's early poems, "Written by the Sea Shore—October, 1784" in the Third Edition, has much suggestion of the language of the sublime. The persona sets the scene "On some rude fragment of the rocky shore," and finds that "the wild gloomy scene has charms for me,/And suits the mournful temper of my soul" (20). Smith uses the language of the sublime in the poem as another approach to establishing correspondences between nature and the melancholy mood of the persona.

In the poems of the Fifth Edition and following editions, Smith would use the language of the sublime much more extensively, and sublime landscapes would become a staple in her novels. "Written September 1791, during a remarkable thunderstorm. . . ," which first appeared in the Sixth Edition, begins with a quatrain describing a sublimely evocative storm:

> What awful pageants crowd the evening sky!
> The low horizon gathering vapours shroud;
> Sudden, from many a deep-embattled cloud
> Terrific thunders burst, and lightnings fly—

The second quatrain contrasts the sublimity of the storm with the beauty of another part of the sky:

> While in Serenest azure, beaming high,
> Night's regent, of her calm pavilion proud,
> Gilds the dark shadows that beneath her lie,
> Unvex'd by all their conflicts fierce and loud.

The two quatrains juxtapose the sublime, which inspires powerful emotion, and the beautiful, which brings tranquility, as defined by Burke. Then in the sestet, Smith uses the contrast of the calmly floating moon with the tumultuous storm to establish correspondence between the scene from nature and the poem's persona:

> —So, in unsullied dignity elate,
> A spirit conscious of superior worth,

In placid elevation firmly great,
   Scorns the vain cares that give Contention birth;
And blest with peace above the shocks of Fate,
   Smiles at the tumult of the troubled earth. (52–53)

The poem's style and content speak to a shift from the late neoclassicism of Smith's earlier work as she moved toward a more authentic romantic voice and achieved a greater mastery of versification. The sonnet goes beyond a description of nature to an identification with it, an approach that would appear more and more frequently in Smith's later poetry. Additionally, the trochaic substitutions that begin lines 12 and 14 and the alliteration that links them emphasize the theme the poem develops, and the mixture of Italian and English sonnet forms shows Smith's willingness to experiment with poetic style.

## THE SEVENTH EDITION OF *ELEGIAC SONNETS*

Seven years would pass before Smith's next addition to *Elegiac Sonnets,* the second volume of the two-volume Seventh Edition subscription publication in 1797. Volume 1 of the Seventh, published in 1795, consists of the poems in the Sixth Edition. The first six editions of *Elegiac Sonnets* and Smith's first two novels are apolitical. But the seven years between the publication of the Sixth and Seventh Editions had seen sweeping changes in Europe and Great Britain; and beginning with the closing chapters in *Celestina,* Smith's novels would reflect those changes.

By the time volume 2 of the Seventh Edition was published, Smith had written *Desmond* (1792), *The Old Manor House* (1793), *The Banished Man* (1794), *The Wanderings of Warwick* (1794), *Montalbert* (1795), and *Marchmont* (1796), novels espousing a liberal political ideology that was called "republican" in Smith's day. The word is difficult to define, but most British republicans of the 1790s were influenced by the political thought that underpinned the French Revolution. More moderate republicans advocated an expansion of the voting franchise, the reform of Parliament, and a constitutional monarchy. Radical voices in the republican camp, however, called for dismantling the monarchy altogether. Republican themes and ideas began appearing in Smith's poems as the century wore on, but never as stridently as in her fiction.

Smith's politics had taken a toll on her popularity.[27] The subscription list for the Fifth Edition boasted 765 names, but the subscription for the 1797 edition had only about one-third as many—287. That the author was well aware of her loss of readers appears in comments from the Preface to this edition. She apologizes for the delay of the second volume's appearance—two years after the first volume of this two-volume publication had been printed—and mentions the death of Augusta, her son's war wounds, and her own health as distractions.[28]

But Smith could no longer confine her anger at some who had suggested that she had taken money without producing the poems. "Surely," she writes in a sentence that reveals her sense of class position, "any who have entertained and *expressed* such an opinion of me, must either never have understood, *or must have forgotten,* what I was, what I am, or what I ought to be" (8). She follows with a bitter tirade against the executors of the Smith estate, then addresses the reduced number of subscribers to this edition. She observes that "party can raise prejudices against the colour of a ribband, or the cut of a cape" and that there are those who cannot forgive authors who "ventured to hint at any opinions different from those which these liberal-minded personages are determined to find the best" (10). She goes on to note rather sarcastically that she thanks those who were her friends when the 1789 subscription was published but have disappeared in 1797, commenting wryly, "Ten years do indeed operate most wonderful changes in this state of existence" (11).

Despite the troubles Smith describes in the Preface, the Seventh Edition saw her largest single addition to *Elegiac Sonnets*—24 sonnets and 13 poems of other types.[29] The best work in these additions demonstrates a pronounced movement toward romantic subject matter and style and a greater mastery of poetic form.

She includes a few sonnets that also appear in her novels—poems spoken in the voices of characters from *The Old Manor House, Montalbert,* and *The Young Philosopher,*[30] as well as one poem from *Conversations, Introducing Poetry,* her first children's book. As in earlier editions, the voice in poems first written for her fiction often reflects the character. Thus, the romantic Walsingham from *Montalbert* speaks "Written in a tempestuous night, on the coast of Sussex" and "On passing over a dreary tract of country, and near the ruins of a deserted chapel, during a tempest," poems replete with the evocative language of the sublime such as a man of feeling might pen. In the latter poem, Walsingham, a victim of hopeless love and one of several Werther figures in Smith's fiction, describes a night in which he courts "the chill horrors of the howling blast." But he finds correspondences between his mood and the scene he describes, for "to *my* heart congenial is the gloom/Which hides me from a World I wish to shun" (59). Walsingham is the alienated romantic, trapped in a society that does not share his capacity for feeling.

Most of the poems in this edition, however, follow the "single subject" for Smith's earlier sonnets, the meditations of the persona on the miseries of her life. A new approach to that theme in this edition appears in references to the death of Smith's daughter, Augusta. In "The winter night," for instance, she describes sleepless nights when the cold winds presage "the last sleep of death." But in the sestet, the poet asks, "Wherefore fear existence such as mine,/To change for long and undisturb'd repose?" In the final lines, she concludes that she will be happy when "By her, whose loss in anguish I deplore,/I shall be laid, and feel that loss no more" (63–64).[31]

The author continues to connect the persona's mood with nature. "Written in October," for instance, describes the close of the year, with the "blasts of Autumn . . . muttering many a sad and solemn sound." The sestet then concludes, "Nature delights *me* most when most she mourns,/For never more to me the Spring of Hope returns!" (74–75). Similarly, "Written at Bignor Park in Sussex, in August, 1799" (first published in the Ninth Edition) celebrates the beauties of the author's ancestral home as she watches "the dark shadows of the threaten'd storm." The clouds pass, returning the sun; but the "visions bright and warm/With which even here my sanguine youth begun" are gone forever. Nature has provided the correspondences that suggest the thought, and the poet concludes with the reflection that her fate "Nor hope nor joy illumines—Nor for me/Return those rosy hours which here I used to see!" (78). The correspondence of nature to the poet's experience and mood is a constant theme in her later work, and the language has moved from the abstractions of post-Augustan poetic diction to a new level of concreteness.

## A NOTE ON THE NEW IDEOLOGY

Readers of the day might have recognized republican sentiments in several poems from the Seventh Edition. "To the shade of Burns," for instance, eulogizes the Scottish poet Robert Burns as a "Bard sublime" whom "Great Nature taught 'to build the lofty rhyme.'" Like others of liberal mind, Smith saw Burns as a child of nature and a fellow romantic, who was "Fired with the love of Freedom" (71). Another poem that would have pleased republicans and rankled conservatives is "To a young man entering the world." Despite the poet's disclaimer in a footnote, the young man addressed might have been her son Lionel, who had been expelled from Winchester College after a student rebellion.[32] The poem addresses a young man who has already experienced "The base controul/Of petty despots"; and the poet says to him, "high disdain/Of Tyrants is imprinted on thy soul." The poet advises him to "raise the shield/Of patriot daring" (65) against oppression, as did John Hampden, a hero of the Commonwealth; and Algernon Sidney, who was executed for opposing Charles II. Both were code heroes among British republicans of the day, and their names recur in Smith's political novels as well as in the writings of others sympathetic to republican ideals.

Most British republicans opposed the wars with France that began in 1793,[33] and the Seventh Edition has a few poems with antiwar themes. "The Sea View" is the best of them, a work that demonstrates Smith's progress in mastering poetic form. The octave describes a pastoral scene. A shepherd "lies/On the soft turf that clothes the mountain brow." He "Marks the Bright Sea-line mingling with the skies" and "The Summer-Sun in purple radiance low." Nature spreads "Even o'er the Rustic's breast a joy serene." But the sestet contrasts the pastoral innocence and beauty of the inland scene with a sea battle in the channel:

> When, like dark plague-spots by the Demons shed,
> Charged deep with death, upon the waves, far seen,
> Move the war-freighted ships; and fierce and red,
> Flash their destructive fire[.]—The mangled dead
> And dying victims then pollute the flood.
> Ah! Thus man spoils Heaven's glorious works with blood! (72)

The soft "s" sounds of the octave and its slow pace reflect unspoiled nature. But the barking consonants of the sestet, the fast-paced rhythm created by the shorter words and "d" sounds, and the violence suggested by the poet's word choice create a harsh contrast. Also, the initial trochaic substitutions ("Move the war-freighted ships" and "Flash their destructive fire") propel the reader into the lines. In Alexander Pope's words, Smith has made the sound an echo to the sense, for this contrast demonstrates the poem's theme—civilization's corruption of nature, a theme that she would develop more fully in "Beachy Head." Also, in Smith's later poetry, she no longer uses the pastoral in the conventional manner, but as a thematic device to state an antiwar theme.

"To a Dead Beggar" confronts republican issues more directly than do other new poems in the Seventh Edition. The poem takes to task an upper-class woman who weeps at the sight of a beggar's funeral: "Swells then thy feeling heart, and streams thine eye . . . . ?" The sort of "feeling heart" cultivated by the cult of sensibility is merely a means of displacing true sensibility, the poet suggests—an empathy that demands a change in the conditions that cause injustice. This condemnation of "fine feelings" experienced for their own sake recurs in Smith's later novels, as it does in the writings of Mary Wollstonecraft and others influenced by republican thought.[34] The poet goes on to tell the lady that "Death, the Leveller, restores to peace" the old man who "living knew not where to rest" and that "in earth's cold bosom, equall'd with the great,/Death vindicates the insulted rights of Man" (96–97).

The reference to the "rights of Man" was a red flag to conservatives, as Thomas Paine's book *The Rights of Man,* a response to Edmund Burke's *Reflections on the French Revolution,* had articulated the republican credo during the pamphlet war between conservatives and liberals (see discussion on page 74). Smith's novel *Desmond* had been a part of that ideological battle, and her republican views no doubt contributed to the loss of favor she cites in the preface to this edition. Thus, she includes a footnote, taking notice of the criticism she has already received for using "terms that have become obnoxious to certain persons." But she states that she has no desire to "obtain the suffrage" of those whose taste is prejudiced by political beliefs or "those who desire that because they have themselves done it, everyone else should be willing to sell their best birth-rights, the liberty of thought, and of expressing thought, for the *promise* of a mess of pottage" (96). She concludes the note by deploring social conditions that permit such misery as the poem describes.

## A NOTE ON BOTANY IN CHARLOTTE SMITH'S POETRY

The Seventh Edition introduces the language of the newly emerging study of botany. Linnaeus (Carl von Linné,) the Swedish naturalist, had established the binomial system of nomenclature in *Species plantarum* (1753) and other works that grouped species of plants according to their sexual systems. Rousseau read Linnaeus, and the French philosopher's last, unfinished work, *Rêveries d'un promeneur solitaire (Daydreams of a Solitary Stroller),* describes his life on an island in the Swiss lake of Bienne in 1765. His experiences in investigating the flora of the island meld the emerging science of botany and the cult of sensibility.[35] It remained for

Erasmus Darwin, the grandfather of Charles Darwin, however, to fully wed science and poetry in *The Botanic Garden,* Part Two of which, *Loves of the Plants,* was first published in 1789.[36] All of these writers influenced Smith's description of nature, both in her poetry and in her fiction.[37]

"To the Goddess of Botany" reflects Smith's fascination with this new science and her adaptation of it to the "single sentiment" of her poems. The study of plants leads the speaker from "the view/Of Violence and Fraud" to the discovery of "All peace from humble life." She would "Find shelter; where my tired, and tear-swoln eyes, . . . . Might rest." Botany takes the poet, as it did Rousseau in *Rêveries,* from her suffering to the simpler joys of nature. In a lengthy footnote, Smith cites the line from "Il Penseroso" in which Milton notes that "rightly to spell . . . of every herb that sips the dew" can heal the sick at heart. She then quotes Rousseau on the benefits of nature to the wounded soul and observes that her situation may be even more pitiable in that she, "chained down to the discharge of duties from which the wearied spirit recoils" (68), lacks even the resource of nature's healing powers. The parallels to Wordsworth's description of his debt to nature for "tranquil restoration"[38] seem obvious.

"To the insect of the gossamer" is the most charming of Smith's poems on the restorative power of nature. The persona addresses the "Small, viewless AEronaut [sic], that by the line/Of Gossamer suspended, in mid air/Float'st on a sun beam." In a note, Smith quotes Dr. Martin Lister on the life cycle of the spider she describes.[39] The insect creates a strand of gossamer on which it floats, driven by air currents. She then cites Erasmus Darwin on the mating rituals of the spider, conducted while aloft on its strands. Rather than dwell on these interesting details, however, Smith moves in the sestet to demonstrate the correspondence between the spider's aerial maneuvers and the poet:

> Thus on the golden thread that Fancy weaves
> Buoyant, as Hope's illusive flattery breathes,
> The young and visionary Poet leaves
> Life's dull realities, while sevenfold wreaths
> Of rainbow-light around his head revolve.
> Ah! soon at Sorrow's touch the radiant dreams dissolve!
> (66–67)

The poems in which the language of botany and zoology appear follow this pattern.[40] Smith shows correspondences that establish the mood of the poem and suggest a parallel or contrast to the persona's life or to the melancholy common lot, and some poems suggest that nature has the power to heal the wounded soul. The striking image of the "sevenfold wreaths/Of rainbow-light" encircling the head of the "visionary Poet" not only demonstrates the author's development as a lyric poet but also reflects the romantic view of the poet as possessing "a more lively sensibility . . . and a more comprehensive soul, than are supposed to be common among mankind."[41] But Smith retains her "single sentiment" in the poem.

### LATER EDITIONS OF *ELEGIAC SONNETS*

The Eighth Edition of *Elegiac Sonnets* is identical to the Seventh and carries the same date, 1797. The Ninth appeared in 1800 and has 12 new poems, 3 of which had been written for *The Young Philosopher* (1798). "Lydia," the most striking of the additions, is a ballad set in the South Downs region near the ocean. The title character awaits her lover, Edward, who had promised to return from the sea within 10 cycles of the moon. Lydia has gone mad and continues to return to the spot, waiting for Edward to return, long after his death.[42] Smith establishes the setting, describing the red glow of lime kilns, the moon's "long bright pathway on the sea," and a legendary phantom horseman, all in vivid language and in imagery that transcends anything in her first six volumes of *Elegiac Sonnets*. The poem's ballad form, intensity of feeling, and correspondence of natural setting and story exemplify Smith's mature romanticism.

## The Endurance of Nature:
### *Beachy Head, with other poems*

Charlotte Smith's first experiment with long narrative poems was *The Emigrants,* published in 1794. This poem, which addresses both British prejudice against French refugees fleeing the chaos in their country and the author's disappointment at the failure of the experiment in France, is discussed in chapter 4 of this book.

In 1805 Smith began negotiating with William Davies for a new edition of the sonnets. She has, she writes, "original and unpublished poems nearly if not quite sufficient to make another volume as large as those you published some years ago" (July 6, Beinecke). The series of letters that follows leaves little doubt that Smith intended the works published posthumously as *Beachy Head, with Other Poems* to be a third volume in a tenth edition of *Elegiac Sonnets*. Two weeks later, she tells Davies that one poem "of considerable length is on a *local* subject. I have made very great progress in it, having had it in hand some years but I wish to be very correct & to leave nothing for criticism to carp at" (July 26, 1805, Beinecke). Still later, she writes to Davies of "a local poem of near 700 lines . . . which is the only part of the work that is not actually ready" (August 18, 1805, Beinecke).[43] Clearly, Smith refers to "Beachy Head," which has 731 lines in its published form.

The correspondence on this proposed three-volume tenth edition, first with Davies and then with the publisher Joseph Johnson, continues to the poet's death. To this point in her writing career, Smith had faced "the humiliating necessity, of accepting whatever price is offered" for her books. Indeed, her letters indicate that she bargained only weakly with Davies. She was usually forced to beg for loans against projected works instead. Now, she tells him, her sons have provided for her and she need not grovel. On September 2, 1805, she writes, "120 guineas is now the price of a very mediocre novel of 11 sheets—, A book of travels (which one might write in a good library, without stirring from the fireside) is 400 guineas—Another more wonderful still, is actually sold for £1500" (Beinecke). She asked £300 for the work, and Davies declined.

Smith continued working on the new poems and seeking a publisher. As always, she thought of the welfare of her children. On July 12, 1806, shortly before her death, she wrote to Johnson mentioning her collection "of all the poems I have written which in my mature judgement [sic] appear worth retaining" and states that the publication is important to her because "I am told that I need only remind certain people of me . . . to obtain a company for my youngest son" as well as for the young man engaged to her daughter (Beinecke).[44]

Johnson published *Beachy Head, with other poems* in 1807, about a year after Smith's death, and the Preface notes that the work is "not completed according to the original design" (Curran, 215). The writer (probably Johnson) no doubt refers both to Smith's intention to publish a final edition of *Elegiac Sonnets* and to the state of the central poem of the collection, "Beachy Head." Smith's letters to Davies had indicated that the shorter poems were ready for publication, but she apparently continued working on the longer one. Internal inconsistencies, moreover, indicate the unfinished nature of the work. The first five hundred lines seem much better focused on the themes of the poem than does the remainder of the work. The author's rapidly failing health apparently prevented her completion of the poem in a form that satisfied her.

The first two-thirds of "Beachy Head," however, shows the culmination of Smith's development as a romantic poet and of her mature poetic
voice. She develops a theme familiar to the Wordsworthian model of
romanticism: the superiority of humble life and its destruction by modern civilization. But the corrupting influences she describes are more
specific than those Wordsworth cites in "Michael," for instance. In
"Beachy Head," Smith addresses specific political and social issues, using
the correspondences of natural phenomena and human life as symbols.
A second and related theme in "Beachy Head" is the timelessness of
human suffering caused by oppressors who will themselves fade away,
just as do those whom they oppress. Only nature endures. Finally,
"Beachy Head" is Smith's last celebration of the romantic beauty of the
South Downs.

This blank verse meditation begins with an apostrophe to Beachy
Head, a landmark that juts over the sea a few miles east of Brighton in
"the hills so early loved."[45] The opening stanza establishes a chronologi-
cal and a historical organization for the poem. First, the poet's reverie on
the "awful hour/Of vast concussion; when the Omnipotent/Stretch'd
forth his arm, and rent the solid hills" (5–7) describes the timelessness of
the land and prepares the reader for the historical perspective that follows. On the one hand, this "vast concussion" is a fine symbol for the
age of revolutions through which Smith had lived. Many of her readers
would have understood that geology, like botany, was associated with
revolution.[46] Thus, the cataclysm suggests the division in political
thought between the continent, where nations were shaken by democratic revolution, and Great Britain, which had resisted change. Also, the
division of England from the continent in this cataclysm prepares for
Smith's musings about the wars that had ravaged England and France,
and the endurance of nature.

When the poet at this early hour observes ships "just emerging from
the arch immense" (37), which include a "ship of commerce richly
freighted" (42), she begins her criticism of civilization's corruption of
nature. The ship is a merchant vessel, bound for India to bring home the
"vegetable down," cotton, as well as the "beamy adamant, and the
round pearl" (51), which the "slave" risks his life to obtain. "These are
the toys of Nature; and her sport," she writes,

> Of little estimate in Reason's eye:
> And they who reason, with abhorrence see

> Man, for such gaudes and baubles, violate
> The sacred freedom of his fellow man. (55–59)

Her country's commercial exploitation of colonial peoples is one example of European civilization's corruption of nature.

Smith establishes these themes in the first 74 lines and intertwines them throughout the next 400. She returns to the historical theme with a description of the wave of invaders who had come to England in the past. She describes the Norman Conquest, accompanying the passage with a patriotic effusion: "But let not modern Gallia form from hence/Presumptuous hopes, that ever thou again,/Queen of the isles! shalt crouch to foreign arms" (143–145). She then describes another battle in which French forces defeated the British during a naval engagement off the English coast in 1690, and notes that the loss has been "Oh! well redeem'd,/Since, by a series of illustrious men,/Such as no other country ever rear'd" (160–162). Smith seems genuine enough in this and other praise for her native land. However much she might deplore faults in the British system of government and law, she acknowledges throughout her works the superiority of her own country's political system over those of other European nations.

In other passages, the poet mentions the invasions of Danes, and preceding them, the Romans, when "the mail'd legion, under Claudius, rear'd/The rampire, or excavated fossé delved." They brought with them elephants, which in the northern climate, "Sunk useless; whence in after ages found,/The wondering hinds, on those enormous bones/Gaz'd" (416–418). The elephant offers a meaningful symbol for the power of the Romans, conquerors whose bones lie in the same ground with the conquered, while nature endures.

In the lines following, Smith focuses these thoughts "By human crimes suggested" (440) on the timelessness of the land into an antiwar statement:

> Hither, Ambition come!
> Come and behold the nothingness of all
> For which you carry thro' the oppressed Earth,
> War and its train of horrors—see where tread
> The innumerous hoofs of flocks above the works

> By which the warrior sought to register
> His glory, and immortalize his name [.] (419–425)

Both the "savage native" of the region and the centurion who "planted
the Imperial Eagle" come to the same end, passing away,

> Even as the clouds, with dark and dragon shapes,
> Or like vast promontories crown'd with towers,
> Cast their broad shadows on the downs: then sail
> Far to the northward, and their transient gloom
> Is soon forgotten. (435–439)

Thus, the cataclysm that "from the continent/Eternally divided this
green isle" (9–10) introduces the central themes of the work—the
human misery wrought by the war between England and France that
had raged intermittently since 1793 and the parallel theme of the quiet
endurance of nature in the face of human savagery. The statesmen
whose egotism sacrifices lives will soon pass away to become part of
nature, in the end coming to the same fate as those their wars destroy.

In the process of establishing these themes, however, Smith presents
a view of nature that few British readers would have understood in
1807. Most would have assumed the biblical explanation of creation,
which held that the earth and its inhabitants were created in the same
physical conditions in which they then appeared. Smith questions this
assumption as she develops her meditation on the timelessness of the
land. She describes the Downs as containing "sea-shells; with the pale
calcareous soil/Mingled, and seeming of resembling substance." She
goes on to consider how such objects could be present on the land, since
surely the ocean "here never roll'd its surge." Then in a passage that
echoes the scientific speculation of the day, she writes:

> . . . Does Nature then
> Mimic, in wanton mood, fantastic shapes
> Of bivalves, and inwreathed volutes, that cling
> To the dark sea-rock of the wat'ry world?
> Or did this range of chalky mountains, once
> Form a vast bason [sic], where the Ocean waves
> Swell'd fathomless? What time these fossil shells,

Buoyed on their native element, were thrown
Among the imbedding calx: when the huge hill
Its giant bulk heaved, and in strange ferment
Grew up a guardian barrier, 'twixt the sea
And the green level of the sylvan weald. (378–389)

The lines reflect the conflict between writers who explained fossils within religious tradition as "mimics" of real species formed by nature or as remnants of the Deluge and those who saw the earth as much older than religious teachings suggested. Smith had done her homework on this poem, and her speculations represent the advanced thought of the day.[47] She reflects on the transitory lives of humans and the timelessness of the land by noting that while scientists quarrel about theories, the peasant and herdsman—as well as the Roman soldiers who first conquered and then became part of the land—ignorant of the past, work the land where "Rest the remains of men, of whom is left/No traces in the records of mankind" (402–403).

Smith returns to her own sad story in "Beachy Head," again following the principle of correspondence. But the correspondence is not with nature. Rather, she posits herself as a symbol of the conquered people of the past. Speaking of her marriage, she writes,

. . . Childhood scarcely passed, I was condemned,
A guiltless exile, silently to sigh,
While Memory, with faithful pencil, drew
The contrast; and regretting, I compar'd
With the polluted smoky atmosphere
And dark stifling street, the southern hills. (287–294)

She follows with a paean of praise for the "Hills so early loved!" memories of which, she writes in language reminiscent of Wordsworth's, enriched her life in later times of trouble. She exclaims, "Haunts of my youth!/Scenes of fond day dreams, I behold ye yet!" (297–298). She recalls climbing a sheep-path,

. . . aided oft
By scatter'd thorns: whose spiny branches bore
Small woolly tufts, spoils of the vagrant lamb

> There seeking shelter from the noon-day sun;
> And pleasant, seated on the short soft turf,
> To look beneath upon the hollow way
> While heavily upward mov'd the labouring wain,
> And stalking slowly by, the sturdy hind
> To ease his panting team, stopp'd with a stone
> The grating wheel. (300–309)

As in Wordsworth's poetry, nature inspires "emotion recollected in tranquillity."

Smith intertwines the themes of oppression by tyrants and the land's endurance with her praise of a life led close to nature. Following her description of the arrival and disappearance of Normans and Danes, she describes "simple scenes of peace and industry,/Where, bosom'd in some valley of the hills/Stands the lone farm" (169–171). But the shepherd who lives there is "one, who sometimes watches on the heights" (176): that is, as the author explains in a footnote, a trafficker in cheap brandy smuggled into the country by sea. She goes on to explain that smuggling is but another kind of commercial exploitation, like the gathering of pearls in Asia, and the shepherds are victims. They may be imprisoned if caught, while those who profit from the commerce remain safe.

Smith contrasts the fear of capture and imprisonment these men must feel with the clear conscience of a shepherd who lives happily with what nature provides, harsh as the life may be. The smuggler's life would be better "If no such commerce of destruction known,/He were content with what the earth affords/To human labor . . ." (190–193). She describes the harsh life of the shepherd in a sort of antipastoral. His life is composed of "(Scenes all unlike the poet's fabling dreams/Describing Arcady)—But he is free" (209–210).

She juxtaposes this simple life with that of the wealthy:

> . . . the child of Luxury
> Enjoying nothing, flies from place to place
> In chase of pleasure that eludes his grasp:
> And that content is e'en less found by him,
> Than by the labourer, whose pick-ax smooths
> The road before his chariot. . . . (245–250)

The contrast between the two classes—those who exploit labor and the slave in Asia or the British peasant—parallels the other themes of the work. Smith portrays a leisure class that finds no happiness in a life divorced from honest labor and nature and contrasts the "sick satiety" (243) that such a life engenders with the honest sufferings and joys of the peasant. But the leisure class she describes is like the oppressors of history. They will disappear, and the land will endure.

"Beachy Head" contains some of Smith's best poetry. But the final two hundred lines seem a departure from the tone of the first two-thirds of the work. The poet describes a melancholy young man who comes to Beachy Head to bemoan his lost love, Amanda. The author makes this sentimental soul the speaker of a poem within the poem, which imitates Marlowe's "Passionate Shepherd to his Love."

Perhaps Smith intended this conventional pastoral to contrast with an antipastoral that follows, as she concludes the poem with the story of a hermit who "long disgusted with the world/And all its ways" (674–66) lived in a cave at the base of Beachy Head. The hermit is a misanthrope but is "feelingly alive to all that breath'd" (688), and he has rescued castaways during storms.[48] The disillusionment of the hermit and his return to nature fit the thematic pattern of the poem, but the lengthy pastoral that precedes it seems intrusive and poorly integrated.

Among the dozen other poems in the *Beachy Head* collection are works written for children. But it also contains one of Smith's finest short lyrics, "St. Monica." A comparison of "To the moon," cited above from the first edition of *Elegiac Sonnets,* with "St. Monica" shows the author's growth from dilettante versifying in the late preromantic tradition to a fine lyric poet and a true romantic voice. In a style modeled on the ballad tradition, "St. Monica" describes an abbey where "twice ten brethren of the monkish cowl" sing requiems for the soul of the abbey's founder. The poem begins with a description of the abbey in earlier days, then establishes its ruined condition as nature overtakes the structure.

Smith then introduces a "pensive stranger" who comes to the abbey not as an antiquarian, but as an observer of nature, one who

> Observes the rapid martin, threading fleet
> The broken arch: or follows with his eye,
> The wall-creeper that hunts the burnish'd fly;
> Sees the newt basking in the sunny ray,

> Or snail that sinuous winds his shining way,
> O'er the time-fretted walls of Monica. (78–84)

He comes to watch "The silent, slow, but active power/Of Vegetative Life, that o'er Decay/Weaves her green mantle" (90–93). For the "pensive stranger," and the reader, St. Monica's is a symbol of the transitory state of humankind and its works, the theme Smith developed in "Beachy Head." But nature endures. The final lines of the poem attest not only to the romantic vision that Smith had achieved in her final years but also to the mature voice of an accomplished poet:

> Oh Nature! ever lovely, ever new,
> He whom his earliest vows has paid to you
> Still finds, that life has something to bestow;
> And while to dark Forgetfulness they go,
> Man, and the works of man; immortal Youth,
> Unfading Beauty, and eternal Truth,
> Your Heaven-indited volume will display,
> While Art's elaborate monuments decay,
> Even as these shatter'd aisles, deserted Monica! (94–102)

William Wordsworth's "Saint Bees" is modeled on "St. Monica."[49] A comparison of the compression, vividness of imagery, minute observation of details from nature, and concise thematic development of "St. Monica" with the rather trite theme and sprawling form of Wordsworth's poem shows that whether or not she is the first romantic poet in England, Charlotte Smith should be remembered for being in her later work a worthy contemporary of the male canonical poets of British romanticism.

## Chapter Three

# Sense and Sensibility in Charlotte Smith's Early Novels: *Emmeline, Ethelinde,* and *Celestina*

Samuel Jackson Pratt, who wrote under his more euphonious stage name Courtney Melmouth, is the epitome of the 18th-century popular novelist. After trying out the clergy and an acting career, he started a circulating library. Pratt had his finger on the pulse of the novel-reading public. When he learned what sort of fiction appealed to his customers, he wrote it himself.

Pratt knew what readers of his day most desired—sentiment. Therefore, he has Raymond, one of his characters from *Emma Corbett,* cry, "O that cursed sentiment!—a term, Frederick, of late invention, to express old emotions in a new way—a term, which many use, more affect, few understand, and still fewer feel,—a term, which,—which,—in short—curse that sentiment!"[1] But properly disposed readers in 1789 surely knew that Raymond would soon receive an education in sensibility. Thus, he later uses the language of sentiment to describe Emma, the title character, in her sickness: "She looks at me sometimes till the heart's soft tear is in her eye. Ah, that tear! It is more worth than the possession of all the reluctant beauty that ever gold, grandeur, or importunity, extorted into their arms. I feel it stream over my senses. Blessed sympathy! Pure effusion! Generous, glorious Emma!"[2] Pratt's style burlesques itself, but his popularity with his reading audience demonstrates that sentiment sold well in novels as well as in poetry.

J. M. S. Tompkins articulates a critical truism when she observes, "There was, in the period that followed the masterpieces of the four great novelists [Samuel Richardson, Henry Fielding, Laurence Sterne, and Tobias Smollett], a real conviction that the novel was played out. The works of Fielding and Richardson were seen as the culmination of a development, not the starting point."[3] But during this time Charlotte Smith, Fanny Burney, Ann Radcliffe, and others advanced the frontiers of the novel and created an audience for writers who followed. Whatever the quality of the fiction produced during this period, there is no denying its popularity. Robert Heilman reports that the number of novels published rose from 81 in 1788 to 117 in 1800.[4] The numbers seem extraordinary for a nation with just under 10 million people and a low literacy rate.

Tompkins finds that as fiction grew in popularity it became increasingly commercial, with the needs of circulating libraries and the demands of readers fueling a lively demand. And since authorship was one of the few acceptable professions for women, many gentlewomen such as Eliza Parsons, Anna Laetitia Barbauld, and, of course, Charlotte Smith entered the lists because writing paid much better than needlework. Although remuneration might be as little as one-half pound per volume, some authors did very well indeed. Fanny Burney received £250 for *Cecilia* in 1782, and as time went on, the top prices increased. Ann Radcliffe earned £900 for *The Italian* in 1797, and Fanny Burney realized £3,000 from a subscription publication of *Camilla* in 1796.[5] Most of the commercially successful fiction in the 1780s and 1790s, moreover, had broad appeal to the sentimentalist.

Readers of the sentimental novel responded to cues similar to those that Smith and other writers used in poetry: simplicity, melancholy, sensibility, sympathetic response to the distress of others, and the alienation felt by those with finely tuned feelings. In fiction, the hero and heroine of sensibility possess these same characteristics. Thus, when they are put in "distress," they become antennae, transmitting those feelings to the properly disposed reader. The sentimental characters' capacity for feeling evokes sympathy from readers who share their sensibility.

Janet Todd notes quite correctly that although authors of "most sentimental novels . . . insist on their instructional nature," still the "feeling responses in the books are paramount."[6] The story inspires tears, and as Harley tells the unfortunate Miss Atkins in *The Man of Feeling* when she weeps bitter tears of repentance for the errors of conduct that led her into prostitution, "there is virtue in these tears; let the fruit of them be virtue."[7] To the British sentimental reader of the period, the pleasure of the passage is the feeling it evokes, but the novel must have a moral tone.

Samuel Richardson's novels, which inspired so many British and continental writers, aroused the feelings of the sensitive reader of his day; but to the author, sentiment was secondary to the didactic purpose of his works. Richardson's continental disciples, however, responded to the intensity of feelings in his novels rather than his insistence of control over them. The Abbé Prévost admired the English novelist's works enough to translate them in a French edition. But in his own fiction, the Chevalier des Grieux in *Manon Lescaut* cries, "Persons of a finer cast can be affected in a thousand different ways; it would almost seem that they had more than five senses, and that they are accessible to ideas and sensations which far exceed the ordinary faculties of human nature."[8] In many continental novels, characters with true sensibility are simply above the rules for ordinary people. In *Julie, ou La Nouvelle Héloïse,* Rousseau's Julie and Saint-Preux consummate their love even though they cannot marry, and one of Rousseau's sentimental characters writes in a letter that she is "beginning to perceive . . . how much your two hearts are above ordinary rules, and how much your love contains a natural sympathy which neither time nor human efforts could efface."[9]

British writers avoided such extreme sensibility. Their readers might enjoy dangerous levels of feeling in continental novels. A translation of *La Nouvelle Héloïse,* in fact, went through 11 English editions during the 18th century alone. But few British novelists—at least very few novelists of the 1780s and early 1790s—ventured into such dangerous waters. Female characters who follow their passions instead of the rules of society are likely to share the fate of the title character in *Ela, or the Delusions of the Heart.* "I fall in the bloom of life," she laments, "the martyr of my own deluding heart."[10] In the British novel of sentiment, feeling must be controlled.

Charlotte Smith, then, inherited an audience for sentimental fiction with a didactic message. Henry Mackenzie, Henry Brooke, Sarah Fielding, Frances Brooke, Fanny Burney, and dozens of other British novelists had turned sentiment into fictional conventions before Smith's career began. Smith's fiction attests to her knowledge of other writers' novels. Her work abounds with literary allusions, including many references to fiction, sometimes in rather unflattering terms. Her faux sentimentalists form their ideas on bad fiction. Clarinthia Ludford in *Ethelinde* tells the heroine that she prefers novels with "a vast deal of white paper" for "people read them so easily while their hair is dressing, that it is quite comfortable" (II, 168).[11] Though Smith might scoff at some of the novels of her time, she understood the power of the genre to delight and, at its best, instruct. Her works brim with references to all of the major British novelists who precede her, as well as to Rousseau and Goethe, and the nature of the allusions suggests admiration for their work.[12]

Charlotte Smith's early novels follow the subject matter and conventions of British sentimental fiction. Her heroines are models of correct behavior. While they have powerful feelings, the moral lesson of each novel is that those feelings must be restrained. The heroines show the proper balance of feeling, and Smith contrasts them with those characters whose sensibility is too powerful or too weak. *Emmeline* and *Celestina* focus on parental authority, a common plot line in the sentimental tradition since Richardson's *Clarissa*. Another theme in each of these three novels is the importance of family loyalty, a topic close to the author's own experience. Above all, these works focus on conservative values and domestic issues: obedience to authority, control of powerful feelings, reliance on reason, parental responsibility, propriety of behavior, and problems that destroy marriages. Smith's first three novels expand the scope of fiction through her descriptions of natural scenery, often presented in the language of the concept of the sublime, and her development of the gothic mode. These novels are the basis from which her later political novels would develop; the subject and themes of her fiction would change abruptly with the conclusion of *Celestina*.

## *Emmeline, or The Orphan of the Castle*

*Emmeline* (1788) earned Smith instant recognition. "We might, perhaps, be censured as too easy flatterers," writes the reviewer for *The Critical Review*, "if we said that this novel equals Cecilia; yet we think it may stand next to Miss Burney's works."[13] The novel's didactic message does indeed resemble that of Burney's *Cecilia;* like Burney's, Smith's story centers on family relationships and control of feelings. As in *Cecilia,* the focus of the work is irresponsible parental authority and the importance of proper education of children.

At the outset, Emmeline is an orphan, described as not yet 16 and living at dilapidated Mowbray Castle in Wales. She is the presumed illegitimate daughter of Viscount Mowbray, who had died abroad. Her uncle, Lord Montreville, who inherited her father's estates and title because of Emmeline's illegitimacy, supports her as a dependent under the care of the housekeeper.

The issues of parental authority and responsibility first arise when Lord Mowbray visits the castle after the death of the housekeeper and brings his son, Delamere, who promptly forms a passionate attachment for Emmeline and declares that he will marry her, despite his father's wishes. Lord Mowbray has a more prosperous match in mind for his son and forbids the union. But Delamere's parents have given him his way all his life, and he refuses to obey his father. For her part, Emmeline is rather frightened of the young man, and when Lord Mowbray asks her to go into hiding, she is happy enough to comply.

And so begins a complicated plot, as Emmeline moves from place to place to avoid the impassioned pleadings of Delamere, who finds her after each move, throwing tantrums when she refuses to marry him and threatening to challenge any man who shows an interest in her. Despite his pride, Lord Montreville rather likes Emmeline and would permit the marriage were he not influenced by his adviser, Sir Richard Crofts, who promotes the interest of his own family at the expense of his patron. Eventually, Lord Montreville agrees to allow Delamere to marry Emmeline if the young man does not see her for one year.

During this time, Emmeline meets Mrs. Stafford, an autobiographical character: a woman with a large family, a foolish husband, and a disputed will in the background. Emmeline travels with the family to southwestern England, where they meet Adelina Trelawny, a sister-in-law to Delamere's married sister Augusta, Lady Westhaven. The young woman has had an affair after being widowed and is in hiding, awaiting the birth of a child. Adelina's powerful feelings have driven her mad, and Mrs. Stafford and Emmeline adopt the young woman. Through aiding Adelina, Emmeline meets her love interest, Captain Godolphin, Adelina's brother.

Smith resolves the plot when Emmeline goes to France with Mrs. Stafford and travels with the Westhavens. There Lord Westhaven's cousin, Bellozane, an impetuous French army officer, falls in love with Emmeline and becomes a nuisance because of his passionate behavior. His parents, like Delamere's, failed to teach him to moderate his feelings. But Emmeline discovers the story of her birth. Her father had secretly married her mother, and she is not only legitimate but the true heir to the estate Lord Montreville had inherited. The action then returns to London, where in a flurry of poetic justice, Bellozane, tiring of Emmeline's rejection, has an affair with Frances Croft, Lord Montreville's married daughter and Delamere's sister. The fiery Delamere challenges Bellozane when he learns of the affair, and the Frenchman fatally wounds him in a duel. Emmeline inherits her father's estate and fortune.

The didactic message of the novel is clear. Montreville's failure in parenting has cost him a son and heir, a daughter, and his wife (who dies, apparently of a stroke, when she hears of Frances' affair); also, because of his pride of birth, he loses a large part of his fortune. Those characters who fail to control their passion—Adelina, Delamere, and Frances Croft, for instance—pay penalties for their behavior. Emmeline, the model of self-control and correct behavior, is rewarded with marriage to Godolphin, the man of her choice.

## Ethelinde, or the Recluse of the Lake

Like *Emmeline, Ethelinde* 1789 charmed the reviewers. *The Monthly Review*'s writer, revealing the usual prejudice against fiction, writes enthusiastically, "We are unwilling to dismiss it by general terms, as is, frequently our practice with this class of production." The reviewer goes on to note that "as she principally aims at a display of character Mrs. Smith is entitled to a rank considerably above the crowd of novelists who have lately come under our review."[14]

While the action in *Ethelinde* centers on family relationships, Smith also focuses on other domestic issues: functional and dysfunctional marriages, forces that destroy families, the dangers of gambling, and, as in *Emmeline,* the impact of poor education. The novel is more loosely structured than *Emmeline.* But as in Smith's first novel, the heroine, Ethelinde Chesterville, stands at the center of the action, the linkage of the various plot lines and the moral norm of the work.

Her father, Colonel Chesterville, a widower, had married a sister of the wealthy Mr. Maltrevors against the will of her family, causing them to disinherit her. The marriage connects Chesterville with Sir Edward Newenden, who married Maltrevors' daughter, Maria. The two men become close friends, and Newenden, a man of feeling, falls in love with Ethelinde. She is a fellow sentimentalist, while Maria Newenden lacks feeling. Although Newenden struggles with his passion, he regularly invites Ethelinde, his wife's cousin, to his home and includes her on a trip to his paternal home in the Lake Country, Grasmere Abbey.

Here Ethelinde meets and falls in love with Montgomery, whose mother has brought him to England to advance his fortunes after his father died in France. Mrs. Montgomery tells their story in a long disgression. The gist of it is, however, that she and her husband had enjoyed a happy marriage—a union of equals. Ethelinde and Montgomery want to wed, but Ethelinde recognizes the folly of marriage without income.

The complications of the story include the difficulties caused by Colonel Chesterville's gambling. His son, Harry, emulates his father and destroys his fortunes. A captain in the army, he impulsively marries Victorine, a beautiful but illegitimate and penniless young woman who is apparently an orphan; however, his compulsive gambling leaves him in debtors' prison while his pregnant wife languishes in a London garret. They are saved when Ethelinde meets Harcourt, Victorine's wealthy father who has been searching for his long lost child after his wife's death. But Harry and Victorine's marriage serves as an object lesson of what can happen when couples wed with no means of support, a counterpoise to Ethelinde and Montgomery's decision to wait until they are established before marrying.

Sir Edward's relationship with Maria is yet another example of a disastrous marriage. It resulted from Newenden's need for money and the Maltrevors' desire to marry their daughter into the aristocracy. Maria lacks feelings, however, and her chief joys are "the ton" (London society) and "deep play" (high-stakes gambling). Since the Maltrevors have pampered the young woman, she is willful and without feelings for others. Her behavior leads to an affair and a duel between Sir Edward and Lord Danesforte, her seducer, in which Danesforte is wounded.

Most of the problems of the novel arise from ill-assorted marriages and faulty education in conduct. Harcourt marries because he is not "entirely indifferent to the splendour of an income of sixteen or twenty thousand" (III, 98–99); for his trouble, he gets a possessive wife whom he cannot love. Sir Edward married for money, and his wife's bad conduct (caused by her parents' failure to teach responsibility and proper morals) made him earn it. Harry Chesterville, another product of faulty education, marries impulsively for love, nearly ruining both his and his wife's lives. Smith establishes Ethelinde as a norm in resisting marriage "without either party having a support for a family" (II, 42).

## Celestina, a Novel

A more tightly structured story than Smith's preceding novel, *Celestina* (1791) focuses once again on the issue of marriage and education of children. But the marriage issue she broaches at the end of the novel signals the change in her fiction from portrayals of family and domestic problems and the display of fine feelings (expressed within the bounds of socially acceptable behavior) to politics.

Mrs. Willoughby, an English widow, adopts the title character, an orphan whom she finds in a French convent as she travels on the continent with her family. She raises Celestina with her son and daughter, Willoughby and Matilda, and as they grow up, Willoughby and Celestina fall in love. But on her death bed, Mrs. Willoughby makes her son promise he will marry his cousin, Miss Fitz-Hayman, the daughter of the wealthy Lord Castlenorth, to repair his estate. Willoughby promises but soon regrets his vow. After much agonizing, he proposes to Celestina, who accepts; and they determine to live on a diminished income.

Just before the ceremony, however, Willoughby receives a message that takes him away from Celestina. Thus, the heroine (and perhaps the less experienced novel reader) remains in doubt for nearly a volume as to why Willoughby has deserted her. He had received an anonymous note (sent by Lady Castlenorth) telling him that Celestina is his half sister, Mrs. Willoughby's illegitimate child. So for nearly two volumes, Willoughby scurries about, first convinced that he should marry Miss Fitz-Hayman and then that he must disprove the rumor about his mother. Celestina, meanwhile, lives for a time with the Reverend Mr. Thorold, whose son Montague falls passionately in love with her. Then she travels with Mrs. Elphinstone, another Charlotte Smith surrogate, and finally lives with Lady Horatia Howard, who more or less adopts her. Throughout this time, both Montague Thorold and Vavasour, Willoughby's friend and an acknowledged rake, besiege the heroine for her hand.

Much of the plot focuses on the evils of arranged marriages. Mrs. Willoughby's insistence that Willoughby marry Lord Castlenorth's daughter and Castlenorth's obsession with maintaining aristocratic lines create most of the problems. But when Willoughby goes to France, hoping to discover the truth of Celestina's parentage, he uncovers a story that, while it follows the novel's theme of parental authority in marriage, creates a bridge to the political works that were to come.

Willoughby meets the Chevalier de Bellegarde, who tells his tale in a digression. He and his brother had fled their home because their father was not only a domestic tyrant but the pattern despotic aristocrat of the ancien régime. He later became friends with an English gentleman, Ormond, and when the Englishman accompanied Bellegarde on a clandestine visit to Genevieve, the Frenchman's sister, he fell in love with the young woman, and they arranged a secret marriage. Bellegarde then married Jacquelina, Genevieve's companion, and the two couples met in the ruined pavilion near the old count's castle.

Eventually, they were discovered. The count detained Bellegarde and Ormond via lettres de cachet and had them thrown into prison. Experienced readers of the day would have known long before the end of the digression that Ormond is Celestina's father, as the "missing heir" theme was a staple in fiction. Genevieve bore her child after she and

Jacquelina were incarcerated in a convent, where Genevieve died. Ormond and Bellegarde were freed when "the glorious flame of liberty . . . burst forth" (III, 256).

The Bellegarde story signals a radical shift in Smith's fiction. The first two novels and even most of *Celestina* offer conservative portrayals of domestic problems and troubles in love relationships. While the novels are sensational enough to titillate the reader of the day, they recommend obedience to authority and observance of traditional behavior. Smith's heroines obey authority figures and are governed by conservative values. The rebellion of young people against a patriarchal aristocrat in the Bellegarde digression, however, signals the dramatic change in the subject and tone of Smith's work from didactic stories of frustrated love to a focus on political and social issues.

## Aspects of the Early Novels

### CHARACTER CONVENTIONS:
### THE DICHOTOMY BETWEEN NATURE AND ART

Character conventions seem the key to the effect of the sentimental novel. Other elements flow from the characters. The sentimentalists transmit their feelings to sympathetic readers. British writers of sentimental fiction organize these characters into two categories: nature and art. Writers key reader response with references to the words "nature" and "art" or cognates when describing characters. In Smith's fiction, the dichotomy underpins the novel's didactic message. Those characters identified with nature are the moral norm of the work. The nature/art dichotomy signals the drift toward romanticism in the closing years of the 18th century, a change that proved subversive not only to neoclassicism but to the social order.

The word "nature" takes on such a bewildering plethora of meanings during the 18th century that it frustrates definition. Basil Willey generalizes that "Nature and Reason are normally associated in the earlier part of the century, Nature and Feeling in the later,"[15] but he goes on to give such a variety of meanings and connotations for the word "nature" during the latter part of the century as to suggest the absence of any generally accepted definition. Pope's discussion of the words "nature" and "art" in *An Essay on Man* might serve as a guide for their meaning to the early part of the century. Pope insists on a balance of the two. But Rousseau's teachings, as Willey so aptly describes them, hold that "the true reforms are those which will lead back to some earlier, simpler, and happier mode of existence,"[16] and the French philosopher's pronouncements on the benevolence of unspoiled human nature dominate the cult of sensibility in the second half of the century.

The words "nature" and "art" appear frequently in the fiction of the late 18th century and help to identify the characters with which they are associated. By the time Smith published *Emmeline* in 1788, a body of conventions for these character types had developed in the works of Rousseau, Henry Mackenzie, Henry Brooke, and Sarah Fielding, to name a few. Elizabeth Inchbald would later write a tour de force on these conventions in her novel *Nature and Art* (1796).

The nature/art dichotomy establishes polar oppositions of values. Characters who follow nature are sentimentalists with values similar to those of the persona in Smith's poems: They have powerful feelings; prefer simplicity in lifestyle to the "ton"; have natural talents rather than learned "accomplishments"; respond to the distress of others; share a congenital sadness and love of what the language of the period calls a "pleasing melancholy" or an "interesting languor" in another person;[17] bond after meeting on a perception of shared sensibilities; and feel a sense of alienation from "the world," which fails to share their values. The words "Orphan" and "Recluse" in the subtitles of Smith's first two novels surely communicate the alienation of the sentimentalist.

Characters who follow art are polar opposites in values: They esteem social status and urban "high life," lack sympathy for others, and fail to relieve the needy. Most important of all, they lack a capacity for feeling and ridicule those who have it. Clearly, the "nature" characters reflect the nascent romanticism of the period, and the contrast with the "art" characters simply underscores their romantic sensibilities. The plot of the novel evokes sympathy for the "nature" character from the reader with sensibility.

These conventions were in place by 1788, and Smith models her characters in *Emmeline* on them. The heroine is a restrained version of the romantic "nature" character. The epitome of simplicity, she has "a kind of intuitive knowledge; and comprehended everything with a facility that soon left her instructors behind her"[18] and demonstrates it for the reader when she goes to France: "To the study of languages, her mind so successfully applied itself, that she very soon spoke and wrote French with the correctness not only of a native, but of a native well educated" (335).[19] She "applied incessantly to her books; for of every useful and ornamental feminine employment she had long since made herself mistress without any instruction" (41). Like all of Smith's heroines, she dresses with minimum ornamentation, so when she lives with Mrs. Ashwood, a lady of fashion to whose home Lord Montreville has sent her, we are told that "The extreme simplicity of Emmeline's appearance . . . and her perfect ignorance of fashionable life and fashionable accomplishments, gave her . . . the air of a dependant," though to some, "The extreme beauty of her person, and the *naïveté* of her manners gave her . . . the attractive charms of novelty" (79). Emmeline is nature's child and expresses an appropriate attitude to the high life: "Formed of the softer elements, and with a mind calculated for select friendship and domestic felicity, rather than for the tumult of fashionable life and the parade of titled magnificence, Emmeline coveted not his [Delamere's] rank, nor valued his riches" (149).

And though Emmeline has no money to assist the poor, she and Mrs. Stafford immediately come to the aid of Adelina Trelawny, despite the latter's suspicion that her husband might be the father of the young woman's unborn child. This incident has particular significance. It was one thing for a male writer such as Henry Mackenzie to allow Harley in *The Man of Feeling* to befriend a prostitute, but quite another for a woman writer to have her heroine not only become intimate friends with a fallen woman but to allow Adelina to marry her seducer at the end of the novel.[20] Emmeline and Celestina have few coins in their purses to give, but they hazard something more valuable to women of the late 18th century—their reputations.

*Ethelinde* and *Celestina* are similarly conventional as "nature" characters. Simplicity is the rule with each. Ethelinde feels out of place when she lives with the Newendens in London and makes every effort to avoid the fashionable soirées which are the focus of Lady Newenden's life. Conventional "nature" characters immediately recognize one another, and Harcourt's comment to Ethelinde about his first impression of her seems typical: "An attraction too powerful to be resisted seemed to impel me towards you . . . ; it was that soft yet deep melancholy which appeared to possess you, and that look which seemed to promise the tenderest pity for the miseries of others" (V, 136). As became the norm for nature characters, Ethelinde has a strong sense of her own difference. At one point Sir Edward Newenden approaches her as she sits pensively beside Grasmere and asks her why she is not part of the "amusing party" inside, and she replies: "For no reason in the world, but because I am like nobody else" (I, 193).

Readers would have responded to the same conventions in *Celestina*. The heroine loves Willoughby because he could never "be quite like those who were called 'other people'" (I, 31). Celestina assists Jessy, an unfortunate young woman—indeed, a servant and beneath the heroine in class—and helps her be united to Cathcart, her sweetheart and a fellow romantic. A counterpoint "art" character in this novel is Matilda, Willoughby's sister and the heroine's childhood playmate, who, when she grows up, becomes a "Bath beauty," a young woman who "knew something of everything, and talked as if she knew a great deal more" (I, 20). She, like Miss Fitz-Hayman, Lord Castlenorth's daughter and another "art" character juxtaposed to Celestina, has "laboured accomplishments" (III, 52), while Celestina is "naturally" creative, as exemplified by the poems she dashes off at odd moments throughout the novel. Another juxtaposition is Lord Castlenorth's preoccupation with aristocratic lineage against the humbler but more satisfying life Willoughby would enjoy in following his heart with Celestina. And in all three of these early novels, first attachments rule, another convention in sentimental fiction. All three heroines are besieged by supplicants for their hands in marriage, but they can only be in love with one man—a person who shares their tastes and capacity for feeling.

## NATURE, LANDSCAPE, AND THE SUBLIME

All of the character conventions described above were in the making before Smith began writing fiction, and they are no doubt part of the romantic consciousness that was then aborning. The enthusiastic response to nature and the use of the language of essays on the sublime and the picturesque were an integral part of that consciousness and had already appeared in poetry. But Charlotte Smith introduced descriptions of natural scenery in fiction and first established a love of nature as one of the conventional features of the romantic characters. In these early novels, the description of nature provides atmosphere and enhances the dramatic situation portrayed. Nature also corresponds to the mood of the scene or the state of mind of the character in similar fashion to the correspondence between nature and persona in Smith's poetry. Nature also keys the reader to character recognition. Romantics, or "nature" characters, love scenery; "art" characters are incapable of enjoying it. Moreover, Smith brings to her landscape description the language of the sublime and the picturesque, which became a staple in her poetry in the third and following editions of *Elegiac Sonnets*.

A few examples of sublime scenery appear in fiction before *Emmeline*. In *Julie, ou La Nouvelle Héloïse,* Rousseau sets a scene among the rocks at

Meillerie that was imitated for the rest of the century. Nature provides a backdrop to Saint-Preux as he walks about the alpine rocks and glaciers: "This solitary place formed a retreat, wild and deserted but full of those kinds of beauties which please only sensitive souls and appear horrible to the others" (335). The passage goes on to give a description of the scene which reflects the developing taste for the horrors of nature. Charlotte Smith loved it so well that she alludes to the "rocks of Meillerie" repeatedly in her novels. Moreover, the setting for the passage corresponds to the passionate relationship between Julie and Saint-Preux. Frances Brooke also uses the language of the sublime in a passage from *The History of Emily Montague* (1769).[21] But these are isolated scenes within the novels, and such passages are rare before the 1790s.

Smith brought her poetic taste in natural scenery to *Emmeline*. A love of nature bonds her sentimentalists. Emmeline, for instance, longs for the scenery around Mowbray Castle after she must leave it, and she prefers the beauties of the countryside to urban settings throughout. But toward the end of the novel, the author sets the scene during a journey through the mountains for a meeting with the old Frenchman from whom Emmeline learns that her birth was legitimate: "In some places huge masses impended over them, of varied form and colour, without any vegetation but scattered mosses; in others, aromatic plants and low shrubs; the lavender, the thyme, the rosemary, the mountain sage, fringed the steep craggs [sic] . . ." (347). The passage goes on at some length, with the "botanizing" so characteristic of Smith's poetry.

*Ethelinde* offers far more abundant examples of sublime and picturesque scenery.[22] The opening chapters, set on the shores of Lake Grasmere, are the first literary evocation of Lake Country scenery, which would become the most celebrated natural beauty in England.[23] Thus, as Ethelinde leaves Grasmere and Montgomery to be with her father in volume 1, nature mirrors her feelings: "They now entered a long and narrow valley, confined on both sides by enormous fells; the few trees that grew on some of them were already faded, and half leafless; the masses of grey rock which composed others, appeared more than usually dark, from a lowering sky; the deep gloom which hung over the face of nature seemed in correspondence with the heavy heart of Ethelinde . . ." (I, 239). Such passages recur throughout the novel. As is the case in Smith's poetry, nature corresponds to the mood of the scene and contributes to its impact on readers with sensibility.

At the end of the novel, Ethelinde, thinking Montgomery has perished in a shipwreck, goes to a bench near Lake Grasmere, where she and her lover had spent a good deal of time. The author sets the scene with some botanizing. "The seat was in a little cave in a soft sand rock; over it's[24] unequal arch, the ivy, mingled with clematis, wild hop, briony, and the woody nightshade, formed festoons which half concealed the entrance" (V, 256). The setting takes on elements of the sublime for Ethelinde in this scene during the late fall, when, as Smith tells us, "The very horrors of the surrounding landscape now afforded her the only gratification she was capable of tasting . . ." (V, 257–258). After establishing the mood and the scene, Smith stages the novel's denouement, with Montgomery returning during Sir Edward's proposal to Ethelinde.

Landscape description is even more plentiful in *Celestina*. The scenes set in the Hebrides offer ample opportunity for the author to create sublime or picturesque backdrops. The incident in which Mr. Elphinstone drowns when his boat founders within sight of land offers an example. When Montague Thorold, who has followed Celestina, appears disguised as a shepherd, Smith describes him in Gilpinian language as "a figure a painter would have chosen to have placed in a landscape, representing the heathy summits and romantic rocks of the Hebrides" (II, 137). Then when Celestina believes that Willoughby has married Miss Fitz-Hayman, she makes for herself "a species of gloomy enjoyment from the dreary and wild scenes around her. . . . She now rather sought images of horror" (II, 142–143). The author creates her most romantic landscapes to date in her description of the Pyrenees, laden with the evocative language of the Burkean sublime as well as more pious reflections on nature and art, during Willoughby's search for Celestina's origin:

> Amid these paths that wound among the almost perpendicular points of the cliffs, he [Willoughby] often sat down; surveying with awe and admiration the stupendous works of the Divine Architect, before whose simplest creation, the laboured productions of the most intelligent of his creatures sink into insignificance.—Huge masses of grey marble, or a dark granite, frowned above his head; whose crevices, here and there, afforded a scanty subsistence to lickens [sic] and moss campion; while the desolate barrenness of other parts, added to that threatening aspect with which they seemed to hang over the wandering traveller, and to bid him to fear, lest even the light steps of the Izard [the wild goat] . . . should disunite them from the mountain itself, and bury him beneath their thundering ruins. (III, 182–183)

The passage goes on to describe all the "wildest horrors" of mountain scenery before introducing the occasional "little green recess" and botanizing at some length. The contrast between "horrors" and the more calming description seems an apparent adaptation of Burke's distinction between the sublime and the beautiful.

In all of Smith's novels, a key element in landscape description is the distinction of characters by "taste," a word that becomes a recognition symbol in sentimental fiction during the 1790s. "Nature" characters possess taste in natural scenery and literature; "art" characters do not. Burke writes that taste is "that faculty or those faculties of the mind which are affected with or which form a judgement of, the works of imagination and the elegant arts."[25] But like the nature/art dichotomy, the word is easier to demonstrate by example than to define. In Smith's novels, the hero and heroine share tastes in natural scenery and literature that bond them. When Emmeline travels in France, she admires a sublime mountain scene, and once again, the landscape and the character's mood are in correspondence: "She knew nobody but Godolphin who had taste and enthusiasm enough to enjoy it. . . . Intent on the romantic wildness of the cliffs with which she was surrounded, and her mind associating with these objects the idea of him on whom it now perpetually dwelt, she had brought Godolphin before her, and was imagining what he would have said had he been with her; with what warmth he would enjoy, with what taste and spirit point out, the beauty of scenes so enchanting" (347–348). Bellozane has no chance of winning Emmeline, because when he sees her admiring his aunt's collection of plants, he thinks it the "most wearisome, or to use the cant of the times, the most *boring* subject in the world" (359).[26]

Each of these first three novels makes similar distinctions. Sir Edward Newenden's attachment to Ethelinde results not only from the heroine's beauty but from their shared tastes—tastes in nature and the arts that he cannot enjoy with his wife. On the road to Grasmere at the outset of the novel, Sir Edward gives Lady Newenden a little lecture on the beauties of the landscape they are passing through, but she replies, "I see but little beauty in those dreary looking mountains. . . . Perhaps you had better apply to Ethelinde. You may teach *her,* as she is a young lady of *sublime taste,* you know, to admire what I, who am a creature without any, really want faculties to enjoy" (I, 31). Similarly, Willoughby and Celestina love the beauties of nature around Alvestone, the hero's estate, while the countryside bores Matilda, Willoughby's unfeeling sister, who prefers the London social scene. Also, Montague Thorold falls in love with Celestina because of their shared taste in poetry and nature.

Charlotte Smith made the recognition and shared taste of hero and heroine popular in sentimental fiction. Ann Radcliffe, Maria Roche, and other purveyors of the sentimental or gothic traditions after her time turned these fictional devices into convention. The convention was so well established by the early 19th century that Jane Austen could spoof it in *Sense and Sensibility* (where the sentimental Marianne regrets that the stolid but dependable Edward Ferrars lacks taste) with confidence that her readers would be in on the joke.

## CHARLOTTE SMITH AND THE GENESIS OF GOTHIC

The chronology of her publications demonstrates that Smith first wrote the sort of gothic fiction that Radcliffe and others made popular in the 1790s. Although her early novels could by no means be categorized as "gothic," at least in the style that the genre would later take, she established the sublimely ruined castle and the picturesque cottage as setting, and against this backdrop placed her beautiful and vulnerable young heroines. Although she portrayed no supernatural incidents, she leads the reader to suspect them before explaining the true cause. Smith created the setting and mood for the gothic. Despite her role as innovator, however, she made clear in her prefaces and elsewhere that she disliked writing such fiction. Yet she understood its appeal to readers, and beginning with *Desmond* in 1792, she used gothic melodrama to lure her largely female audience to read novels that would instruct them in political ideas and social issues.

Jane Austen's fiction offers an excellent springboard for discussing the fiction of the 1780s and 1790s. She read those works as a girl and early began writing what can only be called affectionate burlesques, many of which take aim at the gothic, for the entertainment of her family. A passage from *Northanger Abbey*, Austen's spoof of gothic fiction, demonstrates Smith's part in establishing the ruined castle as an evocative setting for the distresses of hundreds of sentimental heroines. As Austen's heroine, Catherine Morland, travels to Northanger Abbey, which her experience in reading Ann Radcliffe leads her to believe will be a sublime structure from the gothic tradition, the author gives us the young woman's thoughts:

> As they drew near the end of their journey, her impatience for a sight of the abbey . . . returned in full force, and every bend of the road was expected with solemn awe to afford a glimpse of its massy walls of grey

stone, rising amidst a grove of ancient oaks, with the last beams of the
sun playing in beautiful splendour on its high Gothic windows.[27]

Of course, the heroine is disappointed in her expectations.

As is so often the case in Austen's work, the irony of the passage
depends on the reader's familiarity with 18th-century fiction. Knowledgeable readers would chuckle to recall the scene in *The Mysteries of
Udolpho* when Emily St. Aubert reacts to her first view of Castle
Udolpho:

> Emily gazed with melancholy awe upon the castle, which she understood
> to be Montoni's for, though it was now lighted up by the setting sun, the
> gothic greatness of its features, and its mouldering walls of dark grey
> stone, rendered it a gloomy and sublime object.[28]

But *Udolpho* appeared in 1794. Five years earlier, Charlotte Smith
described Ethelinde's approach to Grasmere Abbey in a similar fashion:

> She gave way to the solemn but melancholy species of pleasure inspired
> by the scene around her. It was now evening: the last rays of the sun gave
> a dull purple hue to the points of the fells which rose above the water and
> the park; while the rest, all in deep shadow, looked gloomily sublime.
> (I, 46–47)

The common language of the three passages provides an amusing
insight into the winks and nods between Jane Austen and her reader.
But it also shows the evolution of a new level of evocative language in
the novel of sentiment, passing from innovation, to convention, to bur-
lesque. Allusions in Austen's juvenilia demonstrate that she had read
both *Udolpho* and *Ethelinde,* and the language of her description of both
Grasmere Abbey and Castle Udolpho suggests an awareness of Radcliffe's borrowing and an amalgamation of the two passages.

The dates of their novels show that Smith linked the language of the
Burkean sublime and the Gilpinian picturesque to the castle and cottage settings as well as to landscape before Radcliffe used similar strate-
gies. Such passages appear in Radcliffe's work for the first time in *The
Romance of the Forest,* published in 1791, well after *Emmeline* and *Ethelinde*
and the same year that *Celestina* appeared. Significantly, Radcliffe's earlier novels (*The Castles of Athlin and Dunbayne,* 1789, and *A Sicilian
Romance,* 1790) have little specifically "sublime" description. While
Smith's first three novels are hardly definable as gothic, intimations of

the gothic machinery to come appear in all three. And as Louis Bredvold writes: "In the light of history it appears that the novel of terror was only a variant of the novel of sensibility, exploiting a fresh excitement, trying to push suspense and apprehension to the utmost."[29] Smith's experiments in mild terrors provided the impetus for more powerful thrills in the works of Radcliffe and other purveyors of the gothic.

The tale of terror is of ancient origin, but in *The Castle of Otranto* (1765), Horace Walpole created the universally acknowledged progenitor of all the fictional haunted castles to come. The appeal of the book may seem elusive today, but it set off bells in the psyche of 18th-century readers. The preface to the second edition of Walpole's novel offers a useful explanation of his intent in writing the book: "It was an attempt to blend the two kinds of romance, the ancient and the modern. In the former all was imagination and improbability; in the latter, nature is always intended to be, and sometimes has been, copied with success."[30] Walpole's preface seems an early attempt to distinguish the novel from the romance. In 1785 Clara Reeve discusses the terms in somewhat similar fashion, finding the romance a description of "what never happened nor is likely to happen," while the novel gives "a familiar relation of such things, as pass every day before our eyes . . . and the perfection of it is to represent every scene in so easy and natural a manner, and to make them so probable, as to deceive us into a persuasion (at least while we are reading) that all is real."[31] Sir Walter Scott defines the terms similarly in his "Essay on Romance."[32]

Oddly enough, Walpole's essay on romance inspired few imitations over the next 25 years in England. However, Charlotte Smith had read *Otranto*,[33] and from the first her novels exploit the basic situation and setting of Walpole's work. She uses the castle as setting, and to that setting she brings the evocative language of the sublime and picturesque, not yet in place in Radcliffe's fiction. Yet Smith hews to the "novel," as described by Reeve and Scott, at least. While she knew how to give her readers an occasional sublime shiver, she describes British domestic life in some detail, and she allows no supernatural suggestion to go unexplained. All of the elements of the "sentimental gothic,"[34] though, are in place in these first three novels, the inspiration for Radcliffe's work.

In *Emmeline,* Smith establishes the basic situation of the sentimental gothic in the subtitle: a vulnerable young woman left unprotected in a ruined castle located in a remote area. Emmeline lives in Mowbray Castle, "an old building, formerly of great strength," and "the greater part of it was gone to decay" (1). After the death of Mrs. Carey, the housekeeper, Emmeline is "a being belonging to nobody; as having no right to claim the protection of any one" (6). In a scene that would have caused a shiver for readers unjaded by sensationalism, Emmeline lays out Mrs. Carey's body, performing the "last sad offices," then has dreams of Mrs. Carey calling for her: "her last groan still vibrated in her ears!—while the stillness of the night, interrupted only by the cries of the owls which haunted the ruins, added to the gloomy and mournful sensations of her mind" (7). Smith later sets a scene in which Delamere, smitten by the young woman's charms, literally knocks down the door of her room in the ruined section of the castle to declare his passion: "Emmeline was infinitely too much terrified to speak: nor could her trembling limbs support her" (32). But she breaks away, and Delamere pursues her through the dark corridors of the old castle. The sexual threat to the heroine, at once terrifying and titillating and so much a part of the machinery in the sentimental gothic, seems apparent.

The castle as setting, another element of the gothic, is central to the evocation of the reader's response. Smith's description of Mowbray Castle as Emmeline leaves would echo endlessly in other novels: "The road lay along the side of what would in England be called a mountain; at it's [sic] feet rolled the rapid stream that washed the castle walls, foaming over fragments of rock; and bounded by a wood of oak and pine; among which the ruins of the monastery, once an appendage to the castle, reared it's broken arches; and marked by grey and mouldering walls, and mounds covered with slight vegetation, it was traced to it's connection with the castle itself, still frowning in gothic magnificence" (37). In passages such as this, Smith enhances the level of feeling projected to readers with the addition of mild gothic thrills, sublimely ruined structures as setting, evocative scenery, suggestions of the supernatural (always explained away), and a sexual threat to a vulnerable young woman.

Following this rather sensational opening section, *Emmeline* has only a few gothic passages. With the exception of the heroine's enjoyment of watching a "magnificent and sublime scene" (313) as she observes a storm at sea, while a mysterious figure lurks about Godolphin's home (who proves to be Fitz-Edward, Adelina's seducer, in search of his lover), the novel returns to the conflict and interaction of families and to a resolution of the love relationship.

*Ethelinde* begins with Grasmere Abbey as the backdrop for the action, and Smith's description establishes it as a sister structure to Mowbray Castle, though less ruinous. The author sets no gothic scenes there.

After her father's death, however, Ethelinde visits Abersley, his family home. There she wanders into a room that has "received no alteration for many years" and finds a picture of her father. Smith sets the scene with "cedar wainscoting and rich arras" and "long old fashioned windows in ponderous frames, [which] admitted the twilight reluctantly," all of which create "that gloom and obscurity which inspired and encouraged the most melancholy thoughts." In the throes of the mood that this setting inspires, Ethelinde looks out the window to the family vault, where her father lies, and "invoked his tender and benign spirit to soothe and console her." When a gust of wind rushes through and opens the door to the room, Ethelinde cries, "He hears me . . . surely he hears me, and comes from his grave to meet me!" and then imagines she sees his ghostly figure beckoning her to follow him (V, 209–212). She faints but later realizes that a flash of lightning from the storm outside had created her state. Reason triumphs.

*Celestina* offers many more gothic thrills than Smith's first two novels. Alvestone, Willoughby's estate, is appropriately picturesque, but the author stages no gothic scenes there. The storm at sea in the Hebrides, however, during which Mr. Elphinstone perishes, seems crafted to inspire sublime horror for the susceptible reader, and the description of the ruined chapel where Elphinstone is buried is even more evocative: "The moon, darting for a moment through the ruined stone work of the dismantled window, shewed them a broken table that had once been the altar, on which some pieces of the gothic ornaments of the chapel, and several human bones, were scattered, and near it, the newly turned up earth, on which a few stones were loosely piled, discovered the grave of poor Elphinstone." Celestina then leaves Mrs. Elphinstone to her mourning and "seating herself on one of the ruined monuments near its entrance, yielded to all the gloomy thoughts which the place, the hour, and the occasion inspired," thinking of her feelings should Willoughby die (II, 165–166). The setting reflects the sort of mild horror that readers of Smith's day found agreeable and offers yet another example of correspondence between setting and mood.

Smith intensifies the novel's gothic thrills with the story of Celestina's parents. She sets the scene in the Pyrenees with a long description of sublime mountain scenery and one of her several homages to the rocks of Meillerie when Willoughby recalls the lines, "[I]t seemed that this desart [sic] spot was designed as an asylum for two lovers, who had escaped the general wreck of nature" (III, 184). He then gets lost and finally finds Le Laurier, the peasant who eventually guides him to the

Chevalier de Bellegarde. The latter gives Willoughby his life story, a digression replete with the sensational details readers had begun to crave by 1791, but appropriately distanced from England. The tale has many of the ingredients of the gothic, including the description of the mountain scenery and the castle, imprisonment in dungeons, a tyrannical father, and a sexual threat to Bellegarde's sister (Celestina's mother) from a monk who has ingratiated himself with the old count, Bellegarde's father.

Smith no doubt sets this sensational story in France because readers would object to the sexual suggestiveness of the assignations between the lovers at the "old pavilion" and their secret marriages. Smith had set a similarly passionate tale in France at the end of *Emmeline,* and she surely judged that her readers were not ready for such incidents and such conduct to be acted out on English soil. Mullan cites Richardson's grouping of characters into "Men," "Women," and "Italians" at the beginning of *Sir Charles Grandison* as indicative of a sort of "moral geography" recognized by British readers. ". . . Italy was, as it was to be for Ann Radcliffe, 'the other'. Italy is a convenient place of projection—a location for the excesses of feeling."[35] Similarly, Smith uses France as the setting for such excesses.

Smith, then, was the first British novelist to exploit the gothic setting in the sentimental novel. It would remain for Ann Radcliffe to develop that setting more fully and to create the centerpiece of the gothic reading experience, the hero-villain, the darkly sensual man whose glittering eye and sexual threat titillated readers from the 1790s to the present. Charlotte Smith's best fiction, however, falls within the definition of novel as presented by Reeve and Scott, works that, as Reeve describes them, "deceive us into a persuasion . . . that all is real," as opposed to romance. But she brought a new focus and purpose to the sentimental gothic: She uses it in her later fiction as the framework for presenting political issues.

## "LET US NOT . . . BE THE SLAVES OF PASSION": *CONCORDIA DISCORS* IN CHARLOTTE SMITH'S EARLY FICTION

Smith's works seem well suited, then, to create a response in readers attuned to the language of sentiment. She accepted and refined conventions from the tradition of sentimental fiction, and in the years following the publication of these first three novels, other writers imitated her work. Yet the moral norm emphasizes restraint of feeling. Embedded in each of these three novels is a moral imperative that demands that reason and passion be balanced. Smith repeats the words "reason" and "passion," or cognates, as a key to reader response in much the same way that she repeats the words "nature" and "art."

The term *concordia discors,* Latin for "harmonious discord" or "harmony in disagreement," describes a condition usually assumed by 18th-century thinkers and only occasionally described in detail. The concept, which posits a harmony that can result only from the war of opposites, first appears in classical literature, as well as in the works of English Renaissance writers such as Spenser and Shakespeare. But in Epistle Two of his *Essay on Man,* Alexander Pope defines the *concordia discors* most clearly as it appears in the 18th century and as it came to be applied in sentimental fiction, asserting that passions, including ruling passions, effectively motivate us, while reason restrains these passions.[36]

Charlotte Smith uses the conflict between reason and passion as a structural element for these early novels. Her heroines are models of conduct, always functioning as the moral norm in her works; and the author repeatedly demonstrates that they control their passion with reason. Also, the conflict of reason and passion establishes plot complication.

Each novel portrays a Werther character, one who, in the words of Smith's poem on this figure so endlessly fascinating to the 18th-century reader, is "Passion's helpless slave. . . , scorning Reason's mild and sober light" ("Supposed to be written by Werter," Curran 26–27). Not all of these characters exactly match Goethe's Werther in his community of taste with the object of his obsession, but the similarities seem too close to be accidental. Each has passions that are out of control, and through both the characters' actions and words, Smith demonstrates the error of their conduct.

Delamere is the first and most passionate of her Werther figures. He cannot govern his feelings, and when Emmeline refuses to see him at one point, "He stamped about the room, dashed his head against the wainscot, and seizing Mrs. Watkins by the arm, swore, with the most frightful vehemence, that he would see Miss Mowbray though death were in the way" (64). The "wildness of ungovernable passion" shakes even his father's resolve against the marriage to Emmeline. Later, when Delamere suspects that Emmeline is having an affair with Fitz-Edward, "He could not conquer, he could not even mitigate the tumultuous anguish which had seized him; but seemed rather to call to his remembrance all that might justify it's [sic] excess" (257). Smith makes the Werther parallel clear when, on one occasion with Emmeline and Delamere together, the young woman idly picks up a book, discovers it is a copy of the second volume of "The Sorrows of Werter," then lays it down and with a smile says, "That will not do for me to-night" (170), to which Delamere replies: "O, I have read it—and if *you* have, Emmeline, you might have learned the danger of trifling with violent and incurable passions. . . . Without you, my life is no longer valuable—if indeed it be supportable; and should I ever be in the situation this melancholy tale describes, how do I know that my reason would be strong enough to preserve me from equal rashness. Beware, Miss Mowbray—beware of the consequence of finding an Albert [Charlotte's husband in *Werther*] at Woodfield" (170).

Sir Walter Scott observes that "while his may be a boarding school objection," he and other readers of his time were disappointed that Emmeline would drop a first attachment and break her engagement "with the fiery, high-spirited, but noble and generous Delamere, to attach herself to a certain Mr. Godolphin, of whose merits we are indeed told much, but in whom we do not feel half so much interested as in poor Delamere." Scott's recollection speaks volumes of the power the Werther character held for readers.[37]

In *Ethelinde,* Sir Edward Newenden is an interesting twist on this character type, a reversal of the role. Smith makes him a married man passionately but hopelessly attracted to an unmarried woman, the opposite of the Werther-Lotte relationship. Newenden is a man of honor who knows his error but cannot correct it, and the author cues the reader, repeating the opposites of the *concordia discors*. When Ethelinde insists on leaving his home after he establishes a separation from his wife, Sir Edward "felt the reason of all she urged; but his heart revolted" (III, 261). He constantly must "call himself anew to an account for his unhappy and criminal passion" (II, 63), but at another point in the novel, "He no longer struggled to conquer a passion with which he had so long thought it a point of honor to contend. . . . His heart rebelled against his reason and his principles" (III, 247–248). Smith also underscores Sir Edward's powerful feelings in confrontations with Lady Newenden, contrasting her lack of sensibility and his failure to check his own. He indulges in lengthy fits of weeping, and she displays cold control. Moreover, like Delamere in *Emmeline,* he fights a duel, the ultimate result of excessive passion in Smith's novels and in sentimental fiction, wounding Lord Danesforte, his wife's lover.

The discord between reason and passion seems less prominent in *Celestina,* at least as regards repetition of the terms for character identification. But Montague Thorold, Celestina's failed suitor, shows all the

qualities of a Werther,[38] including a community of taste with the heroine. He falls in love with Celestina and follows her everywhere. Smith
contrasts the young man with Vavasour, Willoughby's friend, who also
becomes a suitor when he believes the latter can no longer think of marrying Celestina. But Vavasour is a self-proclaimed epicurean. Clearly, he
lacks true feelings. In sentimental fiction, virtue and sensibility are part
of a package, and since Vavasour lacks one, he must lack both. Thus,
when he follows Celestina to the Hebrides (as does Thorold) after
Elphinstone's death, his inability "to check for one moment his vivacity
in complement to their [Mrs. Elphinstone's and Celestina's] despon-
dence, seemed to Celestina such a want of sensibility, as gave her a very
indifferent opinion of his heart" (II, 231). This novel gives us yet
another duel by a Werther figure when Vavasour wounds Thorold.

The successful suitors in each novel better regulate the balance
between reason and passion than do the Werther figures, but it is the
heroines' task to show restraint and prevail on their lovers to do the
same. Emmeline is the model of reason and proper conduct. All of
Delamere's pleadings and Bellozane's Gallic ardor fail to inspire a
response, and she tries patiently to reason with each of them. To make
her heroes attractive to the reader of the day, though, Smith must give
them powerful feelings too. Thus, when Godolphin learns that Adelina,
his sister, has borne Fitz-Edward's child out of wedlock, he seems determined to fight the man: "educated with a high sense of honour himself .
. . all his passions were roused and awakened by the injury it had sus-
tained from Fitz-Edward." He has, we are told, "in a great excess all
those keen feelings, which fill a heart of extreme sensibility." Mrs.
Stafford then "represented to him, with all the force of reason" the folly
of risking his own life or killing Fitz-Edward. When Adelina, whom the
excess of passion has driven mad, begs most piteously for his restraint,
he reluctantly agrees not to issue the challenge, and Emmeline exclaims,
"Thank God . . . that you at last hear reason!" (275–282).[39] Godolphin,
unlike Delamere, can control his passion through reason. Moreover, he
waits patiently for Emmeline to settle her business with her uncle before
they make known their attachment, partly because Emmeline knows
that Delamere would challenge her lover.

Ethelinde and Montgomery have more difficulty in controlling their
feelings. At the start of the novel, young Montgomery is inexperienced
in love, and Mrs. Montgomery tells Ethelinde that "his passions, naturally too warm and violent, have here no objects likely to render them
too powerful for his reason" (I, 183–184). The words "reason" and

"passion" occur repeatedly in their dialogue. Montgomery knows that he should seek to make his fortune so that he and Ethelinde can marry without fearing indigence. Yet he equivocates: "such a cottage as this [his mother's] would shelter us," he rationalizes, "and by the time it was proper to make his appearance the next morning, he had persuaded himself it was consistent with his reason and duty . . . to make another attempt to shake the resolution of Ethelinde" (IV, 197). Ethelinde has less restraint than Emmeline, but she pleads with him: "Let us not, my dear friend, be the slaves of passion but exert our reason and prudence to save us from future repentance" (IV, 271). Moreover, in the scene in which Ethelinde invokes her father's spirit, Smith tells us, "Her reason a moment checked the idea; but fancy, so long busied in restoring his countenance, his voice, and gesture, had already the superiority" (V, 211–212). Ultimately, however, reason prevails.

The same war of reason and passion underlies the character relationships in *Celestina*. Willoughby has promised his mother that he will marry his cousin, Lord Castlenorth's daughter, to restore his fortune, but as he tells Celestina, he adores her "with a passion too strong for my reason" (I, 67) and plans to marry her and live a relatively simple life. Celestina agrees, though at first, "her reason, her genuine affection for him, told her that to indulge this tenderness was injurious to him" (I, 68). Willoughby's struggle continues, even when he suspects that Celestina may be his half sister. He frequently falls ill due to "the anxiety of a mind at war with itself" (III, 162) and because he has "long been so harassed between his love and his interest, his honour and his reluctance" (III, 82). Celestina, though, controls her feeling with reason more effectively. When she receives a disappointing letter from Willoughby, "[h]er reason, too, came to her assistance, and strengthened the resolution she had formed" (II, 217).

The passion that Montgomery, Willoughby, and Delamere express for their ladies no doubt adds to the romantic melodrama of the works in which they appear. Moreover, the reasoned restraint of the heroines underscores the didactic core of the novels. Indeed, Smith's emphasis on balance seems characteristic of the works of an 18th-century writer. But it would change in her novels following *Celestina*. While the characters in her later fiction still value their reason, it leads them to a perception of the tyranny of custom. Now they are willing to follow their hearts, even to flaunt the dictates of society. In her later novels, then, Smith gives her heroes and heroines a radical sensibility that leads them to a form of romantic individualism.

## Chapter Four

# The French Revolution in Charlotte Smith's Works: *Desmond, The Emigrants,* and *The Banished Man*

Bliss was it in that dawn to be alive,
But to be young was very Heaven![1]

So wrote Wordsworth of the early days of the French Revolution after he arrived in Paris in 1791, the times that Charlotte Smith describes in volume 3 of *Celestina*. While he is in France, Willoughby mentions "hearing, and *but* hearing, at a distance, the tumults, with which a noble struggle for freedom at this time (the summer of 1789) agitated the capital, and many of the great towns of France" (III, 181). Later, in the digression that tells his life, Bellegarde praises the "glorious flame of liberty"—the fall of the Bastille—which released him from the prison where he was held by his father's lettre de cachet, one of the hated tools of the French monarchy.[2] Bellegarde's story demonstrates what could happen to a "victim of despotism" during the ancien régime, and the old count is the pattern aristocrat to English liberals. A few years later, the language of this passage would have attracted the wrath of the *Anti-Jacobin* and other reactionary voices; but in 1791, the year *Celestina* was published, the reviewers took no notice. Most British liberals believed the French were simply achieving the freedoms that the British had long enjoyed, freedoms that the youthful Wordsworth had seen as "a gift that rather was come late than soon."[3]

But Smith would go on to take the novel to a level of political discourse that this developing genre had not seen. It is a curious fact that she was nearly the only British novelist to address the contemporary events in France that would leave Europe in flames for 20 years and forever change the course of history.[4] In *Desmond,* published in 1792, Smith's hero articulates a moderate republican position. *The Emigrants*

(1793), a long, meditative poem, reflects disappointment with the violence that had marred the revolution and asks for tolerance toward French refugees; but the author's republican views remain unchanged. Finally, *The Banished Man* (1794), while one of Smith's most self-indulgent and least successful works when judged as art, remains an interesting insight into British liberal thought after the French experiment in democracy resulted in anarchy and terror. In the latter two works, Smith condemns the leadership of the revolution but upholds the original ideals.

*Desmond* stands as a turning point in Smith's career. All of her novels following 1792 contain political commentary and criticism of social injustice. Gone is the focus on proper female conduct and domestic problems as central issues. Smith would continue, however, to use the techniques she had established in her first three novels. Her characters fit the nature/art dichotomy, and she uses polarities of thought similar to the *concordia discors* concept. She decorates the novels with her poetry, and she continues to use landscape description to establish scenes or reflect the mood of characters. Although she makes her distaste for gothic paraphernalia all too apparent in asides and prefaces, she felt she had to include the sort of gothic thrills that she had used in her early novels and that Ann Radcliffe and others popularized. But in all of her novels after 1791, Smith adapts the conventions of fiction to present social and political issues from a republican perspective. Although *The Banished Man* and later works show her disappointment with the revolution in France, her republican principles remained intact throughout her life. Her prefaces and occasional textual comments suggest that she used her novels to bring otherwise unavailable political issues (as well as information ranging from history to botany) to her largely female audience. Her political novels evidence a different sort of didacticism from that of her early works.

## Desmond, a novel

*Desmond* is a historical novel, of sorts. The dates of the letters that compose this epistolary work track the recent history of the early 1790s. The first letter is dated June 9, 1790, and the final one February 6, 1792. The author's Preface carries the date June 20, 1792. Thus, the novel's action covers the period following the fall of the Bastille on June 14, 1789, through the early days of reform, the bringing of the royal family and the National Assembly to Paris, the nationalization of the church, the initial war with Prussia and Austria, the attempt of Louis XVI and his family to escape, and the development of the French constitution.

*Desmond* articulates, then, the early euphoria that British liberals felt at the success of the revolution. Ironically, if Smith sent her final copy to the publisher in June, the book must have arrived in bookstores at nearly the same time the Parisian mob massacred approximately 1,200 prisoners on September 2–6, 1792, an event that dismayed many of those in England friendly to the revolution. But the positive reviews, which began appearing in September, show that the reaction against the revolution had not set in. A reviewer for *The Critical Review,* for instance, notes the lack of balance in Smith's presentation of political ideas but concedes that "history may confirm the sentiment and confute ours."[5]

Smith satirizes both the smug conservatism of the British ruling classes and the reactionary ire of the French aristocracy. Against these positions, she juxtaposes the favored liberal views of Desmond, her hero. He is another of her Werther characters, a man dominated by passion. In the context of the novel, Smith balances Desmond's republican ideas against the comments of Bethel, the young man's chief correspondent, who provides something like a center point. But *Desmond* differs from Smith's other novels in that the hero's actions as a Werther character prove to be the norm, despite the fact that his views (or at least his rhetoric) are somewhat more liberal than Bethel's.

Thus, on one level *Desmond* is a novel of ideas, with various speakers contributing to the interplay of political dialogue. On another level, the novel offers much of the appeal of Smith's earlier works. Smith blends the discussion of politics with the story of Desmond's hopeless love and gothic melodrama to keep her readers' interest. She enlists sympathy for republican ideas by putting them in the mouth of conventional characters from the sentimental tradition.

The plot grows from Lionel Desmond's attachment to Geraldine Verney. Desmond is a well-to-do young British landowner who has just come into his patrimony. In this epistolary novel, the hero addresses most of his letters to Erasmus Bethel, his friend and mentor. Geraldine is another autobiographical character: a woman whose family pressed her into marriage with a feckless husband. As the story progresses, Desmond tries to help Waverly, Geraldine's brother, a hopelessly scatterbrained and constitutionally indecisive young man, by taking him to France. There Desmond fights a duel to save Waverly from a disastrous marriage and is wounded. Desmond later lives incognito near Geraldine in England, to protect her, and then goes to France when Mr. Verney tries to sell his wife to the unscrupulous Duc de Romagnecourt, a corrupt French aristocrat who has fleeced Verney in high-stakes gambling. Desmond arrives in time to save Geraldine in a blood-and-thunder sequence with enough gothic thrills for the most avid devotee, and Mr. Verney is conveniently killed, leaving Desmond free to wed his Geraldine.

The love story is quite different from Smith's earlier novels of didactic sensibility. Desmond is in love with a married woman, and he consistently defends his feelings against Bethel's criticism. Moreover, while in France, he has an affair with Josephine Boisbelle, the sister of his friend Montfleuri, a French aristocrat with republican sentiments. Like Geraldine, Josephine is a married woman, separated from her émigré husband. She nurses Desmond after his duel and bears his child.

Smith's comments in the preface show her concern as to how her readers might respond to Desmond's passion for a married woman: "In sending into the world a work so unlike those of my former writings . . . I feel some degree of the apprehension which an Author is sensible of on a first publication."[6] She goes on to defend her hero's behavior: "No delineation of character appears to me more interesting, than that of a man capable of such a passion so generous and disinterested as to seek only the good of its object; nor any story more moral, than one that represents the existence of an affection so regulated" (ii). But she does not mention the affair with Josephine Boisbelle. Were there no political discussions in the work, the love story would seem revolutionary enough for British fiction of the 1790s.

The letters from Desmond describing his political discussions provide the central focus of the novel. In the preface, Smith acknowledges that the political content of the work may offend some and attributes the ideas she presents to "conversations to which I have been a witness, in England, and France, during the last twelve months."[7] She also acknowledges her republican bias when she adds that "if those in favor of one party have evidently the advantage, it is not owing to my partial representation, but to the predominant power of truth and reason, which can neither be altered nor concealed" (ii–iii). Smith's assumption of reason's infallibility echoes the thinking of Thomas Holcroft, William Godwin, and other British republican writers.

The Desmond/Geraldine love story provides the structure of the novel and the opportunity for Desmond to move from place to place and report his conversations to Bethel. His friendship with Montfleuri leads to discussions with both liberals and conservatives on the continent, and he corresponds with the Frenchman when he returns to England. Through these letters, Smith gives her readers insights into both political issues and recent historical events. Despite a spirited defense in the Preface of a woman writing on politics, Smith must have felt insecure in undertaking such subjects. She puts most of the political discussion into the mouths of male characters. Apparently, she felt that while her audience might accept political novels from women writers, the actual ideas were best spoken by male characters.

## *DESMOND* AS HISTORICAL NOVEL

*Desmond* reflects the rush of events in France and the polarities of response those incidents inspired in Great Britain. The events of 1789 and 1790 caused little trepidation there. British liberals had long deplored conditions in France. Six years before the Bastille's fall, William Cowper wrote in *The Task,*

> There's not an English heart that would not leap
> To hear that ye [the Bastille] were fall'n at last; to know
> That ev'n our enemies, so oft employ'd
> In forging chains for us, themselves were free.[8]

Cobban quotes a letter from *The Analytical Review* published after the Bastille's fall that seems typical of the British reaction: "As men, and as Britons, we most sincerely wish them success; and pray that no dissentions amongst themselves may obscure the glorious prospect before them."[9]

Britain, though, had more radical thinkers. Dissenters believed that the Test Act kept them from full political participation, since those who could not subscribe to the "Thirty-Nine Articles" of the Anglican faith were not eligible for government service and there were ambiguities regarding freedom of worship. These individuals, and others concerned about the corruption all too common in government, wanted parliamentary reform. Many organized groups existed, and they became the meeting places for reformers. Agendas varied for those who attended, ranging from the more radical who wanted to do away with monarchy and aristocratic titles to moderates who focused on reforming the parliament.[10]

In 1789 the London Revolutionary Society, named for the Glorious Revolution of 1688, planned a commemoration of the anniversary of the revolution, and on November 4, Dr. Richard Price, a Unitarian minister, presented a sermon entitled "A Discourse on the Love of Our Country." Price celebrated the gains in toleration achieved in 1688 and praised the revolution in France. His conclusion was heady stuff for its time: "Tremble all ye oppressors of the world! . . . Restore to mankind their rights; and consent to the correction of abuses before they and you are destroyed together."[11]

The speech touched off a war of pamphlets. Edmund Burke responded with *Reflections on the Revolution in France,* published in November 1790, attacking Price specifically and republican principles in general. Mary Wollstonecraft replied within a month with *A Vindication of the Rights of Men,* a republican response to Burke's conservative broadside. But the event that polarized the debate was the publication in March 1791 of *The Rights of Man* by Thomas Paine (a second volume followed in 1792). Both Paine's and Wollstonecraft's titles come from the French General Assembly's *Declaration of the Rights of Man and the Citizen* on August 26, 1789.

Paine, an accomplished propagandist,[12] attacked Burke's defense of monarchy in a work with great popular appeal, by one estimate selling more than two million copies.[13] Paine's book won him friends in Paris, where he was elected to the General Assembly, taking his seat in 1792. But he was tried for sedition and found guilty in absentia in England, an ominous note for the British revolutionary movement. Dozens of books and pamphlets appeared siding with Paine or Burke (primarily the latter as repression deepened).

*Desmond* is a fascinating historical novel in its own right. But the work is also a shot fired in this war of pamphlets, books, and magazine articles, and it is the only novel to address the subject. Smith attacks Burke through the comments of Desmond and Bethel. Thus, the Burke/ Paine controversy is part of the recent history that the novel reports, as well as a central point in the discussion of ideas.

If, as was her usual practice in producing a novel, Smith spent approximately one year in composing *Desmond,* it is possible that she adapted the novel's discussions to events as she wrote it. Her surviving letters provide no evidence, so whether she might have responded to current events cannot be proved. Yet the novel is a unique amalgam of fiction, events of the day or very recent history, and political discussion.

One looks in vain for a specific reason for the sudden change in Smith's work. Her letters provide few clues. She does write to Joel Barlow on November 3, 1792, complementing him on his tracts "Advice to

the Privileged Orders" and "Letter to the National Convention" (Huntington). An American, Barlow was a well-known sympathizer with
republican France, and perhaps he is the sort of person to whom Smith's
sister, Catherine Anne Dorset, refers when she mentions that at
Brighthelmstone (Brighton) Smith "formed acquaintances with some of
the most violent advocates of the French Revolution, and unfortunately
caught the contagion, though in direct opposition to the principles she
had formerly professed."[14] William Hayley, her mentor, was of the
republican camp. And Smith's acquaintance with Helen Maria
Williams,[15] a friend of the revolution in its early stages whose *Letters from
France,* which presents an idealized view of revolutionary reforms, is the
only other solid evidence of connections with those sympathetic to the
revolution.

Smith borrowed from Williams's *Letters* in *Desmond* at several points.
The two writers certainly express similar ideological views on the French
Revolution, but there are more specific points of comparison. In 1785
Williams became friends with the wife of the Comte du Fosse, who had
married against his father's will, leading to persecution similar to that
which Smith's Montfleuri describes in *Desmond* and Bellegarde in
*Celestina.* Both of Smith's characters are aristocrats who support the revolution and utter the same sentiments as those that Williams reports
from du Fosse. Also, Smith's portrayal of happy peasants dancing on the
village green at Montfleuri's estate closely resembles passages in
Williams's letters describing a visit to du Fosse's estate. A more precise
bit of borrowing is the passage in *Desmond* in which the hero reports on
"the furious manner in which the carriages of the *noblesse* were driven
through the streets, where there are no accommodations for the foot
passenger—and where the proud and unfeeling possessors of those
splendid equipages . . . have been known to feel their rapid wheels
crushing a fellow creature . . ." (I, 108). The passage goes on at some
length, as does a similar report in the *Letters:* "One subject of complaint
among the aristocrates [sic] is, that, since the revolution, they are
obliged to drive through the streets with caution. . . ."[16]

Williams first went to France in July 1790 and returned to England
in September; later that fall she began publishing her *Letters.* Textual
parallels suggest that Smith read the first volumes of the *Letters,* and
perhaps her acquaintance with that work gave her ideas for the development of Montfleuri and Bellegarde as characters. Certainly Smith's and
Williams's political sentiments run parallel. Both admire the Comte de
Mirabeau,[17] express views consistent with republican moderates on par-

liamentary reform and war, and defend the general effectiveness of the British constitutional system, if improved.

## TWO PERSPECTIVES ON DINING WITH A FOOTMAN:
## POLITICAL DIALOGUE IN *DESMOND*

In her review of *Desmond* for *The Analytical Review,* Joseph Johnson's publication, Mary Wollstonecraft praises the novel's subordinate characters because they are "sketched with that peculiar dexterity which shoots folly as it flies."[18] Wollstonecraft alludes to the variety of individuals with whom Desmond reports dialogues, showing that the folly Smith describes comes from both British conservatives opposed to the revolution and aristocrats in France.

The dialogue begins when Desmond visits the Fairfax home while waiting for Waverly to arrive for their projected tour. General Wallingford decries the National Assembly as "a collection of dirty fellows" who have "abolished all titles and abolished the very name of nobility" (I, 60). Mrs. Fairfax's addition to the discussion is especially interesting because it reflects the kind of sensibility that Smith and other British liberals had come to reject: "Heavens! how my sympathizing heart bleeds, when I reflect on the numbers of amiable people of rank, compelled thus to the cruel necessity of resigning those ancient and honorable names which distinguished them from the vulgar herd!" (I, 63). In Smith's later poetry and novels, true sensibility brings empathy for victims of social injustice. Mrs. Fairfax is a false sentimentalist.

Desmond expresses satisfaction with the overthrow of the feudal system. But Mrs. Fairfax's response focuses squarely on the basic fears of the English middle class: "Good Heaven! I declare the very idea is excessively terrific; only suppose the English mob were to get such a notion, and in some odious riot, begin the same sort of thing here!" Desmond's response is that of British moderate republicans: "Perhaps there may never exist here the same *cause:* and, therefore, the *effect* will not follow" (I, 68–69). He goes on to demonstrate that the British and French aristocracy are quite different and that many of the abuses being corrected in France do not exist in England.

Smith does not allow the withers of British aristocracy to go unwrung, however. Lord Newminster is a republican's portrayal of the aristocrat, a rude, ignorant lout to whom the middle-class Fairfaxes compulsively genuflect. In one scene, he comes into the Fairfax home while the family is having tea, stretches out on a sofa with his boots on, and embraces a dog, cooing "Oh! thou dear bitchy—thou beautiful bitchy—damme, if I don't love thee better than my mother or my sisters." He then feeds the dog chocolate, crying, "[W]as it hungry? . . . was it hungry, a lovely dear?—I would rather all the old women in the country should fast for a month, than thou shouldest not have thy belly full" (I, 57). The double-edged satire hits not only the bad manners of the aristocrat but the toadying attitude of the middle-class Fairfaxes to a titled boor.

Desmond's letters report similar debates with conservatives in France. When a young abbé defends the old way, Montfleuri responds by saying that "the antiquity of an abuse is no reason for its continuance" (I, 123) and lectures the abbé on the *taille,* the *gabelle,* tax farming, lettres de cachet, and other abuses. Smith follows with a long passage that amounts to a history lecture from Montfleuri, tracing the events that led to the Revolution, replete with quite erudite allusions to Millot, Voltaire, Rousseau, and others. Part of Montfleuri's lecture involves references to the French king, Henry IV, a name that appears often in the writings of British republicans.[19] The founder of the Bourbon line stood as a symbol for liberals of the good king.

A visit to Montfleuri's uncle, the Count de Hautville, provides an opportunity for another lengthy conservative/liberal dialogue, capped by an interesting allusion to James Boswell's *Life of Samuel Johnson,* which had been published in 1791. Smith must have read the *Life* either immediately before beginning *Desmond* or during the book's composition. In a bit of historical irony, Johnson's attacks on republicans made him a target of opportunity in the pamphlet wars long after his death. Under the date of 1763, Boswell writes, "He [Johnson] again insisted on the duty of maintaining subordination of rank." He then quotes the Great Lexicographer as follows:

> Sir, there is one Mrs. Maccaulay in this town, a great republican. One day when I was at her house, I put on a very grave countenance, and said to her, "Madam, I am now become a convert to your way of thinking. I am convinced that all mankind are upon an equal footing; and to give you an unquestionable proof, Madam, that I am in earnest, here is a very sensible, civil, and well-behaved fellow-citizen, your footman; I desire that he may be allowed to sit down and dine with us." I thus, Sir, shewed her the absurdity of the leveling doctrine. . . .[20]

Mrs. Catherine Maccaulay remained "a great republican" from 1763 until her death, ironically in the year of the *Life's* publication. She wrote a number of histories of England (particularly of the Stuarts) from a republican perspective, and even wrote one of the many pamphlets by republicans attacking Burke's *Reflections.*

Smith alludes to Johnson's antirepublican sentiments during a conversation between Desmond and de Hautville, a typical aristocrat of the ancien régime. Desmond asks de Hautville "whether you really think, that a dealer in wine, or in wood, in sugar, or cloth, is not endued with the same faculties and feelings as the descendant of Charlemagne" (I, 236). In a passage that echoes Johnson's put-down of Mrs. Maccaulay, de Hautville asks why Desmond's footman is a servant if they are equals. Smith explains in a footnote that this question had previously been called unanswerable. But Desmond has a ready response:

> Because—though my footman is certainly so far upon an equality with me, as he is a man, and a free-man; there must be a distinction in local circumstances; though they neither render me noble, or him base—I happen to be born heir to considerable estates; it is his chance to be the son of a labourer, living on those estates.—I have occasion for his services, he has occasion for the money by which I purchase them: in this compact we are equal so far as we are free.—I, with my property, which is money, buy his property, which is time, so long as he is willing to sell it.—I hope and believe my footman feels himself to be my fellow-man; but I have not, therefore, any apprehension that instead of waiting behind my chair, he will sit down in the next.—He was born poor—but he is not angry that I am rich—so long as my riches are a benefit and not an oppression to him. He knows that he never can be in *my* situation, but he knows also that I can amend *his.* (I, 237–238)

The lecture goes on for almost two more pages, concluding with a quotation from Voltaire that supports the speaker's conclusions.

The word "compact" explains Smith's answer to the vexing questions that the existence of a servant class must have posed to British republicans. Smith no doubt agreed with the views of Rousseau, the author of *The Social Contract,* that the third essential duty of government is to fill citizens' wants. But not as a gift. In his *Discourse on Political Economy,* Rousseau writes: "This duty is not, we should feel, to fill the granaries of individuals and thereby to grant them a dispensation from labor, but to keep plenty so within their reach that labour is always necessary and never useless for its acquisition."[21]

The letter from de Hautville's estate is rich in ideological dialogue of the day. Desmond, for instance, carries on a discussion with a member of the high clergy, who execrates the General Assembly not only for its confiscation of church property and establishment of civil status for clergy but also for leveling the incomes of all ecclesiastics, an action that increased the income of local priests but greatly diminished that of the hierarchy. This long letter is another example of Smith's practice of matching recent historical events with fictional scenes, as it is dated September 30, 1790, about two months after the Assembly's reconstitution of the church.

## *DESMOND*, BURKE, AND PAINE

*Desmond* abounds with references to the controversy that arose over Burke's *Reflections*. The first appears in a letter dated January 8, 1991, two months after the publication of the book. After reading the *Reflections*, Desmond writes to Bethel, "I own I never expected to have seen an elaborate treatise in favor of despotism written by an Englishman, who has always been called one of the most steady, as he undoubtedly is one of the most able of those who were esteemed the friends of the people" (II, 62). The tone of disappointment may arise from Burke's opposition to the British war with the American colonists, an opposition shared by Smith and other republicans. But Desmond goes on to accurately, if hyperbolically, predict, "I foresee *that a thousand pens will leap from their standishes* (to parody a sublime sentence of his own) to answer such a book" (II, 63) In an April 10 letter, Desmond writes, again to Bethel, "Leave him then, my friend, to waste in swinish excess, sums, which he has earned by doing dirty work, at the expence of those who are now called the 'swinish multitude,' hundreds of whom might be fed by the superfluities of his luxurious table" (II, 114).

Smith attributes the phrase "swinish multitude" to Burke. She uses it satirically in a variety of contexts in *Desmond* and other works that follow, as did many republican writers. *Politics for the People: or A Salmagundi for Swine,* a republican magazine published in 1794 and 1795, used "swinish multitude" as something of a logo, publishing satirical poems and essays signed by "Old Hubert" or "a brother grunter." There were many other responses to "swinish multitude," including "The Rights of Swine: An Address to the Poor" (1794).[22] The satirical sallies on his unfortunately chosen phrase characterize Smith's attacks on Burke in the novel, which come up again and again in the dialogues between Desmond and Bethel. The attacks become more vitriolic as the novel progresses, with Desmond labeling the British statesman "the champion of the placeman—and the apologist of the pensioner" (III, 209).

References to Paine's *The Rights of Man* turn up on schedule from a historical perspective when Bethel sends Desmond a copy with a letter dated March 18, 1791, the month when the book appeared, noting that it is written by an "obscure individual, calling himself the subject of another government" and that it "could never have attracted so much attention, or have occasioned to the party whose principles it so decidedly attacks, such general alarm, if there had not been much sound sense in it, however bluntly delivered" (II, 92). Desmond answers on April 10, responding that he is "forcibly struck with truths, that either were not seen before, or were (by men, who did not wish to acknowledge them) carefully repressed" (II, 115–116). Desmond goes on to predict the attack that will be (and was) mounted against Paine and notes that "those who feel the force of his abilities, will vilify his private life, as if that was any thing to the purpose" (II, 117). Smith, who would have written the passage a few months after volume 1 of *The Rights of Man* appeared, thus acknowledges the ad hominem attacks on Paine's marital difficulties and his failure as an exciseman before immigration to America. In the same letter she predicts the government's sedition trial of Paine in 1792 by having an effete British lordling whom Desmond meets in France cry, "I wonder they don't punish the author, who, they say, is quite a low sort of fellow." He goes on to articulate, as does Mrs. Fairfax in England, the underlying fear of the privileged classes in England: "I hope our government will take care to silence such a demagogue, before he puts it into the heads of *les gens sans culotes* [sic], in England, to do as they have done in France, and even before he gets some of the ragged rogues hanged—*They* rights! poor devils, who have neither shirts nor breeches!" (II 121).

Part 2 of *The Rights of Man* appeared in February 1792, and Paine's attack on the monarchy provoked government reaction. Wilson and Ricketson report that "Prime Minister Pitt undertook a smear campaign against the character of Paine and initiated court action which eventually resulted in the libel conviction."[23] Thus, Smith's letters in *Desmond* dated April 1791, may be reactions to the events that continued into the spring and summer of 1792. It is worth noting that *Desmond* appeared at almost the same time that Paine left England for France, with a writ out for his arrest.

Other historical milestones come up in the letters between Bethel and Desmond. In a letter dated June 28, 1791, Bethel notes "the flight of the King of France and his family" being reported in England, and on July 2, Desmond responds, calling attention to the "magnanimity shown by the French people, on the re-entrance of the King into Paris: This will surely convince the world that the *bloody democracy* of Mr. Burke, is not a combination of the swinish multitude, for the purposes of anarchy, but the association of reasonable beings, who determine to be, and deserve to be, free" (III, 89). He goes on to compare the moderation of the French people in receiving the returned king with what might have happened had the monarchists succeeded in overthrowing the revolutionary government.

Also, war with Austria and Prussia impended in 1791, the date of the final letters in the novel. Desmond takes note of this possibility, deploring the actions of the "Northern Powers" but asserting that such actions will hardly "destroy the lovely tree that has thus taken vigorous growth in the finest country in the world." He goes on to regret that despite the pacific intentions of the French toward their neighbors, "its root must be manured with blood" (III, 207–208). The tree metaphor was rather common in France at the time. Doyle notes that in 1789, peasants planted liberty trees on land owned by aristocrats. "They called them *Mays,* from a much older tradition, festooned them with symbols of seigneurialism, and claimed that if they stood for a year and a day their lord's rights would be extinguished."[24]

Some of the most interesting letters reflect differences between Bethel and Desmond. Bethel's given name, Erasmus, alludes to the author of *The Praise of Folly,* a work that proposes a sane, balanced view of life, and the name suggests his political position. Bethel speaks with the authority of experience (Smith tells his history in a long letter at the outset) and reason. In a letter dated July 6, 1791, Bethel begins by suggesting that Desmond is "far gone . . . in what are called (but, I think, improperly called) the *new doctrines,* that you would contest this opinion with me," and goes on to praise the English constitution, which though flawed, is "undoubtedly the best in the world." He insists that "it may, I believe, be truly asserted, that in no age or country, has there existed a people, to whom general happiness has been more fairly distributed, than it is among the English of the present day." Moreover, he reads trouble on the horizon in France. He hopes the French will find a government superior to the British, but, "I am compelled to say," he writes, "that the proceedings of the National Assembly, since the death of Mirabeau, gives [sic] me too little reason to believe they will." He regrets the absence of "some great leading mind" to guide the revolution, because "[t]he *despotism* of superior ability is, after all, necessary; and it is the only despotism to which reasonable beings ought to submit" (III, 101–103). Bethel's republicanism is of the most moderate sort, and he lacks Desmond's passion.

Desmond soon answers, with a criticism of the English constitution. He quotes Boswell's *Life* on the subject of the British Parliament, in which "any question, however unreasonable or unjust, may be carried by a venal majority," and he goes on to answer Bethel's assertion that the British system brings general happiness more effectively than any other by saying that "this rather proves that their condition is very wretched, than that ours is perfectly happy." He deplores British attitudes toward slavery, and concludes with a statement that ends up not very far from that of Bethel and seems a good summation of British liberal—as opposed to radical—thought of the period:

> I think that our form of government is certainly the best—not that can be imagined—but that has ever been experienced; and, while we are sure that practice is in its favor, it would be most absurd to dream of destroying it on theory.—If I had a very good house that had some inconveniences about it, I should not desire to pull it down, but I certainly should send for an architect. . . . But I should be very much startled if my architect was to say, "Sir, I dare not touch your house—If I let in more light, if I take down those partitions, and make the other changes you desire, I am very much afraid that the great timbers will give way, and the *party-walls* crush you beneath their ruins" (III, 165\*–166\*).[25]

Neither Bethel nor Desmond articulates a specific political agenda, and their comments about change differ more in Desmond's impassioned rhetoric than in substance. Both support moderate reform, and the dialogue between them provides a springboard for Smith's presentation of republican ideas.

## *DESMOND* AND FICTIONAL CONVENTIONS

Despite the ideological tone of *Desmond,* Smith relies on the fictional conventions that she had both inherited and created in her earlier novels. Moreover, she juxtaposes opposites as she does in those works, cues the reader with the repetition of words and the evocative language of the sentimental novel, and includes a bit of gothic melodrama at the conclusion.

In volume 3 Desmond follows Geraldine to France, where she has been lured by her husband. In scenes that would do justice to Radcliffe at her best, Desmond rescues her from banditti who glower "with the

terrific look which Salvator gives to his assassins" (III, 274–275).[26] The
scenes abound with ruined castles, hollow groans, and all the paraphernalia of the developing gothic mode—considerably intensified from
Smith's earlier novels.

Smith's characters are cut from the cloth of the sentimental-gothic
tradition and the nature/art dichotomy. Geraldine admires Desmond
because he "has so much taste, and so much genuine enthusiasm" (II,
217). Despite his revolutionary fervor, Desmond can admire a picturesque ruin on Montfleuri's estate, even though it reflects the ancient
tyranny of the church, commenting to Bethel, "I, who love, you know,
every thing ancient, unless it be ancient prejudices, have entreated my
friend to preserve this structure in its present state—than which, nothing can be more picturesque" (I, 171). Both Geraldine and Desmond
display the alienation of the hero and heroine of sensibility. Desmond,
for instance, confesses in one of his letters to being "a strange, eccentrick
being, and not much like any other" (II, 233). Like the conventional
sentimental characters in so many other novels, both Geraldine and
Desmond eschew the materialist lifestyle, and both respond to the needs
of the unfortunate. Geraldine, for instance, writes to her sister that the
"only pleasure I have lost in losing high affluence, is that of having the
power to befriend the unhappy, to whom I can now give only my tears"
(II, 197). The properly disposed reader would respond to Desmond and
Geraldine as fellow sentimentalists.

In his powerful feelings, at least, Desmond is a lineal descendant of
Delamere and Sir Edward Newenden, an "English Werter" (III, 60), as
his friend Bethel calls him. In the *concordia discors* of reason and feeling,
Desmond fails to control his passion. When he follows Geraldine into
the countryside, he writes to Bethel that "much eloquence will be necessary to supply the defect of *reason,* which I know you will think my conduct betrays" (II, 233–234). But, as he later writes, "I find, that seven-
and-twenty is not the age of reason, or, at least, where the heart is so
deeply concerned" (II, 235–236). When Smith has him quote Saint-
Preux from *La Nouvelle Héloïse,* Desmond's identification with passion is
complete: " 'There are,' says St. Preux, in those enchanting letters of the
incomparable Rousseau, 'but two divisions of the world, that where
Julie is, and that where she is not' " (II, 240). He goes on to compare his
feelings for Geraldine to these sentiments.

Other characters reflect an excess of passion over reason. Perhaps
Smith panders to a British audience's cultural assumptions about the

French or perhaps she shares them. But her Gallic characters, Josephine Boisbelle and her brother Montfleuri, are at the mercy of their passions. Although Josephine writes no letters, the novel suggests that she initiated the affair with Desmond. And while Montfleuri may follow sweet reason in his politics, his letters after meeting Fanny Waverly, Geraldine's sister, demonstrate a stereotypical Gallic impetuosity.[27]

Smith counterpoises Desmond's apparent excess of passion with Geraldine (who remains a dutiful wife despite her obvious attachment to Desmond) and Bethel. The latter expostulates with Desmond throughout the novel over his conduct, and the word "reason" recurs consistently in his letters, identifying his position for the reader. He advises Desmond, for instance, to "sit down for some months, at least, quietly in Kent, where I hope you will recover your reason" (III, 85). Desmond's powerful feelings contrast with what the younger man calls Bethel's "cold and calm philosophy" (I, 161). Later, when the Duc de Romagnecourt arrives in England, insisting that Geraldine accompany him to France, she fears that Desmond will challenge the Frenchman. She reasons that if she persists in refusal, Romagnecourt will go away. But, she writes to her sister, "nor would Desmond be persuaded that I ought patiently to endure this transient evil—I saw consequences attending *his* applying to Monsieur de Romagnecourt, of which I could not bear the idea without terror" (III, 19). The fiery Desmond has already fought one duel at this point and seems ready for another.

Smith's presentation of a Werther figure who becomes the moral norm of the work reflects the dawning of a romantic sensibility in Great Britain and on the continent. Schama writes:

> The drastic cultural alteration represented by this first hot eruption of the Romantic sensibility is of more than literary importance. It meant the creation of a spoken and written manner that would become the standard voice of the Revolution, shared by both its victims and its most implacable prosecutors. The speeches of Mirabeau and Robespierre as well as the letters of Desmoulins and Mme. Roland and the orchestrated festivals of the Republic broadcast appeals to the soul, to tender humanity, Truth, Virtue, Nature, and the idyll of family life.

Schama goes on to quote Mercier: " 'Reason with its insidious language can paint the most equivocal enterprise in captivating colors but the virtuous heart will never forget the interests of the humblest citizen. Let us place the virtuous statesman before the clever politician.' "[28] Charlotte

Smith's novels never display the distrust of reason that characterizes French radical thought, but in *Desmond* and the novels that follow, the feelings become an ever more important guide to her virtuous characters.

## "The Sacred Flame of Liberty Becomes a Raging Fire": *The Emigrants*

Since the Preface to *Desmond* carries a date of June 1792, we can assume that the novel could not have reached bookstore's or circulating libraries until at least late summer. By then the swirl of events in France had taken a new direction. In early September, the Parisian mob killed approximately half of the 2,600 people held in nine prisons, nearly all of the deaths outright murders or executions after proceedings in kangaroo courts.[29] The Jacobin clubs—revolutionary groups that met across France—insisted on the removal of the king and the establishment of a republic. And after the king's attempted escape, despite the attempts by moderates in the Assembly to justify keeping Louis on the throne, radicals demanded that he be brought to trial, a demand supported by the ever more powerful Parisian mob. The trial and subsequent execution of Louis XVI took place in December 1792 and January 1793. The *sans culottes* of Paris dominated the Legislative Assembly, sometimes by terror, and the nation veered toward chaos.

Long before the Reign of Terror, thousands fled the country. By 1791, half of the officer corps had left France. Many stayed on the French borders, and Koblenz was a center of émigré activity. A far larger number of aristocrats, terrified at the castle burnings in the countryside, and priests who refused to accept the civil constitution of the clergy (designated as "refractory") also left. The émigrés were a source of concern in the Assembly from the beginning, and on November 8, 1791, it passed a decree threatening them with a death penalty if they did not return by January 1. Many of these emigrants came to England, where they sometimes received a cool welcome.

English liberals were shocked at the turn of events. Charlotte Smith's poem *The Emigrants,* the Dedication for which is dated May 10, 1793, at Brighton, less than a year after the publication of *Desmond,* is a response to the changed situation.[30] It expresses the disappointment that British republicans must have felt at the chaos in France, attempts to enlist readers' sympathy and understanding for émigrés, and warns of what can happen if people are denied liberty too long.

Undoubtedly, Smith spoke with both the Chevalier de Faville, her son-in-law, and other exiles during the months before Augusta's marriage. Thus, *The Emigrants* is in part a plea for tolerance of those who fled the troubles in France, albeit a rather cool one. Smith demonstrates ambivalence in her feelings about those who fled France, however, and in some respects, the poem can be read as another entry in the pamphlet war.

In her dedication to William Cowper, Smith notes that in Britain, "those who are the victims of the Revolution, have not escaped the odium which the undistinguishing multitude annex to all the natives of a country where such horrors have been acted." The phrase "undistinguishing multitude" is surely an ironic allusion to Burke's "swinish multitude." She continues in a passage that reflects the uneasiness republicans must have felt in a time of building repression:

> ... by confounding the original cause with the wretched catastrophes that have followed its ill management; the attempts of public virtue, with the outrages that guilt and folly have committed in its disguise, the very name of Liberty has not only lost the charm it used to have in British ears, but many, who have written or spoken, in its defence, have been stigmatized as promoters of Anarchy, and enemies to the prosperity of their country.[31]

The author sets the poem on the beach at Brighton on "a morning in November, 1792." She establishes the meditative and elegiac mood by writing "Alas! how few the morning wakes to joy!/How many murmur at oblivious night/For leaving them so soon" (I, 8–10). As in *Elegiac Sonnets,* Smith establishes herself as narrator and generalizes about the woes of the world before introducing a group of émigrés.

> Behold, in witness of this mournful truth,
> A group approach me, whose dejected looks,
> Sad Heralds of distress! proclaim them Men
> Banish'd for ever and for conscience sake
> From their distracted Country, whence the name
> Of Freedom misapplied, and much abused
> By lawless Anarchy, has driven them far
> To Wander. . . . (I, 95–101)

She makes her republican sympathies and ambivalence about the French emigrants apparent when she notes that their sole hope is that German armies may scourge France, "that pleasant land" (I, 104), and continues, "Whate'er your errors, I lament your fate" (I, 107–108).

In the lines that follow, she introduces four clerical figures: a monk, a high churchman, an abbé, and a parish priest. Smith's republican principles do not permit her to describe them with much sympathy. The monk, "in a moping cloister long comsum'd" (I, 114), had thought that "To live on eleemosynary bread,/And to renounce God's works, would please that God" whom he worshiped (I, 118–119). Next she describes the high official of the church who "declines/The aid he needs not" (I, 125–126), while he looks back to what he had lost, services "Where, amid clouds of incense, he held forth/To kneeling crowds the imaginary bones/Of Saints suppos'd, in pearl and gold enchas'd" (I, 132–134). In France, he was believed "To hold the keys of Heaven, and to admit/Whom he thought good to share it" (I, 137–138). The higher clergy in France was almost exclusively composed of younger sons of the aristocracy.[32] Thus, this priest can afford to decline aid. She next describes the abbé (a priest who would serve in a well-to-do family) in only marginally sympathetic fashion. She then praises the selfless devotion of the parish priest, but notes that he "Taught to the bare-foot peasant, whose hard hands/Produced the nectar he could seldom taste,/Submission to the Lord for whom he toil'd" (I, 172–174). She goes on establish a tone of disapproval that he has left and some justification for the violence in France:

> . . . even such a Man
> Becomes an exile; staying not to try
> By temperate zeal to check his madd'ning flock,
> Who, at the novel sound of Liberty
> (Ah! most intoxicating sound to slaves!),
> Start to license[.] (I, 190–195)

Smith includes disclaimers in footnotes, noting that "nothing is farther from my thoughts, than to reflect invidiously on the Emigrant clergy," but the description of them strikes a decidedly negative tone.

She introduces two other émigrés, an aristocrat and his wife. The latter dreams of the glories of Versailles, where "Beauty gave charms to empire" (I, 226). Neither she nor her husband in their "high consciousness of noble blood" can see the true cause of the revolution, because "luxury wreathes with silk the iron bonds,/And hides the ugly rivets with her flowers" (I, 278–279). Smith asks of the aristocrat,

> . . . could *he* learn,
> That worth alone is true Nobility?
> And that *the peasant* who, "amid the sons
> Of Reason, Valour, Liberty, and Virtue,
> Displays distinguish'd merit, is a Noble
> Of Nature's own creation!" (I, 239–244)

In a footnote that reflects the growing mood of repression in Great Britain, Smith credits James Thomson for the quoted lines (from his adaptation of *Coriolanus*), noting that many now view the egalitarianism of Thompson's lines not as "commonplace declamation but sentiments of dangerous tendency."

Smith describes tax farmers (*fermiers generaux*) who have also become émigrés and ". . . unlamented sink,/And know that they deserve the woes they feel" (I, 294–295). She then addresses "Fortune's worthless favorites" in England, "Who feed on England's vitals" (I, 315–316), and in a passage whose tone foreshadows Thomas Carlyle's *The French Revolution: A History* and Charles Dickens's *A Tale of Two Cities* writes,

> Study a lesson that concerns ye much;
> And, trembling, learn, that if oppress'd too long,
> The raging multitude, to madness stung,
> Will turn on their oppressors; and, no more
> By sounding titles and parading forms
> Bound like tame victims, will redress themselves! (I, 332–337)

The phrase "raging multitude" in this passage refers once again to Burke's "swinish multitude" and warns that when the masses are treated as "swinish," they are likely to react as did the French.[33]

Book 2 opens on the South Downs in Sussex and is dated April 1793. The narrative reflects the changes that time had wrought. Smith again establishes the persona from *Elegiac Sonnets* as narrator, noting that, like her, the emigrants have known better times; and while she asks for tolerance and humanity in their treatment, most of Book 2, like Book 1, reflects the reaction of British republicanism to the chaos in France. She asks what promise the young year will bring those "who shrink from horrors such as War/Spreads o'er the affrighted world" (II, 45–46). Referring to French moderates, she observes that they see the "Temple, which they fondly hop'd/Reason would raise to Liberty, destroy'd (II, 48–49). She refers to "The headless corse of one, whose only crime/Was being born a Monarch" (II, 54–55) and to the war that had begun in February 1793. She hopes that when France revives, a free people will choose a king, speculating that such a ruler will be like the much-admired Henry IV.

But Smith still speaks for the original goals of the revolution, while the world "shrinks, amaz'd,/From Freedom's name, usurp'd and misapplied" (II, 80–81), and sees tyranny the greater evil. Before rejecting liberty, the reader, she writes, should consider the "black scroll, that tells of regal crimes/Committed to destroy her" (II, 88–90). Book 2 contains a lengthy description of the horror of war in France and closes with a meditation on the human condition:

> . . . my soul is pained
> By the variety of woes that Man
> For Man creates—his blessings often turn'd
> To plagues and curses: Saint-like Piety,
> Misled by Superstition, has destroy'd
> More than ambition; and the sacred flame
> Of liberty becomes a raging fire,
> When Licence and Confusion bid it blaze. (II, 412–419)

In this poem, Smith, as she observes in her Preface, imitates the blank verse style of Cowper's *The Task*. But *The Emigrants* resembles *Elegiac Sonnets* in its description of natural scenery, the general tone of melancholy, and the ubiquitous autobiographical persona. *The Emigrants* stands apart from early editions of *Elegiac Sonnets,* however, in its powerful political statement. While the poem's ostensible subject is the unfortunate plight of those who have left France, it offers at best a mixed sympathy. The aristocrat has failed to understand what caused his fall, as have the refractory clergy she describes. Much of the poem is an apology for the early phases of the Revolution, mixed with the disappointment of a British republican that it had failed, resulting in yet another tyranny.

## The Banished Man

Smith's seventh novel,[34] published in 1794, a year after *The Old Manor House* and within months after *The Wanderings of Warwick,* is one of her least satisfying from an artistic standpoint. It is her seventh novel in six years, and during the same time period she had published *The Emigrants* and three editions of *Elegiac Sonnets,* a remarkable production under any circumstances, but especially impressive considering the author's family obligations. In *The Banished Man,* however, she seems written out. The novel has a numbingly long autobiographical digression, in the form of Mrs. Denzil's story, and an aimless plot. Also, the text of the first edition is riddled with typographical errors.[35] The only real interest the work holds is the author's interpretation of events in France and the British reaction to them.

The story again reflects recent history, beginning in October 1792, in Austria near the French border at the castle of the Baron de Rosenheim. The baron is away, and the baroness and her daughter fearfully await the arrival of the French troops after their victory over the Prussian-Austrian army. Smith may refer to the battle at Valmy, in the passes of the Argonne, on September 20 of that year, although it did not precipitate the sort of wholesale retreat the novel describes. The baroness hears groans outside and eventually discovers the Chevalier d'Alonville and his father, the Viscount de Fayolles, both of whom had fought against the revolutionary forces. Fayolles is fatally wounded, and after his death, d'Alonville escorts the ladies to Koblenz, where they rejoin their husbands.

After d'Alonville returns to the castle and retrieves an important legal document for the baroness, he meets the Marquis de Touranges, an embittered aristocrat searching for his wife and mother and accompanied by the Abbé de St. Remi. He also meets Ellesmere, a young Englishman with whom he forms a friendship. After traveling about the German states, the group eventually goes to England with Ellesmere.

While d'Alonville ponders his future, he visits Ellesmere's family, meets Henrietta Denzil, another autobiographical character, and falls in love with her daughter, Angelina—a parallel, of course, to Augusta Smith. But d'Alonville feels he has to visit his brother in France, who has gone over to the revolutionary side and adopted the name du Fosse.[36] D'Alonville is caught, but his brother saves him, hoping to convert him to the revolution. D'Alonville steadily refuses and eventually, with his brother's help, escapes and returns to England, bringing jewelry given him by du Fosse for safekeeping. He briefly serves as a tutor to the children of Lord Abedore, fights a duel with a rake who has designs on Angelina, and marries his true love. With Mrs. Denzil, the couple then move to the continent, where they can live on d'Alonville's modest income from the sale of the jewelry given him by du Fosse, who was guillotined during the Terror.

Despite the work's artistic flaws, it has historical interest in its treatment of incidents of the time. Like *Desmond,* the novel describes recent events, the action beginning in 1792. The Abbé de St. Remi, for instance, tells of Madame de Touranges being held in prison during the September massacres, spattered with the blood of the slain, and released by the whim of the mob. Coblenz, where d'Alonville spends some time, was an important rallying point for emigrants, and the description of their community rings true. In volume 2, d'Alonville's captivity in Paris and his experience of seeing from his prison window 11 prisoners (three of them women) guillotined resembles contemporary accounts. The times were stormy in Paris in 1793, with the mob gaining ever greater control of the Assembly.

Smith introduces another historical allusion in Carlowitz, the Polish patriot whom d'Alonville and Ellesmere meet in Dresden. The revolutionary fervor of the times inspired a movement toward greater freedom in Poland, and the Poles were able to establish a constitutional monarchy in 1791. Later, Russia, Prussia, and Austria invaded. From the spring of 1794 until the fall, the Poles, led by Kosciusko, put up a determined resistance.[37] But the superior armies of the enemy and the nation's internal class divisions brought about eventual defeat, and the three powers partitioned Poland out of existence.

The Polish revolution would have been in progress as Smith wrote *The Banished Man.* Thus, the novel is yet another instance of the author's introduction of topical material. The peaceful revolution in Poland was inspired by the American and French experiments in democracy. However, we hear very little about Carlowitz's specific philosophy. He insists, "While I have any remains of strength I must use it, though my country exists no longer" (I, 163), but he addresses no issues. The Polish people and their friends abroad must have known that national extinction would be the result of defeat, and the novel surely reflects liberal sympathy for Polish Jacobinism during the days in 1794 when Poles fought for independence. Thus, the Carlowitz character instructs readers on current history.

In addition to using Carlowitz to introduce contemporary historical events, Smith juxtaposes his political liberalism against d'Alonville's hatred of republicanism and gives the Polish patriot the most stirring arguments. Even d'Alonville is nearly convinced, saying, "Had I been a Polonese, I might have thought and have acted as you have done. Had you been a native of France, you would have seen her monarchy exchanged for anarchy infinitely more destructive and more tyrannical, with the same abhorrence as I have done" (I, 164). And so it goes, when Carlowitz eventually makes his way to Paris seeking help for his country. D'Alonville meets him on his way back to England after his adventure in France, where the Pole was imprisoned for debt. Carlowitz tells of his disappointment:

> I thought I should have found in the new land of freedom, persons in whom I should meet congenial sentiments, and be admitted to serve the cause in which my whole soul was engaged; but how cruelly I was disappointed, you may imagine, when I tell you that I quitted almost immediately a place where I saw and heard actions and language more inimical to the cause of the real liberty and happiness of mankind, than could have proceeded from the united efforts of every despot that had ever insulted the patience of the world. (II, 163)

But Carlowitz remains a republican, and at the end of the novel, Smith describes him engaged in friendly discourse with d'Alonville: the Pole convinced that "worth alone is true nobility and true honor" and intent on returning home to "rouse the dormant or timid virtue of his country" (II, 172); d'Alonville remaining equally adamant against republican philosophy. Ellesmere, who had been wounded in battle on the continent, speaks the position of the author. He adheres "to that system of government as the best under which his own country had become the most flourishing in the world," but "he seldom thought the bold assertions of Carlowitz were carried too far" (II, 172–173). Through Ellesmere, Smith sums up the views of moderate British republicans in a letter to d'Alonville: "*You* think, that even in its first germination it [the French Revolution] threatened to become the monster we now see. . . . I still think, that originating from the acknowledged faults of your former government, the first design, aiming only at the correction of these faults, at a limited monarchy and a mixed government, was the most sublime and most worthy [purpose] of a great people" (II, 321).

Smith provides an amusing political polarity in Sir Maynard Ellesmere, who is a Tory of the old school, and Mr. Nodes, "whose money was obtained by making buttons." Much to the disgust of Sir Maynard, Nodes "impudently built a better house than Eddisbury Hall itself; placed a bust of Franklin in his vestibule; . . . had Ludlow among his books, quoted Milton to his companions, and drank to the rights of

man" (II, 151). He also has pictures of Richard Price and Joseph Priestly
in his house, two heroes of the British republican movement. Nodes
seems the sort of republican one might have met at meetings of the local
revolution society.

The conservative magazine *The British Critic,* which reviewed few
novels, took note of *The Banished Man,* welcoming Smith back into the
fold of correct politics. "We must not close this article," the reviewer
writes, "without congratulating the lovers of their King and the constitution, in the acquisition of an associate like Mrs. Charlotte Smith. . . .
She makes full atonement by the virtues of *The Banished Man,* for the
errors of *Desmond.*"[38] Both the fact that such a magazine would review
Smith's novel at all and the tone of respect for the author demonstrate
Smith's status, even though the political views expressed in her novels
had damaged her reputation.

Yet the reviewer surely responds only to the sentiments of the novel's
hero and ignores those of Carlowitz and Ellesmere. The political dialogues in *The Banished Man,* while not so effectively embedded in the
plot as are similar passages in *Desmond,* demonstrate no real difference in
the writer's politics. D'Alonville is the most charismatic character in the
work, and he expresses political principles appropriate for a French émigré. Smith balances liberal against reactionary views, however, and the
tone of the work favors the liberal.

Smith is never specific in her republicanism, and she creates no real
political agenda. Her ideas come from Rousseau, Voltaire, Diderot,
Montesquieu, and certainly John Locke. She valued liberty and hated
tyranny. *Desmond, The Emigrants,* and *The Banished Man* show sympathy
for the early ideals of the French Revolution and with the reform movement in England. Her heroes express the sentiments of moderate British
republicanism; and one suspects that while Charlotte Smith might not
care to dine with her footman (if she had had one), she would certainly
have defended him as a fellow citizen and member of the social compact.

## Chapter Five

# The Condition of England Question: *The Old Manor House, The Wanderings of Warwick, Marchmont,* "The Story of Henrietta," and *The Young Philosopher*

The 1790s saw the inception of a discussion on reform in Great Britain that continued through most of the 19th century as, in Thomas Carlyle's words, "the condition of England question." Republican groups such as the London Corresponding Society and the Constitutional Information Society called for reform. The agendas of these organizations and their members varied widely, but common demands included parliamentary reform, extension of the voting franchise, and peace. While most members of the reform societies sought only moderate changes, a small radical wing of the movement plotted the overthrow of the monarchy.[1]

As France descended into chaos in the months following the execution of Louis XVI in 1793, a strong reaction to the reform movement developed in Great Britain, spawning groups such as the Association for Preserving Liberty and Property against Republicans and Levelers. Reactionaries labeled those of republican persuasion Jacobin. And John Thelwall wrote that republicans accepted the name "Jacobin" not because they espoused the politics of terror but because "it is fixed upon us, as a stigma, by our enemies."[2]

A small group of British writers, most of them associated with liberal printer and publisher Joseph Johnson, expressed the ideology of British Jacobinism in their works during the 1790s. William Godwin, whose *Political Justice* (1793) had considerable influence among intellectuals, stood as nominal leader. Thomas Holcroft, Mary Wollstonecraft, Elizabeth Inchbald, Mary Hayes, and, during the time he was in England, Thomas Paine also articulated republican ideals in their works to one degree or another. William Blake and Robert Bage were peripherally associated with the Godwin circle.

Charlotte Smith's family situation and her distaste for London prevented her active participation with the members of this group, but she knew many of them or had read their work. She wrote a preface for Godwin's play *Antonio* (1800), and her letters refer to conversations with Elizabeth Inchbald. Also, she wrote homages to Wollstonecraft in the Preface of *The Young Philosopher.*

All of Smith's fiction is didactic. Her early novels teach lessons: duties of children and parents to one another, restraint of feeling, the necessity of education for children, and most of all, proper conduct for young women. But the lessons changed in the years following the publication of *Desmond* in 1792. Smith continues to employ sentimental and gothic fictional conventions to hold her readers' attention, and she balances the demands of the plot with the moral lesson more effectively than do most of the writers in the Godwin circle. Yet in each novel, she integrates political issues of the day—presented from a republican perspective— and history lessons to make her fiction an education for the reader as well as an entertainment.

## The Old Manor House

Most critics have accounted *The Old Manor House,* Smith's fourth novel, published in 1793, her best. Sir Walter Scott writes, "The *chef-d'oeuvre* of Mrs. Smith's works is, according to our recollection, the *Old Manor-House.*"[3] And in his history of the novel, Walter Allen comments, "It is odd that so good a novel should not have been reprinted since 1820."[4] In this novel, Smith integrates her political message in a coherent story with none of the lengthy digressions that mar her later works and with a minimum of weeping sentiment.

Temporarily freed from the day-to-day worries of family care and her legal problems, Smith wrote her best novel during an idyllic stay at Eartham, William Hayley's estate, in the late summer and fall of 1792. A letter to Joseph Cooper Walker dated February 20, 1793, suggests that it was published in March. "The Old Manor House is not yet published here," Smith writes, ". . . . but it will be probably quite the end of the month first" (Huntington). William Cowper was also there at the time and writes in a letter, "None writes more rapidly or more correctly—twenty pages in a morning, which I have often read and heard read at night, and found not a word to alter."[5]

The novel blends romantic melodrama, history, and political consciousness. The melodrama focuses on the relationship between Orlando Somerive, the younger son of a country gentleman of limited means, and Monimia,[6] the niece of the housekeeper in the home of Mrs. Rayland, Orlando's wealthy aunt. Mrs. Rayland, whose ruling passion is social status, disapproves of Orlando's father because he married beneath him. But she likes Orlando, and he has some prospects of inheriting her estate. The lovers meet surreptitiously in Monimia's room, and if Mrs. Rayland or Monimia's aunt should discover them, Orlando would lose hope of his inheritance. A comic sidebar concerns the elderly General Tracy, who visits Mr. Somerive, ostensibly to help Orlando get a commission in the army; his true agenda, however, is the seduction of Isabella, Orlando's pretty sister. His plan failing, Tracy proposes marriage. But Isabella elopes with Captain Warwick, the general's handsome nephew.

Smith introduces her political theme, and a lesson in recent history, when Orlando receives his commission and goes to America, permitting the author to comment on the injustice of the British action against the colonists and on the horrors of war. Orlando is wounded and captured by Indians but eventually escapes and returns to England, where he finds and marries Monimia. In a nicely plotted sequence, Orlando finds Mrs. Rayland dead and her estate in the hands of a Church of England bishop. He proceeds to break into the Rayland manor, finds a will that had been suppressed, and inherits the estate.

*The Old Manor House* is Smith's best work in terms of character development. The secondary characters are particularly effective. Cranky old Mrs. Rayland ranks as one the author's most original creations. Smith turns the old lady's fixation on the virtues of the aristocracy into excellent satire. The superannuated General Tracy, who has wooden teeth and requires at least two hours of cosmetic work before he can appear in the mornings, is a fine comic Lothario. Some of Smith's lower-class characters also come alive, providing comic relief to the political issues which dominate the novel. Smith demonstrates a deft hand in writing a variety of dialects. The lines she gives Betty, the pretty servant girl at the Rayland manor who feathers her nest with gifts from the enamored butler, is a good example of Smith's ability to write servant-class speech. The young woman's response to Orlando when he threatens her with Mrs. Lennard's displeasure is a jewel: "'As to *her* favour,' answered the girl pertly, 'I values it no more than that; and she had better keep her tongue within her teeth about me, I can tell her that; and as for places, there's more in the world. One should have a fine time on't, indeed, to pass all one's life in this here old dungeon, among rats, and ghosts, and old women.'" *The Old Manor House* has many amusing bit players, and Smith's ability to move from the dialogue of the sentimental hero and heroine to the speech of servants or of a young roué like Warwick suggest that she could easily have written the multiple voices of *What Is She.*

The novel has its faults. The clandestine meetings between Orlando and Monimia, which are long, numerous, and tearful, will tax the patience of a modern reader. Moreover, the work has some amusing factual errors. Smith, for instance, describes savannas and swamp plants along the St. Lawrence, which she says is as one and a half miles wide. But despite its faults, *The Old Manor House* remains her best-plotted novel and contains her most memorable characters.

## THE ANTIWAR THEME IN *THE OLD MANOR HOUSE*

As Smith wrote *The Old Manor House,* Louis XVI was still alive; and although moderate British republicans were distressed by the actions of the unruly mob in Paris, they retained hope that the revolution would yet succeed in achieving its early goals. However, there was much talk of war against France in Great Britain (finally declared in February 1793), and most republicans were ardently opposed.[7] Smith sets her story during the American Revolution to present her antiwar theme.

The conflict with the colonists had been unpopular in Great Britain. Edmund Burke had spoken and written against it. And even the ubiquitous Samuel Jackson Pratt took a stand in *Emma Courtney,* when old Courtney, who has lost his two children to the American war, cries "I am childless, sir Robert. . . . Behold what CIVIL WAR has done for me."[8] Thus, Smith could use the British response to a democratic revolution in America as a parallel to a war against a democratic revolution in France.

Like *Desmond,* then, *The Old Manor House* is a historical novel. Smith makes the time line clear (from September 1776 to September 1779). Despite the historical backdrop, though, *The Old Manor House* should be read in the context of events in 1792. Although Smith criticizes the British ministry's conflict with the colonists that had ended 10 years earlier, she uses the American war to plea for peace at a time when hostilities with France seemed inevitable.

In *The Old Manor House,* then, Smith suggests parallels between past wars and possible future ones with minimum authorial intrusion. She underscores the unpopularity of the American war in Great Britain. At one point Orlando ponders: "He had always been told, that the will of the people was the great resort in the British Government; and that no public measure of magnitude and importance could be decided upon, but by the agreement of the Three Estates. Yet the present war, carried on against a part of their own body, and in direct contradiction of the rights universally claimed, was not only pursued at a ruinous expence, but in absolute contradiction to the wishes of the people who were taxed to support it" (358). The American conflict was indeed unpopular in Britain, but in the contemporary context, Orlando's remark carries implied criticism of a possible war with France.

The novel emphasizes the inhumanity of war through descriptions of atrocities committed in America and the treatment of British soldiers. Soon after he arrives in the colonies, for instance, Orlando discovers that the British hire Indians to kill the colonists. One native named "the Bloody Captain" shows him 11 scalps, "some of them evidently those of women and children, others of very old, and consequently defenceless men; many of them fresh, which he said, with an air of triumph, he had taken from the enemies of the King of England within three weeks . . ." (360–361). But the Ministry treats its own soldiers little better. On the transport ship, the provisions are spoiled, and "nothing could equal the inconvenience to which his [Orlando's] soldiers were subjected, but that which the miserable negroes endure in their passage to slavery." In a footnote, Smith observes, "It has lately been alleged in defence of the Slave Trade, that Negroes on board Guineamen are allowed *almost* as much room as a Soldier on a Transport.—Excellent Reasoning" (345). Disease then breaks out because of overcrowding, killing numerous soldiers.

Smith connects the experience on the transport to her antiwar theme. Orlando perceives that war is good business for some, even if as many soldiers die of sickness as by the sword. Those who profit are "messieurs the contractors," for the most part members of Parliament, "who under other names enjoyed the profits of a war, which, disregarding the voices of the people in general, or even of their own constituents, they voted for pursuing" (349). Orlando's uncle, Mr. Woodford, a London merchant, is such a war profiteer. He has "a very lucrative contract, which he held to so much advantage as reconciled him to the necessity of relinquishing a seat in parliament for a Cornish borough, with which he obliged some of his powerful friends" (495). Smith had some knowledge of "lucrative contracts" to supply the military, as her husband had held one for a year before the Peace of Versailles in 1783.

Reform of Parliament was a basic demand of British republicans. Smith connects it to the antiwar movement through her description of Woodford. His "Cornish borough" is an example of the "rotten boroughs" that scandalized republicans.[9] After Woodford becomes wealthy from his contract, he is forced to give up being "*a representative of twenty or thirty electors, who had been paid for their suffrages at so much a head*" (495).

By 1793 the mood of reaction against events in France had set in, and Smith refers to the revolution only briefly in *The Old Manor House*. At one point, however, she includes a footnote referring to a bloody punitive British expedition against the colonists that had been described in the *Annual Register:* "Those who have so loudly exclaimed against a whole nation struggling for its freedom, on account of the events of the past summer (events terrible enough, God knows!) are entreated to recollect how much the exploits of this expedition . . . exceed anything that happened on the 10th of August, the 2d of September, or at any one period of the execrated Revolution in France—and own, that there are savages in all countries—even of our own" (360).

Smith's tone in referring to the revolution in France would change over the next two years, which would see the publication of both *The Emigrants* (six months after *The Old Manor House*) and *The Banished Man* (1794). A letter to Charles Burney (August 20, 1793, Beinecke) shows her disillusionment with the French experiment in democracy. She refers to "the horrid conduct of the men [in France] who dare to violate under the pretense of Republicanism every law of God and Man."[10] But her antiwar principles would remain constant, as did those of most British republicans. Doyle writes, "By the end of 1793 the corresponding societies, stunned into silence momentarily when their French inspiration became the enemy, had recovered their verve and were campaigning against the war in favour once more of radical parliamentary reform."[11]

As the mother of two sons in the British armed forces, however, Smith had reasons other than her political persuasions for opposing the war; thus, the irony of her reference in *The Old Manor House* to an old soldier who served his country in "fighting the battles of its politicians" and has "been deprived of his leg to preserve the balance of Europe" (461) is especially striking. Her own son Charles would be deprived of a leg at the siege of Dunkirk in September 1793.

## SATIRE OF CLASS CONSCIOUSNESS
## IN *THE OLD MANOR HOUSE*

Revolutionary thought from France caused many people in Britain to reassess their assumptions about class privilege. Smith's response to Johnson's put-down of Mrs. Maccaulay in *Desmond* (see pages 72–73 above) shows her republican views on this subject in 1792. *Emmeline,* written four years earlier, is a pageant of aristocratic high life. However much the heroine values simplicity, she moves within these circles, and Smith suggests no criticism of that, beyond the pride of Emmeline's uncle. Similarly, except for Lord Danesforte, the rake who seduces Lady Newenden, she portrays no disagreeable aristocrats in *Ethelinde.* But in *Celestina,* Lord Castlenorth's preoccupation with quartering[12] has become as much an object of satire as Baron Thunder-Ten-Tronckh's in *Candide,* and Old Bellegarde is the typical ancien régime tyrant.

Smith is even more egalitarian in her creation of characters for *The Old Manor House.* Monimia, for instance, is surely the most unusual of heroines in novels of the 1790s. Such characters are always of gentle birth, or discovered to be a child of the gentry in the last chapter. But Monimia has minimal connection to the gentry (her father was an attorney but an apparently unsuccessful one) and is little more than a servant in Mrs. Rayland's home. In one scene, Orlando enters his aunt's room and sees Monimia close beside a fire preparing medicine for the old lady in a saucepan, "her beautiful arms exposed to its scorching heat, while she was employed in watching the important preparation that was boiling" (165). After her marriage to Orlando, Monimia actually gets a job (unbeknownst to her husband) with a "very considerable linen warehouse" making articles of clothing on a piecework arrangement, and "by the neatness and punctuality of her performance, entered soon into constant employment" (494).[13]

Smith's satire of class prejudices contrasts with the respectful portrayals of aristocrats in *Emmeline* and *Ethelinde.* Mrs. Rayland assumes that General Tracy must be a heroic and virtuous person because of his aristocratic heritage, but he is really a geriatric Lovelace. Smith also refers to the death of Lord Carloraine, Mrs. Rayland's neighbor, and the inheritance of his estate by a grandson who is "completely the nobleman of the present day" and cares nothing about the land of his ancestors. He has "parliamentary interests . . . in a northern county," so he sells the estate to a wealthy young man whose father "had very lucrative contracts" during the Seven Years' War (35–36). Smith shows that there is little difference between the aristocracy of her day and the great merchant families.

## "Misery . . . The Certain Concomitant of Slavery": *The Wanderings of Warwick* and "The Story of Henrietta"

By mid-1793 Smith had done her best work in fiction. In 1793 and 1794 she published three novels and *The Emigrants,* helped Augusta and de Faville establish themselves, worked hard to settle the Smith estate, and cared for Augusta, whose illness had begun in 1794. It is little wonder, then, that the quality of her fiction should suffer.

*The Wanderings of Warwick* appeared in 1794. At the end of *The Old Manor House,* a footnote promises that the author will tell the stories of Warwick and Isabella in a novel soon to be published. Smith had taken an advance from J. Bell for *The Wanderings of Warwick,* which was to be a two-volume production, but wrote only one, and that later than promised. Bell was piqued and inserted a statement in the advertisement of the book, attributing the abbreviated form and tardiness of the work "solely to the Author—to whom he leaves the task of justifying her conduct."[14]

*The Wanderings of Warwick* is Smith's weakest novel. She has transformed Warwick and Isabella from the sprightly and witty characters of *The Old Manor House* to a conventional sentimental hero and heroine. She frames the story with an afternoon conversation between Warwick and Orlando in which the former relates his adventures. The novel is in part a travel narrative in fictional form. But it is also an adaptation of *Manon Lescaut,* the French novel that Smith had translated but withdrawn from publication. One of the characters, the Conde de Villanova, is hopelessly in love with a dissolute woman who makes his life too miserable to endure.

As in *The Old Manor House,* Warwick and Isabella leave England for America after Orlando's convoy has departed. They undergo a variety of perils, including storms, pirates, and sea battles, staying for a time in Barbados before eventually arriving in Lisbon, where a retired British admiral helps them. When they discover that he has designs on Isabella, they leave with the Conde de Villanova, a Spanish nobleman whom they had met earlier. After Villanova kills himself because of his doomed love, Warwick and Isabella return to England, where Warwick tries his luck as a writer before his friends persuade General Tracy to forgive him.

Even so slight a work as *The Wanderings of Warwick* has its interest as a reflection of political and cultural issues of the day. By 1795, the British antislavery movement had gained followers among a diverse cross section of political and religious groups. Quakers and others had long spoken out against slavery, as had republicans.[15] The movement eventually succeeded in three stages: abolition in England and Ireland in 1772 (Scotland in 1778), prohibition of British participation in the slave trade in 1806, and abolition in the colonies in 1833.[16] Despite the family estates in the West Indies, Smith makes a strong antislavery statement in her fiction.

*The Wanderings of Warwick* and "The Story of Henrietta" both address the issue of slavery through the experiences of the characters. Isabella and Warwick find themselves in Barbados when their ship is blown off course by a storm, and Warwick has "an opportunity of observing the state of the negro slaves" (44). He then digresses to tell of his earlier experience in Jamaica, where he saw slave gangs driven with whips to work in the fields. "When I considered that these were creatures endued with a portion, and, as some have contended, an equal portion, of that reason on which we so highly value ourselves," he comments, "I turned with horror and indignation from such a spectacle" (45).

The discussion of slavery is short in *The Wanderings of Warwick,* but Smith focuses on the discrepancy between the general decency of many slave owners and their indecent treatment of slaves. Warwick notes that he "used to listen with wonder to orders I frequently heard given by a man I was often with, who was in every other instance reasonable and humane, for the punishment of his slaves for faults, which were in my apprehension so trifling that I should hardly have reprimanded a servant in England for committing them" (46). He then tells of a young woman in Jamaica, Miss Shaftesbury, who is engaged to a fellow officer. She is one of Smith's faux sentimentalists, who can "weep over the fictitious distresses of a novel, and shrink from the imaginary sorrows of an imaginary heroine" (53). But Warwick's friend sees this sensitive soul direct the punishment of a 10-year-old slave girl and reports, "I heard the shrieks of the miserable little victim;—I saw her back almost flayed; and Miss Shaftesbury seemed to me to enjoy the spectacle" (54). Smith's story reinforces a common charge of the abolition movement: Slavery degrades the owner as well as the slave.

"The Story of Henrietta," in *Letters of a Solitary Wanderer* (1799–1800), a collection of four individual tales, offers Smith's most telling commentary on the slavery issue. As is the case with so many of Smith's novels, this story should be read in the context of the times, the late 1790s. William Wilberforce had repeatedly introduced bills in Parliament calling for the abolition of the slave trade. The measure nearly passed in 1791, but with the reaction against the violence in France, support for abolition abated. In 1799 when *Letters* was published, the prospects looked dim for such a law because of the war with France. But the antislavery forces still pushed their agenda enthusiastically. Thus, "The Story of Henrietta" can be read as a reflection of that movement.

Moreover, Smith gives her readers another history lesson in this tale. The last Maroon war in Jamaica was fought in 1796, three years before "The Story of Henrietta" was published. The Maroons were runaway slaves who had married indigenous people in the West Indies and had taken refuge in the interior.[17] In some places they cooperated with landowners by capturing and returning escaped slaves, but they also sometimes sided with slaves during uprisings.

"The Story of Henrietta" is Smith's best adventure story. The Wanderer, a melancholy young man who travels from place to place and reports the stories he hears, meets George Denbigh, whose story is composed of events leading up to his marriage to the Henrietta of the title. Her father is a Jamaican planter who sent her to England to be raised. After Denbigh and Henrietta Maynard are engaged, her father summarily demands her return to Jamaica. Denbigh follows, but when he arrives he discovers that Mr. Maynard intends to force Henrietta to marry one of his hirelings. The story has plenty of thrills, with Henrietta first kidnapped by an enamored slave and then captured by Maroons, who wound Denbigh when he pursues her. Both are saved by Henrietta's uncle, whose life story, told in a digression, forms the bulk of the volume. His miseries have disenchanted him with humanity, and to avoid his species, he lives in a cave, much like Parson Darby in "Beachy Head."

Most of the antislavery sentiment comes from Maynard, Henrietta's uncle, when he tells his story. Born in Jamaica, he had been sent to England for an education. His older brother, Henrietta's father, brutalized him, which caused, he says, "that abhorrence of tyranny and injustice which I have invariably felt through the rest of my life."[18] The elder brother's treatment of the younger resulted from his inability to cope with English public schools, where he himself was beaten as he had

beaten slaves in Jamaica. Henrietta's father is an example of the theme
of this story, as Maynard articulates it: "Misery . . . is indeed the certain
concomitant of slavery. It follows with undeviating step the tyrant who
imposes, and the slave who endures the fetters" (II, 133).

Maynard's digression tells of his unhappy marriages and the deaths of
both a beloved son and a best friend. When he goes through the papers
of the latter, he finds "many manuscripts, as well as printed tracts, on
the condition of the Africans and their state of slavery in the American
colonies" (II, 281). Maynard endures a shock of recognition regarding
his own behavior to slaves and returns to Jamaica to alleviate their lot.

There he finds himself stymied by other planters, who discover legal
means to prevent his manumission of the slaves. Freeing his slaves only
makes the lot of those owned by other planters harder. As a result, Maynard retires to the cave where he had taken Henrietta and Denbigh. At
the end of the story, Denbigh has sold his Jamaican estates at a considerable loss because he deplores the exploitation of black people.

Charlotte Smith was a woman of her times. Her works reflect both liberal
positions on issues of the day and many of the cultural and racial stereotypes held by even the most enlightened. While she takes a firm stand
against slavery at a time when Anti-Jacobin sentiment made such a position unpopular, her portrayal of blacks in both *The Wanderings of Warwick*
and "The Story of Henrietta" will seem racist to a modern reader. Both
Warwick and Denbigh comment on the vanity of "house negroes," who
wear the most colorful imitations of their masters' clothing they can find.
Both describe them as childlike and unteachable. In "The Story of Henrietta," much of the melodrama comes from what Smith calls the Maroons'
"fierce inclination for European women" (II, 114).

Indeed, in *The Wanderings of Warwick,* Smith's attitude toward black
people and to slavery seems ambivalent at first glance. The Smith family
had estates in the West Indies where slave labor would have been used.
Thus, Warwick's comment that it is in "the interest of the planters to be
careful of the lives of their slaves," and "in general they are not ill
treated" (59–60) sounds like a justification for slavery. Most of the
abuse, he says, comes from those who hire the slaves of others. He continues this discussion by comparing the lot of slaves to that of British
peasants. After describing the hard life of a representative laborer, who
ends his life in the workhouse, Warwick concludes, "Let any one who
has ever inspected a work-house compare his *then* situation with that of
the negro, who it is true is a slave; but for whom all the necessaries of

life are provided in his old age" (64). Smith goes on to depict the final
days of the slave to be far more comfortable than those of the workman.

The comparison, however, should be read as Smith's sympathy for
the British laborer rather than as a defense of slavery. Warwick's final
comment makes that point clear: "Let me, after having enumerated all
these circumstances or palliation, declare against every species of slavery: let me protest my belief that it brutalises, while it degrades, the
human character, and produces at once servility and ferocity" (66). In
"The Story of Henrietta," furthermore, Smith describes slavery as an evil
that must be ended.

## "The Iron Plowshare of Oppression in the Form of Law": *Marchmont*

Although *Marchmont* has no autobiographical characters so identifiable
as Mrs. Stafford in *Emmeline* or Geraldine Verney in *Desmond,* the didactic message of the work focuses squarely on the problem in Smith's life
that most preoccupied her: injustices of the law. The novel was published in 1796, one year before the Seventh Edition of *Elegiac Sonnets,*
with its attack in the Preface on the executors of her children's estate.
Augusta had died in 1795, and the period following must have been
especially trying for Smith.

Indeed, the reviewers often took note of such public pillorying of enemies. The conservative journal *The British Critic,* for instance, which had
welcomed her back to the fold of political respectability in its review of
*The Banished Man,* nonetheless observes that "the only reprehensible
part of the work before us, is the extreme eagerness with which our irri-
tated and perhaps injured novelist introduces her own story [through
Mrs. Denzil]. . . . Private history should not be introduced for public
perusal."[19] And in its review of *Marchmont, The Critical Review* first chas-
tises the author for the improprieties of the hero and heroine, which "are
not calculated to operate upon young minds as a warning against similar imprudence,"[20] then takes the author to task for introducing her own
troubles and describing lawyers in epithets.

Unscrupulous lawyers cause the distress of the hero and heroine in
*Marchmont.* Althea Dacres, Smith's heroine,[21] resembles the youthful
Charlotte Smith. Her father is widowed, then remarries for money.
Althea's stepmother parallels Smith's, and the young woman is similarly
alienated from her father. Moreover, Althea lives with an aunt, Mrs.
Trevyllian, after her mother's death, as did the author. But there the

similarities between author and character end. The aunt dies when the young woman is 17, leaving her niece a small legacy.

Althea's father insists that she marry Mohun, a powerful attorney. Althea refuses; to force her into obedience, Dacres sends her to live in a ruined manor house formerly owned by the Marchmont family. After a number of gothic episodes there, she learns that young Marchmont, whom she had met in Mr. Dacres's home, is hiding in the deserted portion of the building after attorney Mohun tricked him into signing papers by which he assumed his father's posthumous debt. Vampyre, an attorney with a name that Smith no doubt thought appropriate for those of his profession, trails Marchmont without mercy, planning to imprison him for debt. During their clandestine meetings, Althea becomes attached to Marchmont. Eventually, however, he leaves for France, where he has a relative who might relieve his financial distress.

When Althea's father dies, the young woman feels spurned by her stepmother and decides to live with Marchmont's mother and sisters, who are so poor that they plan to start a business to sell their needlework.[22] Her residence there gives her, and the reader, an opportunity to see Marchmont's letters from the continent detailing the horrors of France under the Directory. When Marchmont returns, he and Althea marry, but Vampyre, at the instigation of Mohun, casts him into debtors' prison. The novel goes into great detail on life there, as Althea insists on living in prison with her husband.

The machinations of lawyers continues when Althea inherits £2,000 from her father and a yet larger estate from a relative of Mrs. Trevyllian, the woman who raised her. But her stepmother, aided by Mohun, outright refuses to permit the inheritances. Smith resolves the plot with a sort of deus ex machina when Marchmont meets Mr. Desborough, yet another kindly misanthrope, who recognizes the injustice of British debtors' laws and helps those in need. A distant relation to Marchmont, Desborough assists in freeing the young man and in forcing Mohun and Mrs. Dacres to release Althea's estate.

Like all of Smith's novels following *The Old Manor House*, *Marchmont* is a flawed work. The plot moves ponderously, and the villains are melodramatic stick figures. Vampyre, for instance, is "the Satanic agent of abused law" (III, 38). But Smith's criticism of the British legal system in a time of political repression makes the novel unique to the fiction of the mid-1790s.

The Preface leaves little doubt as to what will follow. The author mentions that in the days before Augusta's death, "those men who *then held,* who *still hold,* the property of my family" gave only "refusal of the most necessary assistance, taunts, and insults" (viii). She then launches into a diatribe against lawyers. Beginning her remarks with a ironic admission that there are "honest and good men in the profession I believe, for I know *two,*" she notes that since "the great master of novel-writing, Fielding" had failed to reform the profession, "my feeble pen can do nothing but prove that other Murphys and Dowlings [lawyers in Fielding's works] exist in the present day" (xiii–xiv). She follows with a scathing attack on the profession and notes that "the character most odious" in the novel (presumably Mohun) "is drawn *ad vivum*" (xi–xii). This "most odious" character is probably a reference to John Robinson, the estate trustee she hated.

Such criticism had become dangerous by 1796, when *Marchmont* was published. The sedition trials of John Thelwall, Thomas Holcroft, Horne Tooke, and nine others began in 1794. All were acquitted. But after two mass meetings sponsored by reform societies in 1795 that reportedly drew 100,000 people and an incident in which the royal carriage was first stoned and then (after the king had left it) destroyed by a mob, Parliament passed the "Two Acts" in December. Cone writes that this legislation "in effect introduced a new law of treason so extended as virtually to forbid discussion of constitutional and public grievances."[23] But unrest continued, most ominously expressed by insurrections in the armed forces.[24]

Considering the atmosphere of repression at the time, Smith is remarkably explicit about the flaws of the British legal system. She refers to the devastation of the Marchmont estate by the "iron plow-share of oppression in the form of law" (I, 265). Furthermore, she condemns debtors' law, which "confounds innocence with guilt, and equally punishes intentional fraud and inevitable misfortune; yet which exists no where in such force as in a country boasting of its enlarged humanity and perfect freedom" (II, 21–22). Also, repeated allusions to Voltaire's *Candide* offer ironic criticism of the British legal system. In one of his letters from the continent, Marchmont rants: "War, earthquake, pestilence, famine, tempest, all the calamities of this best of all possible worlds . . . do not, I am convinced, occasion more anguish to '*the poor creature of the earth,*' than these locusts, which we ourselves arm with stings and claws—because it is the custom" (IV, 44).[25]

As in both *Desmond* and *The Old Manor House,* Smith traces injustices of the law to the British political system. Althea's father, we are told, is a member of Parliament: "He possessed two boroughs in right of Lady

Dacres: and having thus acquired a nomination of three voices, together with his own, in parliament, he of course became a man of consequence in the political world: and though he had yet no ostensible post, it was believed that he had ample compensation for the expences of the sort of open house he kept, as well in London as in Capelstoke, for the accommodation and resort of that party which adhered to the *existing powers* in administration" (I, 229–30). Smith alludes to the "rotten boroughs" that British reformers would point to as symptoms of political decay well into the 19th century.

In *Marchmont,* Smith offers yet another lesson in recent history for readers, told from the perspective of a British republican moderate. As noted in Chapter 4, the Reign of Terror in France had begun in 1793 and lasted through most of 1794. The constitution of 1795 created a Convention to replace the Assembly and a five-person Directory with executive power. Order had been restored to Paris in 1794, but at the expense of personal freedoms.

Marchmont goes to Paris, looking for his relative. But he writes to his sister Lucy that he leaves because "my very soul was sick of the wild assemblage of ideotism and phrensy [sic] which I every day saw," and he longs to leave, he writes, for these people's "folly called for my contempt, while their ferocity excited my abhorrence" (III, 185). In a passage that dates the action of the novel, he describes the rape of Toulon,[26] which occurred in December 1793, painting a picture of life in France that would have warmed the heart of any British anti-Jacobin.

Yet even in describing the devastation of France, Smith does not leave British withers unwrung. Her republican sympathies remain firm. The failure of the revolution, Marchmont writes, resulted from its leaders, not the original ideal. And tyranny is the same in England or France. Marchmont writes, "Whether I am to exist under the tyranny of Robespierre, or a victim of the chicanery of Vampyre, seems to me a matter so immaterial, that it ought not to induce me to cross the water to embrace the one, or escape the other" (II, 163). Smith links injustices under British law with the tyranny that had evolved in France when Marchmont writes, "The same obnoxious professional men [lawyers] are accused by the French nobility of having been the cause of, and the chief gainers in, the revolution" (IV, 45).[27]

Smith retained her sympathy for the goals of republican moderates, even after she recognized the failure of the French Revolution. She used her novels to bring both knowledge of recent events and the republican perspective on them to her readers. Her next novel would combine the discussion of political and social issues raised in *Marchmont* with a debate between liberal and conservative characters on the philosophical questions that underpin her social criticism.

## "Radical Sensibility": *The Young Philosopher*

In *The Young Philosopher,* published in 1798, Smith addresses the issues raised in her earlier novels: abuse of the law, parliamentary reform, anti-war sentiment, and hatred of all forms of tyranny. The letter in which she proposed the project to William Davies (June 22, 1797; Beinecke) suggests that she intended it to be a work with some substance: ". . . from the nature of the plan it will require books and leisure. I meant to have called it 'The Young Philosopher' and I thought some of the ideas that occurred to me, both of characters and incidents were likely to be worked up in a composition of more solidity than the usual crowd of novels." The title alludes to Rousseau's description of Saint-Preux in *La Nouvelle Héloïse,* to whom Claire refers in a letter to Julie as "your young philosopher."[28]

*The Young Philosopher* is loosely constructed, nearly a third of the novel consisting of digression. It does, however, have Smith's best opening chapter, with a party going astray in southern England—clearly Smith's "beautiful and beloved spot"—and trapped in a storm after their carriages overturn. In the accident, Dr. Winslow, "a dignified clergyman, who, besides an affluent private fortune, possessed very considerable church preferment," and his wife are slightly injured. His niece, Miss Goldthorpe, an orphan with a fortune of £50,000, breaks her arm.

The accident adroitly introduces the hero, George Delmont, who lives nearby and comes to the rescue of the party. They stay with Delmont while Miss Goldthorpe's arm heals, a visit made longer by the young woman's attraction to the hero. Dr. Winslow intends his ward to marry his son and is quite upset over her declared intent to give her hand and fortune to Delmont. But George declines both, and the party eventually leaves his home.

Delmont is the hero and philosopher of the novel's title, a young man who has has been taught "to reason on everything he learned, instead of seeing all objects, as they are represented, through the dazzling and false medium of prejudice, communicated from one generation to another" (I, 86–87). Armitage, his neighbor and mentor, introduces him to Laura Glenmorris and her daughter Medora, who becomes the love interest for Delmont. Laura tells her story in a volume-long digression, detailing reasons why she and her husband had moved to America. She had returned to claim an inheritance, and lawyers for her father's estate provide the plot incidents of the novel, which is replete with an abduction (sparking another long digression) and a sequence with Laura running mad in the streets. At the end of the novel, George Delmont goes to America with the Glenmorrises.

Blended with the melodramatic plot of *The Young Philosopher* is a potpourri of the social criticism from Smith's other novels, presented through long discussions between conservative and liberal speakers, with those presenting republican views receiving the most stirring lines. The political content is powerful enough that Smith saw fit to distance herself from the liberal characters. In the preface, she writes: ". . . there may be many traits, many ideas, and even many prejudices, which may be necessary to support or render these characters natural, that are by no means those of the composer of the book; I declare therefore against the conclusion, that *I* think either like Glenmorris or Armitage, or any other of my personages" (I, vi). Perhaps the climate of repression by 1798 made Smith cautious. Yet both of these characters express approval of the American Revolution and anti-war sentiments, criticism of abuses of the law, and hatred of all types of tyranny. Both, moreover, articulate a perspective on the French Revolution consistent with Smith's earlier works: that the original goals were admirable but had been corrupted.

As in all her political novels, Smith defends the original ideals of the revolution in France. Armitage was "present at Paris at the taking of the Bastille" (I, 175–176) and had written a pamphlet in which he cautioned the French people against excesses. However, he "hazarded a few opinions on the rights of nations, and the purposes of government" (I, 176), which made him an outcast in Great Britain. When Dr. Winslow tells George that philosophers caused the bloodshed in France, the young man responds: "The truth is, that the gloomy and absurd structures, raised on the basis of prejudice and superstition, have toppled down headlong; many are crushed in their fall; . . . but the bastilles of falsehood, in which men's minds were imprisoned, are levelled with the earth, never, never to rise again!" (I, 147)

Like other British republicans, Smith saw both the successful revolution in America and the fall of the ancien régime to be blows against tyranny. Glenmorris calls the former "the unnatural war they [the colonists] had been driven into" and says that "the noble flame of liberty seemed to have purified their [the Americans'] minds from every narrow and unmanly prejudice" (II, 241). In a time of political repression, praise for the American war was no doubt safer than praise for the early ideals of French republicanism.

Smith's letters show her disillusionment with British political institutions. On March 25, 1794, she wrote to Joseph Cooper Walker: "I assure you that I have neither naturally nor artificially the least partiality for my native Country, which has not protected my property by its boasted Laws; & where if the Laws are not good, I know nothing that is" (Huntington). Characters in her novels reflect her cynicism. Several become misanthropes. Parson Darby in *Beachy Head,* Maynard in "The Story of Henrietta," and Desborough in *Marchmont* are examples. In *The Young Philosopher,* Glenmorris leaves Britain forever, because there "the miseries inflicted by the social compact greatly exceed the happiness derived from it" (IV, 394). The recurrence of such characters reflects the author's growing despair that reform could succeed.

Lionel Stevenson calls *The Young Philosopher* Smith's "most visionary [novel] in its proposal of a utopian substitute for contemporary culture."[29] Indeed, the work is closer to those of Bage and Holcroft in its philosophical tone than are her other novels. In her fiction, she juxtaposes reason and feeling, beginning with the *concordia discors* in *Emmeline. Desmond* signals a new approach to this dichotomy of qualities. True sensibility in Smith's later works is not the fine feelings of the heart that confer virtue on those who possess them. Rather, it is the capacity to feel for those in need or for the victims of injustice. In *Marchmont,* Althea has this radical sensibility. She reads "Rousseau, and some other authors not usually making part of the studies of young women" (III, 60). After Althea's long rumination on the horrors of war, the author steps forward to address her character: "Ah! candid and unadulterated mind! You have learned early to reflect. . . . By imagining yourself in the place of others, as you now continually do, you will learn to feel for all the unhappy, or even for those who appear so; whereas it might save a good deal of (for the most part useless) pain, if you could contrive to feel only for yourself" (III, 64–65). Feeling is the automatic response to distress, but reason is the capacity to perceive the root causes of that distress.[30]

Smith's conception of a radical sensibility based on a combination of reason and feeling underpins her critique. In her preface to *The Young Philosopher,* she defines her theme as "the ill consequences of detraction. . . , the sad effects of parental resentment, and the triumph of fortitude in the daughter [Medora], while too acute sensibility, too hastily indulged, is the source of much unhappiness to the mother" (I, vi–vii). These themes do emerge in the melodramatic adventures of Laura and Medora Glenmorris, but they are decidedly secondary to the novel's criticism of British society and institutions. Smith demonstrates the proper blend of reason and sensibility in two important dialogues, each pitting a liberal hero against an opponent who uses religion to justify a conservative position.

In the first, Armitage confronts Mrs. Crewkherne, Delmont's aunt, whom Smith describes as a Methodist, a Blue Stocking, and an anti-Jacobin. The French Revolution is anathema to her, and Edmund Burke is "the great and commanding writer and orator, who had enacted Peter the Hermit, and . . . preached a crusade against 'the Gallic savages'" (I, 180–181). She praises Burke's idea "that France, republican France, could, by a single blow, be struck from among the nations of the earth" (I, 177). Yet all her beliefs, as Smith describes the woman, are based on prejudice, not reason. The author exposes those prejudices in a long debate with Armitage. The passages seem patterned on the trial of Socrates, with Crewkherne first accusing Armitage of being an "atheist, a deist, a freethinker, an illuminy;[31] I don't know what, not I; a jacobin, and a republican" (IV, 5).

In his defense, Armitage denies being an atheist and articulates his faith: "I imagine that our way to please God is, to do all the good that is in our power to all his creatures" (IV, 7).[32] He denies having "an horror of kings and of nobility," and says he "would die, were it necessary, for a good king, for a king shewing himself worthy of the sacred charge, by devoting himself to the real happiness and prosperity of the people." He goes on to maintain that he holds "all the wild schemes of universal equality as utterly impracticable, and altogether absurd" because other inequalities would quickly emerge. He further denies the charge of Jacobinism, which, he says, has "polluted the cause of freedom" in France (IV, 15–16).

Through this character, Smith establishes a model for a radical sensibility: a balance of reason and feeling that leads to the perception of social injustice and a desire to effect change. George Delmont's philosophy seems essentially similar, one based on "plain reason and common sense" (I, 153).[33] And in dialogues between Delmont and Dr. Winslow, who "had no other weapons than the wretched ones furnished by that inveterate prejudice and selfish interest which hood-winked all enquiry" (I, 153), Smith uses the clergyman as a foil. He "had never thought of any object but exactly as his predecessors, his masters, had told him to think" (I, 155). His love for "'ancient opinions' . . . saved him the trouble of forming any new ones," and he fears new ideas because they might "diminish or do away [sic] the emoluments which the regular professors of them enjoyed" (I, 156). The argument between Delmont and Dr. Winslow mirrors the debate between Paine and Burke: Burke's condemnation of Price's sermon focused on the inviolability of tradition, and Paine spoke for "plain reason and common sense" as a guide to change.

Delmont, Armitage, and Glenmorris, the ideological centers of the novel, are preeminently men of reason. But they balance reason with feeling to achieve the radical sensibility the author attributes to Althea in *Marchmont*. When Delmont hears the sad stories of poor people whom he assists, "his heart swelled with indignation against those whom these real or apparent sufferers described as having been the cause of their wretchedness, and against the systems through which only they could be inflicted." Because of his passion for those in distress, "he was led to enquire if the complicated misery he every day saw . . . could be the fruits of the very best laws that could be framed in a state of society said to be the most perfect among what are called the civilized nations of the world" (I, 54). In another scene, George tells his brother Adolphus he could not live in Ireland where he "must daily witness, without having the power materially to alleviate, the miseries of the lower classes of people." Adolphus, a man of the world and a counterpoint to George's humanitarianism, replies, "The people! . . .—the people—what the devil hast thou to do with them?" (III, 138). George, who has a properly disposed mind, balances reason and feeling. Adolphus clearly lacks the capacity to feel for the needs of his fellow humans.

Other British republican writers of the late 18th century employ the words "reason" and "feeling" in a fashion similar to Smith's usage. Paine, for instance, begins his argument in *Common Sense* with a request that the reader "divest himself of prejudice and prepossession, and suffer his reason and his feelings to determine for themselves."

## Seven Castles in Bohemia: The Gothic Mode in Charlotte Smith's Political Novels

Smith begins a section from *The Banished Man* that is set off from the preceding narrative and labeled "Avis au Lecteur" with a quotation from Sterne: "'There was, an please your honor,'" said Corporal Trim, 'there was a certain king of Bohemia, who had seven castles'" (I, i). She goes on to write, "I find that Mowbray Castle, Grasmere Abbey, and the castle of Rockmarch, the castle of Hautville, and Rayland Hall, have taken so many of my materials to construct, that I have hardly a watch tower, a gothic arch, a ceder [sic] parlour, or a long gallery, an illuminated window, or a ruined chapel, left to help myself" (I, ii). She adds that, "*Le vrai*. . . , or even *le vrai semblance,* seems not to be the present fashion" and that it is time for her to resign the field before she has to mine apparition books for "a dismal tale of an haunted house" (I, v–vi).

The tone of the passage no doubt results from the time when it was written (1794), when Augusta was ill and money in desperately short supply. The frantic pace at which she had to produce her work surely drained any joy from the process. This passage and others in Smith's works, however, reflect a recognition that she had to give her readers gothic thrills and melodramatic plots to hold their attention.

Kelly admits Smith, along with Mary Robinson, to his list of "English Jacobin novelists" only peripherally because her work lacks a "philosophically motivated search for 'unity of design,' which was central to the techniques" of these writers.[34] Kelly's comments suggest a criticism of Smith's work—namely, that her novels focus on character and plot rather than the ideological issues that drive the works of Godwin, Holcroft, Inchbald, and Wollstonecraft. Indeed, in her best work, Smith deftly blends a discussion of political and social issues with a story designed to capture and retain her readers' attention. Thus, the qualities of her work that Kelly criticizes should rather be viewed as strengths.

Writing an engaging story, however, was a matter of necessity for Smith. She wrote for "the novel market" to support her family; she had to give her readers what they wanted. Moreover, for her novels to have the potential for educating her audience, she had to offer them conventional thrills. For all their emphasis on social and political issues of her time, Smith's political novels have the structure of the sentimental gothic.

In *The Old Manor House,* for instance, the dilapidated Rayland manor is a surrogate ruined castle. It has secret passages, such as the one that leads Orlando to Monimia's turret bedroom. The old library where the lovers meet offers a splendid setting for one of Smith's most conventional gothic passages. On a "night, dark and tempestuous" (91) they are startled by noises in the chapel nearby. When they investigate, they are "struck motionless by a sudden and loud crash . . . and a deep hollow voice pronounced the words, 'now—now'" (95–96). Orlando demands to know the speaker's identity, and the description that follows demonstrates Smith's skill in establishing the gothic ambience and situation:

... in the dread pause between Orlando's question and his awaiting an answer, the old banners which hung over her [Monimia's] head, waving and rustling with the current of air, seemed to repeat the whispers of some terrific and invisible being, foretelling woe and destruction; while the same wind by which these fragments were agitated hummed sullenly among the helmets and gauntlets, trophies of the prowess of former Sir Orlandos and Sir Hildebrands, which were suspended from pillars of the chapel. (96).

The intruder, however, turns out to be a smuggler.

Smith uses this and other incidents that at first seem supernatural to give readers yet another lesson: not to fear the supernatural. After the timorous Monimia has been frightened by a similar incident a few days earlier, Orlando tells her that he will select books that describe the "best authenticated" sightings of ghosts and that he will give her "reason an opportunity to decide for itself." He describes one such sighting and asks: ". . . shall we therefore believe, that an all-wise and all-powerful Being shall suffer a general law of nature to be so uselessly violated, and shall make the dead restless, only to terrify the living?" He continues, if "sanguinary monsters who are stained with crimes" returned to perse- cute the living, "I am afraid not one of our kings or heroes could have slept in their beds" (48–49).

*Marchmont* and *The Young Philosopher* also offer gothic entertainment with a similar pointed moral embedded. When Althea becomes appre- hensive about mysterious incidents at Eastwoodleigh, the sublimely ruined Marchmont estate, she reasons with herself: "From supernatural agents she could have nothing to apprehend, did they really exist; but against their existence it was with her an unanswerable argument, that the Director of the world would never violate a known law of nature to answer no possible end" (II, 32). Similarly, in *The Young Philosopher,* Smith tells the story of Laura Glenmorris's life in a digression replete with abductions, gothic castles and abbeys, and suggestions of the supernatural. But Smith balances these passages with a spoof of gothic fiction. A silly young woman, a novel reader, tells Laura, "I assure you, people of consequence *do* believe in spirits, and if you would but read some sweet books I met with just before I came from town . . . , I'm sure you would never be such an infidel . . .—all about tapestry waving in the wind, a bloody dagger, and voices calling at midnight, howlings in the air, and dark passages" (II, 42).

Smith knew the power of gothic thrills to hold her readers' interest. In *Desmond,* Geraldine's last-minute rescue from banditti seems tacked on, with little connection to the political theme of the work. But in *The Old Manor House* and the novels that follow, she uses gothic melodrama to entertain her readers and then lectures them on both the foolishness of belief in the supernatural and the effect of bad fiction.

Thus, in her political novels, Smith created stories intended to entertain her audience, blended with the issues of the reform movement as well as lessons on history, geography, botany, and other topics. In her prefaces, particularly for *Desmond* and *Letters of a Solitary Wanderer,* and in occasional passages from her novels, she makes her purpose clear. Smith knew that her audience was primarily female, and she sought to bring her readers knowledge on matters to which they would otherwise have little access.

## Chapter Six
# The Wrongs of Woman:
# *Montalbert* and Other Works

A small but vocal movement for women's rights grew from the intellectual ferment in Britain during the 1790s. Indeed, a realization of the inequities women faced before the law and in the home seems a natural product of egalitarian republican rhetoric. A parallel movement began in France, as exemplified by Olympe de Gouges's *Declaration of the Rights of Women and the Citizen,* which paralleled the Assembly's *Declaration of the Rights of Man and the Citizen.* But French men proved no more ready to extend *égalité* to women than were British men to extend them constitutional rights.[1]

### British Jacobin Feminism

If British republicanism of the 1790s can be labeled English Jacobinism and the fiction of the Godwin circle termed the Jacobin novel,[2] Mary Wollstonecraft's *A Vindication of the Rights of Woman* might justly be called the manifesto of Jacobin feminism. Wollstonecraft had responded to Burke's *Reflections* in 1790 with *A Vindication of the Rights of Men. A Vindication of the Rights of Woman,* published in 1792, should be read as both an allusion to her previous work and an extension of its argument. "In whatever light I view the subject," writes Wollstonecraft of women's place in society, "reason and experience convince me that the only method of leading women to fulfill their peculiar duties, is to free them from all restraint by allowing them to participate [sic] the inherent rights of mankind."[3] In her final book, which appeared the year after her death in 1797, Wollstonecraft would carry the logic of her arguments in *Vindication of the Rights of Woman* to a novel whose title, *Maria, or The Wrongs of Woman,* is a word play on those of the earlier works, and apply her thoughts on the subjugation of women to a fictional example.

In *Vindication,* Wollstonecraft focuses on women's education, or rather the lack thereof. She had written *Thoughts on the Education of Daughters* in 1787, and she returns to the topic in *Vindication,* attributing the vanity, artfulness, and penchant for petty gossip displayed by some women to the influence of men, who dictate women's education and self-concept. She attacks Dr. Gregory[4] and Rousseau, and assails the latter for his insistence on women's obedience to men in *Émile*. She speaks forcefully for a national school system and coeducation. A proper education, she writes, would bring women "domestic taste" and make them better mothers, the role that Wollstonecraft sees as most important to them. She cites revolutionary France as a model: "Let an enlightened nation then try what effect reason would have to bring them [women] back to nature, and their duty; and allowing them to share the advantages of education and government with man, see whether they will become better as they grow wiser and become free."[5]

Other writers of the 1790s also trace the subjugation of women to their lack of education. In her *Appeal to the Men of Great Britain on Behalf of Women,* Mary Hays asserts that prejudices established and perpetuated by men create the mental subordination of women. Education, Hays writes, is a key to improving women's status. Although they are "—an oppressed,—a degraded,—and an excluded portion of the human race," they are "fully equal to the perfecting of many of the arts, from which they are by the tyranny of fashion debarred." Like Wollstonecraft, Hays admits that women's primary role lies in domesticity and child care, but there "women shine with most lustre, if their natural talents have been at all improved by a proper education; or even if indeed they have not been quashed or perverted by an improper one."[6]

Mary Robinson, a woman who had suffered even more than had Hays and Wollstonecraft from the tyranny of men,[7] also focuses on education in her *Thoughts on the Condition of Women and on the Injustice of Mental Subordination.* Her intent, she writes, is to remind her countrywomen "that they are not the mere appendages of domestic life, but the partners, the equal associates of man: and, where they excel in intellectual powers, they are no less capable of all that prejudice and custom have united in attributing, exclusively, to the thinking powers of man."[8] Robinson also proposes higher education for women: "Had fortune enabled me," she writes, "I would build [a] UNIVERSITY FOR WOMEN," where those most gifted would receive classical educations.[9]

Many writers—Catherine Maccaulay, Elizabeth Inchbald, and Helen Maria Williams, for instance—contributed to the nascent women's rights movement of the 1790s. But no more striking example of the inequality that British and French women writers attacked could be cited than the gender discrimination established as law, which permitted

Benjamin Smith to take most of the income from his wife's fortune and even some of the money she earned from her books while he ignored his responsibilities as husband and father. Because of her own experience, Smith used her pen to educate her readers on women's condition.

Smith makes her awareness of women's powerlessness quite plain. In her preface to *Desmond,* for instance, she writes, "Knowledge, which qualifies women to speak or to write on any other than the most common and trivial subjects, is supposed to be so difficult of attainment, that it cannot be acquired but by the sacrifice of domestic virtues." Thus, when she observes that her fiction results from the "proud man's contumely, th' oppressor's wrong;/The law's delay, the insolence of office," she surely uses the word "man" advisedly. The performance of her own "domestic duties" must include the support of her family through writing, a condition that results from "the power of men who *seem to exercise all these with impunity*" (I, iv–v). Smith's practice of referring to John Robinson and the other trustees of the Smith estate as men in *Desmond* and elsewhere—which, of course, they were, since only men were allowed to fill such roles—surely reflects her awareness of the helplessness of women before the law. Thus, in her Preface to the Sixth Edition of *Elegiac Sonnets,* she rails against "The Honorable Men" who block her children's inheritance.

In her letters, Smith is also explicit about the gender of her tormentors. On January 20, 1794, she complains to Joseph Cooper Walker, "I struggle in vain against the Men, who have by cunning possess'd themselves of all the effects, and by fraud keep that possession" (Huntington). On March 25, 1794, she refers to her children's estate being in the "tenacious talons of the worthy gentlemen who keep it" (Huntington). And Smith no doubt refers to her own situation when she writes to Sarah Rose, "But even if you should meet, in that respect with the usual fate of the unfortunate, & learn from sad experience, that there is little good among Men, still *your* solicitudes are for the children of a Man you love" (dated February 7, apparently 1804, Huntington).

As we will see, Smith's fiction and poetry gave her female audience lessons in geography, history, botany, and geology, as well as politics and current issues. But she also brought to her readers an awareness of the "wrongs of woman." In her fiction, she satirizes male characters who express misogynist views and describes the suffering of women that results from domination by husbands or fathers. In the novels following the publication of *Desmond* in 1792, she presents strong, independent heroines as role models. And she shows that even men who love their wives value them as private possessions that would be damaged beyond repair if they are defiled by another man, even through rape. This critique of male domination of women closely parallels those of other Jacobin feminists.

## The Gender of Gothic: Fiction and Knowledge

In her own fiction, Smith repeatedly expresses her contempt for most novels, which were often, as she comments through Geraldine Verney in *Desmond,* a "rivulet of text running through a meadow of margin" (II, 147). Such comments reflect the low regard in which fiction was held in her time, and Smith's letter makes no secret of her feelings about writing it. She laments to William Davies in a letter dated October 20, 1797, that she is "doomed from year to year to invent fables for the public & to take as a favor any price offered because I am necessitated to ask advances" (Beinecke).

Although she admired the great novelists of her day, Smith's letters suggest that the books she preferred were poetry and nonfiction. She avidly read history and science as well as discussions of politics. All of the profits of Smith's "literary business" went to support her family, however, and she could have had little time to engage in the unprofitable market in prose polemics. Instead, she used her novels to bring her audience knowledge of a wide variety of topics from her reading.

That the novel was a genre for women was a common assumption in the 18th century, often reflected in comments by reviewers. Two of the reviewers of *Desmond* praise the novel because it brings information as well as entertainment to women. The writer for *The Critical Review,* for instance, observes, "the opportunities of modern fine young ladies for information are so few, that every means of their obtaining it, incidentally should be approved of."[10] The presumption of a female audience for fiction recurs endlessly in reviews of novels during the period.

Comments from Smith's prefaces and novels confirm her understanding that she wrote for a female audience. In the Preface to *Desmond,* for instance, Smith's answer to an anticipated criticism of a woman's writing about politics shows both her awareness of her audience and her concern for using fiction to educate her readers:

> But women it is said have no business with politics—Why not?—Have they no interest in the scenes that are acting around them, in which they have fathers, brothers, husbands, sons, or friends engaged—Even in the

commonest course of female education, they are expected to acquire some knowledge of history; and yet, if they are to have no opinion of what *is* passing, it avails little that they should be informed of what *has passed,* in a world where they are subject to such mental degradation; where they are censured as affecting masculine knowledge if they happen to have any understanding; or despised as insignificant triflers if they have none. (I, iii–iv)

She goes on to anticipate that some will "exclaim against the impropriety of making a book of entertainment the vehicle of political discussion" (I, viii), which is exactly what she does in *Desmond* and, indeed, in all of her remaining novels.

Letters from Geraldine Verney, the heroine of *Desmond,* to her sister echo the author's comments on women's education in the Preface. Fanny complains that her mother will not allow her to read novels on the grounds that they might "convey the poison of bad example in the soft semblance of refined sentiment" (II, 146), a common objection to fiction in essays and reviews.[11] Smith implies exactly this criticism in both *Emmeline* and *Ethelinde* through her presentation of silly young women who model themselves on novel heroines. But in *Desmond,* Geraldine tells Fanny that if every work of fiction were proscribed, "I really know not what young people (*I mean young women*)[12] will read at all," and goes on to defend novels that "represent human life nearly as it is" (II, 166). If novels "do no good, they do no harm"; and, she continues, "There *is* a chance, that those who will read nothing, if they do not read novels, may collect from them some few ideas, that are not either fallacious or absurd, to add to the very scanty stock which their usual insipidity of life has afforded them" (II, 173).

Smith again defends the potential of fiction to educate readers in her Preface to *Letters of a Solitary Wanderer:* "Books of entertainment, usually described as Novels, are supposed to be, if not exclusively, primarily read by young persons; and much has been said of the inutility and the danger of that species of writing" (I, vi). By "young persons," Smith clearly means here, as she did in the Preface to *Desmond,* young women, as she specifies when she asserts that any woman who would imagine herself a heroine would be silly and frivolous "though she had never heard of a circulating library" (I, vi).

Smith then follows with a passage that shows, as does Geraldine's letter in *Desmond,* her belief that a novel—clothed in the trappings of the sentimental gothic to attract and retain her readers' attention—could bring useful knowledge and political awareness to women:

That novels are at least useless where they are not pernicious I cannot allow: if they do not instruct, they may awaken a wish for useful knowledge; and young persons, who have no taste for anything but narrative, may sometimes, by the local description of a Novel, learn what they would never have looked for in books of Geography or Natural History. The dangers and distresses that are expected to form the greater part of a story in every Work of this kind, may be imagined amidst the most interesting period of history, without, however, falsifying or misrepresenting any material or misleading fact. I have endeavoured to construct these volumes in some degree on this plan. (I, vi)

Smith's comments seem especially appropriate for *Letters of a Solitary Wanderer* because of the work's contents, which range from a tale culminating with the ascension of "Good King Henry" Bourbon (the republican model for kingship) in "The Story of Corisande," to the narrative of a contemporary Jamaican slave rebellion in "The Story of Henrietta," to an account of a revolution by the Hungarians against their Austrian overlords in "The Hungarian." But the history lessons, as well as the discussion of the evils of slavery, are dressed out with the conventional plots, settings, and characters of sentimental fiction as the sugar on the pill. In fact, the first volume, "The Story of Edouarda," is a quite conventional gothic in the Radcliffian mode, perhaps intended to lead women readers into the more thematic tales to follow.

## "Where the Intentions Are Perfectly Pure . . .": Didactic Fiction

Smith's early novels of domestic sensibility have a didactic core. They establish heroines who are models of correct behavior. These characters obey patriarchal authority figures and regulate their conduct according to accepted stereotypes. As demonstrated in Chapter 3 of this study, their strength of character arises from a balance of reason and sensibility. Other women writers of the period echo Smith on the dangers of following the feelings. Wollstonecraft finds that "soft phrases, susceptibility of heart, delicacy of sentiment, and refinement of taste, are almost synonymous with epithets of weakness."[13] Reason, she writes, places humankind above the beasts, and God gave humans passions that "by struggling with them [they] might attain a degree of knowledge denied to the brutes."[14] Similarly, in the advertisement for her novel *Julia* (1792), Helen Maria Williams describes the purpose of her book as to "trace the danger arising from the uncontrouled [sic] indulgence of strong affections; not in those instances where they lead to the guilty excesses of passion in a corrupted mind—but, when disapproved by reason, and uncircumscribed by prudence, they involve even the virtuous in calamity."[15]

Writers such as Smith, Wollstonecraft, and Williams no doubt respond to a sexual stereotype of the period.[16] As a response to this stereotype, Jacobin feminist authors insist that women's reliance on feelings is not innate. They deny the assumptions of a patriarchal society, which assumes, like Mandeville, that women are "unfit . . . for abstruse and elaborate thoughts, all Studies of Depth, Coherence and Solidity, that fatigue the Spirits and require a Steadiness and Assiduity of Thinking."[17] Wollstonecraft argues that a male-dominated culture educates women to accept this stereotype, and like those of other writers of her time who advocate women's rights, her works emphasize the need for a balance of reason and feeling, both for men and women.

In *Emmeline* and *Ethelinde,* both written before the spread of revolutionary thought, Smith's repetition of the words "reason" and "feeling" (or cognates) and the emphasis on balance suggest a similar position. But this early emphasis on the *concordia discors* of reason and passion as a guide for female conduct changes somewhat in the novels following 1791. Her heroines still rely on reason, but they do not allow social prejudices to keep them from happiness. Unlike Emmeline, Althea in *Marchmont* and Laura Glenmorris in *The Young Philosopher* defy authority figures. Desmond's triumphant justification of his behavior toward Geraldine signals this shift toward trust in feeling. "The Event has shewn," he writes to Bethel, "that, where the *intention* is perfectly pure, it is not always wrong to follow the dictates of the heart, even when they impel us to act contrary to the maxims of the world, and even in defiance of its censure" (III, 245). The *concordia discors* has given way to romantic individualism. Reason and sensibility still work together in Smith's characters with radical sensibility. Yet reason does not lead those characters to accept society's dictates. Rather, it explodes social stereotypes and unmasks injustice, while feeling leads to behavior appropriate for the individual and to a desire to correct the faults of society.

Ideals such as Desmond's might be acceptable to conservative British readers when spoken by a male character, especially one modeled on the popular Werther. Geraldine Verney, after all, remains a slavishly dutiful wife, even though her husband is a monster. In the novels that follow, however, Smith's heroines share Desmond's rejection of convention and social prejudice. In *Marchmont,* Althea meets the hero unchaperoned in his hiding place. "It was true," she reasons, "that young women of her age are not, according to the established rules, to trust themselves with persons who may presume upon their condescension:—but Althea considered herself as placed in a singular situation, where mere forms might be dispensed with" (II, 115). Later, Smith writes of Althea that she "had also that strength of mind that enabled her to be decided when her understanding and conscience told her she was right" (II, 150). Laura Glenmorris's justification of Medora's actions in *The Young Philosopher* offers another example of individualism:

> If it be romantic to dare to have an opinion of one's own, and not to follow one formal tract, wrong or right, pleasant or irksome, because our grandmothers and aunts have followed it before; if not to be romantic one must go through the world with prudery, carefully settling our blinkers at each step. . . ; if a woman because she is a woman, must resign all pretensions to being a *reasoning* being, and dares neither look to the right nor to the left, oh! may my Medora still be the child of nature and simplicity, still venture to express all she feels, even at the risk of being called a strange romantic girl. (II, 14–15).

The passage parallels Mary Wollstonecraft's perception: "It is, however, sufficient for my present purpose to assert, that, whatever effect circumstances have on the abilities, every being may become virtuous by the exercise of its own reason. . . . In fact, it is a farce to call any being virtuous whose virtues do not result from the exercise of its own reason."[18] Both Smith and Wollstonecraft extend the philosophy of the age of reason to womankind and show that "rules to regulate the behaviour, and to preserve the reputation . . . too frequently supersede moral obligations."[19] Althea and Laura Glenmorris are models of a radical sensibility in which the balance of reason and feeling creates individualism. Those possessed of this true sensibility reject social stereotypes and desire to remedy social injustice.

## "The Virtue of Fortitude": Smith's Heroines

In the Preface to *Marchmont,* Smith writes that "my purpose has been to enforce the virtue of fortitude; and if my readers could form any idea of the state of my mind while I have been writing, they would allow that I practice the doctrine I preach" (I, xvi). She also stresses the importance of fortitude in the Preface to *The Young Philosopher,* stating that her theme is "the ill consequences of detraction; . . . the sad effects of parental resentment, and the triumph of fortitude in the daughter [Medora Glenmorris]" (I, vi–vii).

All of Smith's heroines demonstrate the fortitude she describes. Even Emmeline and Ethelinde, whose conduct is exemplary even by Dr. Gregory's standards, have the grit to take care of themselves in adversity. Her later heroines' behavior, however, reflects the romantic individualism that was soon to emerge. They resist tyrannical parents—and husbands—to create their own lives, and Smith offers them as role models whose actions demonstrate the fortitude that enables women to endure in a male-dominated society.

Like other British Jacobin feminists of her time, Smith believed that women's behavior was the result of an education that did not inculcate the virtue of fortitude. In "The Story of Henrietta," for instance, Maynard digresses on his life and describes a friend's comment on the character of women while comforting him on his wife's elopement with another man:

> I believe, my friend, it is a melancholy truth, that women have no character at all; and what is called their education gives none: it only helps to obliterate any distinguishing traits of original disposition which here and there may rise by chance into higher styles of character. We set out with saying that women *must* do so and so, and *think* so and so, as their grandmothers and mothers thought before them. If any of them venture even to look as if they had any will of their own, or supposed themselves capable of reasoning, how immediately are they marked as something monstrous, absurd, and out of the course of nature! . . . What then are we to expect from women, who, flattered into angels in their youth, forget that age will come; and sickness, perhaps, even sooner than time blast the perfections on which all their vanity is founded?[20] (II, 213–214)

The misogyny of the opening line, an allusion to Pope's "Of the Character of Women,"[21] reflects the speaker's disgust with women who are products of a traditional education, and Smith shows that when women lack character, the fault lies with men, who teach them to value themselves only for their beauty.

Smith establishes her heroines as role models who educate themselves through reading and thus learn the virtue of fortitude. A long passage from *The Young Philosopher* in which Medora tells of her experience during her abduction seems intended as a lecture on the author's view of female fortitude:

For my mother I determined to exert that resolution, which she had often told me was a virtue as becoming in a woman as in a man. It is not firmness, Medora, she has often said, that gives an unpleasant and unfeminine character to a woman; on the contrary, the mind which has acquired a certain degree of reliance on itself, which has learned to look on the good and evil of life, and to appreciate each, is alone capable of true gentleness and calmness. . . . She who has learned to despise the trifling objects that make women who pursue them appear so contemptible to men; she who without neglecting her person has ornamented her mind, and not merely ornamented, but has discovered that nothing is good for any human being, whether man or woman, but a conscientious discharge of their duty; . . . these are the acquisitions that will give tranquility to the heart and courage to the actions. (IV, 226–228)

As Smith knew from personal experience, women would need fortitude to survive in a male-dominated society where many believe that they are the slaves of their feelings and incapable of reason. Her novels abound with such misogynists. In *Desmond,* Bethel reports Geraldine Verney's comment that her husband has "for the understanding of all women . . . the most contemptible opinion; and says, 'that we are good for nothing but to make a shew while we are young, and to become nurses when we are old.' " Geraldine opines that "more than half the men in the world are of his opinion; and that by them, what some celebrated author has said, is generally allowed to be true—that a woman even of talents is only considered by men with that sort of pleasure with which they contemplate a bird who speaks a few words plainly" (II, 32–33). Mrs. Verney describes her father as similarly contemptuous of women: "*We* were always brought up as if we were designed for wives to the Vicars of Bray.[22] . . . I cannot help recollecting that he was a very Turk in principle, and hardly allowed women any pretensions to souls, or thought them worth more care than he bestowed on his horses, which were to look sleek, and do their paces well" (III, 133).

Men such as Geraldine's father, Smith suggests, are intimidated by intelligent women. In *The Banished Man,* Carlowitz, after describing his daughter Alexina as lacking in the qualities most men admire, says, "I am convinced there is nothing that is so repulsive to the generality of men, as the appearance of unusual strength of intellect in a woman.— Men who have talents are afraid of finding a rival in a mistress: and weak men, conscious of their own inferiority, dread lest they should make themselves liable to be governed or despised" (II, 171). Mohun, the villain in *Marchmont,* is similarly insecure with intelligent women.

He has "so thorough a contempt for the understandings of women, that he thought her [Althea's] mind not worth conciliating" (I, 211). And while "he thought the young and handsome highly honoured in being allowed to become objects of his notice and favour; . . . those who had (on whatever pretensions) acquired the name of sensible women, he vehemently declared them to be his aversion" (I, 224).

The heroines of Smith's novels following *Desmond* have the fortitude and self-reliance to survive in a world dominated by men like Mohun. In addition to the independence she shows in meeting Marchmont unchaperoned, Althea, in *Marchmont,* stands up to the tyranny of her father when she refuses the arranged marriage to Mohun. Medora (in *The Young Philosopher*) ultimately defeats the man who abducts her. And the Marchmont sisters show courage and self-reliance in planning a business that will support them and their mother.

Characters like Medora, Althea, Monimia (in *The Old Manor House*), and other Smith heroines are models of Jacobin feminism: women who have strong sensibilities but who, unlike Ethelinde and Emmeline, follow their own feelings, balanced by reason, rather than the dictates of a patriarchal society. Marchmont refers to a particularly interesting role model for women, from a historical perspective, in a letter to his friend Eversley:

> I believe that women, whom we have proudly called but children of a larger growth,[23] have, when they possess good understandings, more fortitude than men. Not to recall to observation the heroines of Antiquity, I feel ashamed of my Impatience, when I contemplate the most illustrious woman* of modern times, sitting in her dungeon amidst the most degraded of the human species . . . yet such was her firmness of mind, that she could arrange her miserable apartment, and call off her attention from the present horrors that surrounded her . . . and apply herself to botany and to music. However, the part this extraordinary woman took in the republican government of France may have raised prejudices and hatred against her. (IV, 342–343)

The asterisk leads to a footnote which identifies Mme. Roland, wife of a minister in the revolutionary government in France. Roland was a model of the strong, intelligent woman of her day, a woman whom Smith could admire.[24]

## "The Most Dreadful of All Fetters": Marriage and Slavery

In her political novels, Smith often uses slavery as a metaphor for marriage, both implicitly and explicitly. *Desmond* has several such references, perhaps because Geraldine Verney is a surrogate for Charlotte Smith, whose husband resembles Benjamin Smith. Geraldine, for instance, tells Bethel she doesn't fear going to France because even if she gets " 'among the wildest collection of those people, whose ferocity arises not from their present liberty, but their recent bondage, is it possible to suppose they will injure *me,* who am myself a miserable slave returning with trembling and reluctant steps, to put on the most dreadful of all fetters? Fetters that would even destroy the freedom of my mind?' " (III, 71). Her husband tries to dispose of her as property to the Duc de Romagnecourt, and she writes to her sister that "there is no humiliation to which I had not rather submit, than that of considering myself as his [Verney's] slave" (III, 142). She later refers to Verney as "the unfortunate man whose property I am" (III, 148).

Passages that compare the treatment of women to slavery recur in other novels and poems. Althea's father uses her as a pawn, trying to force a marriage to Mohun in order to get more political power. Kilbrodie holds Laura Glenmorris captive after pirates kidnap Armitage, also attempting to force a marriage and make himself master of the estate her husband left. In "The Story of Henrietta," Smith approaches the subject of woman as slave even more explicitly. Henrietta's father tries to make her marry one of his underlings, and she comments: "Lawyers have been some days in the house drawing the bill of sale, for what else can I call it. He has been used to purchase slaves, and feels no repugnance in selling his daughters to the most dreadful of all slavery" (II, 76–77). Henrietta later refers to the "detested sale, which my father means to make of his unhappy child" (II, 89). And in "Written at Bignor Park in Sussex, in August, 1799," Smith describes her lost dreams before referring to her separation from Benjamin Smith: ". . . too late/The poor Slave shakes the unworthy bonds away/which crush'd her!" (Curran, 78).

In *Maria, or the Wrongs of Woman,* Wollstonecraft describes marriage in a similar fashion. Maria perceives "the world as a vast prison, and women born slaves."[25] She also notes, "Marriage had bastilled me for life."[26] Darnford, her lover, declares that "till divorces could be more easily obtained," marriage is "the most insufferable bondage."[27]

In a few passages in her letters and novels, Smith goes beyond a comparison of marriage with slavery to equate arranged marriages with a form of prostitution. In "The Story of Henrietta," for instance, Denbigh inveighs against Henrietta's father, who would force her "to throw herself into the arms of a man she abhors, to become a legal prostitute to a contemptible wretch whom she must loath and abhor!" (II, 108). In a letter dated June 15, 1804, to Sarah Rose, Smith refers to her husband as the monster "to whom I was sold, a legal prostitute, in my early youth, or what the law calls infamy" (Huntington).

On the other hand, Smith's fiction shows no indication that she regarded all marriages as slavery. The Glenmorrises in *The Young Philosopher,* the Montgomeries in *Ethelinde,* and the Somerives in *The Old Manor House* have marriages that are, if not exactly unions of equals, as least happy, though Glenmorris at one point experiences some quite adolescent sexual insecurity (see pages 128–129 below). But, perhaps because of her own experience, Smith often shows marriage to be a form of tyranny for women. *Montalbert,* her sixth novel, focuses on a subtler form of tyranny: that exerted by a man who truly loves his wife.

## Tyranny and Marriage: Male Attitudes and Marital Relationships in *Montalbert*

Published in 1795, *Montalbert* shows signs of the chaos of the author's life at the time. Her daughter Augusta's long illness had ended in death, and the expense of her treatment brought penury to the family. In the Preface to *Marchmont,* published a year later, she writes that after Augusta died, "it was absolutely necessary for me to sit down to finish a novel for which I had received money from my present publisher, who would have been injured if I had not forced myself to fulfill my engagement. Could I *then* have written a preface, this apology for the defects of *Montalbert* would have been in its place; but I was at that time quite unable to ask the indulgence which it was impossible a book written in such circumstances should not have occasion for" (I, ix).

Like most of Smith's later novels, *Montalbert* seems hurriedly written. The characters are woodenly conventional, and the plot is implausible. The work relies too heavily on weeping sentiment and lacks the interesting secondary characters that enliven Smith's best fiction. Unlike the other novels following *Ethelinde, Montalbert* has no overtly political content: no references to reform of Parliament, no antiwar sentiments, and no specific criticism of British law. But it presents Smith's most cogent analysis of marital relationships and the tyranny of love, as well as a powerful, if understated, criticism of male attitudes toward women.

The novel begins with the parental authority theme Smith uses so often in her works. The heroine, Rosalie Lessington, is the daughter of a well-to-do clergyman, but was raised in the home of Mrs. Vyvian, a neighbor. This lady's parents had forced her to marry against her will, despite her love for Ormsby, a distant relative. After a multitude of hints, Smith finally reveals that Mrs. Vyvian is really Rosalie's mother and Ormsby her father. Mrs. Vyvian had borne her child secretly and given it to the Lessingtons to raise. Thus, Mrs. Vyvian is a victim of parental tyranny, and the theme reemerges when Mr. Lessington, Rosalie's presumed father, tries to force her to marry a man she dislikes. The language of the novel suggests that women are slaves to their parents' whims. Mrs. Lessington refers to her brutal husband as "the man to whom she had been sacrificed"[28] (I, 222), and Rosalie speaks similarly of her treatment. When her father orders her to dress to meet the husband he proposes for her, she ponders, "Gracious Heaven . . . , I am thus to be dressed up, and offered like an animal to sale" (I, 75). Mrs. Vyvian reminds her that "it is sometimes not in the power of young women to resist parental authority" (I, 237).

Rosalie meets Mrs. Vyvian's nephew, Montalbert, a young man who was brought up in Italy after his father married there. He falls in love with Rosalie, and she returns his sentiments. Unfortunately, his strong-minded mother[29] has a wife in mind for him, and she would be unlikely to accept a woman who is not only portionless but the daughter of a Protestant minister. Montalbert, though, persuades Rosalie to marry him secretly before he must return to Italy.

Montalbert's jealousy, a ruling passion, becomes apparent early in the novel. Before their marriage, he cannot bear to return to Italy and leave Rosalie "exposed to the persecution of lovers, which it distracted him only to think of" (I, 164). After their marriage, when he sees her at a play with her mother in a box with another family, whose sons vie for Rosalie's attention, "[h]is impetuous spirit could ill submit to a longer course of such punishment" (I, 218), and he improvises a scheme to get her away from the playhouse.

That Montalbert loves Rosalie is obvious, but his love makes him a tyrant. When Rosalie finally leaves England to meet him, they travel through France, where Rosalie's beauty inspires admiration. Such behavior from other men causes Montalbert pain: "He not unfrequently was sensible of something like jealousy, for which he failed not to reason with himself; but still his dislike of the adulation which he saw likely to be offered to his wife, wherever she appeared, conquered the sense he had of the absurdity of feeling such a sentiment in regard to her" (II, 135).

They settle in Messina, where they live in a palace owned by the Count de Alozzi, and Rosalie bears Montalbert's son. Montalbert commutes to Naples to keep his mother happy and unaware of his marriage, and de Alozzi shows signs of passion for Rosalie. A catastrophic earthquake forwards his plans. A chain of melodramatic adventures follows, as de Alozzi abducts Rosalie after he finds her. She is a captive for some time, held at the instigation of Montalbert's mother, who has discovered her son's marriage. Eventually, Rosalie escapes, and a sentimental Englishman, Walsingham, rescues her and returns her to England.

Although Walsingham falls in love with Rosalie, he is the soul of honor. Of necessity, however, she travels with the man and accepts support from him when they arrive in England.[30] But when Montalbert finally finds her, he listens to local gossip about Rosalie and Walsingham and assumes the worst. Thus, when he meets Rosalie accidentally and she tries to embrace him, he rejects her without asking for an explanation: "Lovely, lost creature!—art thou, indeed, lost to me?—Yes—for ever lost! and here—too well convinced that all I have heard is true— here we part for ever!" (III, 193). He then exercises the power of a father and sends the local authorities to take Rosalie's child away from her, authorizing them with a note:

> THE father of the unfortunate child, known by the name of Henry Montalbert, requires to have him immediately delivered to the two persons who attend for that purpose, and who will conduct him to H. MONTALBERT (III, 199)

The letter drives Rosalie into a fit of madness.

Even the hint of improper conduct is enough to poison the minds of all men who know Rosalie: Vyvian, her half brother (Mrs. Vyvian has died during her absence); Lessington, presumed to be her brother until the discovery of her true parentage; and Ormsby, her true father. When they find her, their minds are easily poisoned by the same gossip that turned Montalbert against her. And because Rosalie is unable to speak for herself, they believe her an adulteress. Then in a cleverly plotted case of mistaken identities, Montalbert first contacts Walsingham's brother by mistake and challenges him but meets Rosalie's savior first; a duel ensues in which Montalbert wounds the man who had saved his wife.

Even Ormsby, her father, is so jealous "for the honor of his daughter" (IV, 264) that he is ready to fight first Walsingham and then Montalbert. And Lessington tries to soothe Montalbert after the duel by saying, "Which of us . . . might not have acted as you did?" (IV, 310).

Smith consistently portrays women as possessions for men to fight over. Almost all of the many duels in her novels are fought by men who want to own a woman and resent any other man's attention to her. Delamere is prepared to challenge men who notice Emmeline and is eventually killed in a duel; Thorold and Vavasour fight over Celestina; and Sir John Belgraves challenges Orlando Somerive (*The Old Manor House*), to name a few instances. Duels are the stuff of melodramatic fiction, of course, and perhaps some women readers of the day might have experienced a certain wish fulfillment in dreaming of fiery young lovers fighting over them.

In *Montalbert,* however, the duel between the title character and Walsingham and the attitude of the men who love Rosalie are clearly criticisms of male behavior. Smith portrays Montalbert's jealousy as a fault that leads to the tyrannical abuse of his wife. On the basis of malicious talk about Rosalie, he sets out to claim his son and takes a lawyer with him (III, 298). The reference to the presence of an attorney brings to mind Smith's feelings about injustices perpetrated under British law by those with wealth and power, but it also offers a quiet comment on the powerlessness of women. Smith had good reason to know that she had little status under British law and that a husband could do with his wife what he would.

Rosalie's helplessness even when dealing with men who love her is apparent in other ways. After she makes a dramatic recovery and her child and husband are restored to her, even though she knows of the duel and Walsingham's condition, she is afraid to inquire about the man who had saved her: "Too well aware from the slight and half-stiffled narrative she had received from her brother and her father, that Montalbert's jealousy had been the cause of the step he had taken as to her child, she feared to awaken it anew by naming him [Walsingham]" (IV, 312).

Mary Anne Schofield observes quite correctly that "*Montalbert* is a story of mothering—of the loss and then the discovery of a mother figure." Schofield points out that Mrs. Vyvian, Mrs. Lessington, and Signora Belcastro (Montalbert's mother) are failures as parents, for "all exhibit the capitulation of female decency to unworthy male demands."[31] But the primary focus in Smith's fiction remains on the

tyranny of fathers, husbands, and male authority figures in general. Rosalie Lessington, Geraldine Verney, Althea Dacres, and Henrietta Maynard have tyrannical fathers who insist on marriages that would make
their daughters miserable but would bring financial benefit to themselves. Rosalie Lessington suffers the same sort of tyranny, even from a
husband who truly cares for her, because of his failure to control his passion with reason and to seek an explanation of rumors.

Montalbert's jealousy, of course, stems from his fear that Rosalie has
known another man. This preoccupation with female chastity is yet
another aspect of the tyranny that men exercise over women in Smith's
novels. She shows women to be possessions of men who are so fiercely
jealous of possible contamination by other men that they are ready to
fight on the even slightest provocation. In several novels, Smith uses the
jealousy theme to illustrate men's control of women, even when they
love them. This tyranny focuses to an irrational degree on reputation.

## "A Fate Infinitely Worse Than Death": Rape and Women as Property

While Rosalie Lessington is held prisoner at Formiscusa in Italy, she
learns that Algerian pirates occasionally raid the coast and carry off
women as slaves, which she describes in the journal she writes throughout volume 2 as "a fate infinitely worse than death" (II, 256). The
phrase recurs elsewhere in Smith's novels, as do the rape threats that
they suggest. In *Desmond,* when Geraldine is in the hands of banditti,
she writes her recollections to her sister, describing herself as ready to
faint, but aware that unconsciousness might "subject me to the most
hideous insults" (III, 278). And it is Desmond who uses the familiar
phrase after he rescues her when he acknowledges that they are still in
danger and he dreads "ten thousand times worse than death, the consequences to you, if superior numbers should render my endeavours to
guard you fruitless" (II, 284–285).

The phrase "fate worse than death" does not occur in *The Young
Philosopher,* but the certain future of the woman raped does. George Delmont and Glenmorris may be philosophers, but their adherence to reason does not extend to a willingness to accept defilement of their
women by other men. When he returns after his kidnapping, Armitage
immediately takes Laura to task on her conduct during her residence
with Lord Macarden, who had fought a duel with Kilbrodie after the
latter had tried to force her to marry him. "If I have lost my peace,"

Glenmorris tells his wife, "if I have lost my honour, tell me, Laura, who can restore *them?* where shall I find my peace, my honour again?" (II, 228) And after Medora is abducted, Delmont worries as much that she might have been deflowered as that she might be dead. He goes to Sir Appulby Gorges to settle his uncle's estate because he needs money to seek Medora and marry her "if he regained her, such as his fond hopes sometimes suggested (the same lovely, innocent, and blameless creature he left)" (III, 272–273). But the conditional tense leaves no doubt as to what would happen had she been raped or seduced.

An even more obvious instance of patriarchal attitudes toward women as property occurs in "The Story of Henrietta." Denbigh's primary concern after Henrietta's captivity with the Maroons is her virginity. When he finds her in her uncle's refuge, he describes his sensations as "vague, tumultuous, confused, and painful beyond any that I had hitherto experienced" (II, 152), and he fears "evils worse than death" have befallen her (II, 171). His first question to Maynard is, "What has she suffered?" (II, 149). He determines that he will not abandon her, "though I believe myself the most wretched of human beings" (II, 156). He goes on, "Disgraced, undone, as perhaps she is, I will now stay near her till—My fate at least will soon be decided, after hers is known" (II, 163). He plans to find an asylum for Henrietta if she has been raped, but not to marry her.

The phase "a fate worse than death" would soon become a cliché; and, clearly, Smith uses the fear of rape as a part of the melodramatic plots of her novels. But the exaggerated response of her male characters to the possibility that another man might defile their beloved shows why rape could truly be described as "worse than death." In addition to the pain and humiliation of the act itself, rape meant social ostracism. Surely the hysteria of Smith's male characters at the prospect of their beloved's impurity is a criticism of the patriarchal insistence that female virtue transcend all other qualities of womanhood.

Smith's criticism of male attitudes toward female purity parallels those of other Jacobin feminists. Mary Robinson, for instance, writes, "The laws of man have long since decreed, that the jewel, Chastity, and the purity of uncontaminated morals, are the brightest ornaments of the female sex. Yet, the framers of those laws are indefatigable in promoting their violation."[32] Mary Wollstonecraft's analysis of gender discrimination is similar: "If the honour of a woman, as it is absurdly called, be safe, she may neglect every social duty; nay, ruin her family by gaming and extravagance; yet still present a shameless front."[33]

## "A Female Band": Smith and Wollstonecraft

The works of radical women writers did not go unnoticed. In 1798 the Reverend Richard Pohlwele published his poem *The Unsex'd Females,* an attack on women who spoke out against gender discrimination. Pohlwele expresses regret that "charming SMITH resign'd her power to please,/Poetic feeling and poetic ease." In one of his voluminous footnotes (which considerably outweigh the work's verse), Pohlwele praises Smith's sonnets: "Sweetly picturesque, she creates with the pencil of a Gilpin, and infuses her own soul into the landscape." He also has praise for *Ethelinde* and *Emmeline,* as might be expected from so conservative a reader. But why, he asks, "does she suffer her mind to be infected with the Gallic mania? I hope, ere this, she is completely recovered from a disorder, of which, indeed, I observed only a few slight symptoms."[34]

Pohlwele directs the brunt of his attack at Mary Wollstonecraft, with side glances at Mary Hays, Mary Robinson, Helen Maria Williams, and Anna Laetitia Barbauld, women whom he calls an "Amazonian band— the female Quixotes of the new philosophy."[35] Pohlwele was an arch conservative, and his attack focuses on women who protest against male dominance: "Survey with me, what ne'er our fathers saw,/A female band despising NATURE'S law."[36] He contrasts these women with the conservative Hannah More, whom he describes in a note as "a character, in all points, diametrically opposite to Miss Wollstonecraft."[37]

Pohlwele's pairing of Smith with Wollstonecraft was more appropriate than he knew. That the two women were personally acquainted cannot be demonstrated but seems likely. Neither mentions the other in surviving letters. But they knew each other's work. Wollstonecraft had reviewed *Emmeline* and *Desmond* for *The Analytical Review,* and Smith was well acquainted with Godwin.[38] Furthermore, in *The Young Philosopher,* Smith offers three homages to Wollstonecraft. One occurs following Delmont's discovery of Sir Harry Richmond's treatment of his mistresses and his daughter, when he muses: "These are indeed . . . among the wrongs of woman" (IV, 166). The reference is to Wollstonecraft's posthumously published novel *Maria, or The Wrongs of Women,* which had appeared only five months before *The Young Philosopher.*[39] At another point, Smith quotes "Letters written from Norway, Sweden, and Denmark, by Mary Wollstonecroft [sic]" in a footnote (II, 197).

The third reference appears in the Preface to *The Young Philosopher.* Smith notes that she had written the scenes describing Laura Glenmorris's captivity in a madhouse before she had read *Maria,* in which the heroine is confined in an insane asylum by a husband who has taken that opportunity to put her out of the way (as does Laura Glenmorris's mother). Still sensitive to charges against her *Manon Lescaut* translation, Smith writes, "As I once before heard the charge of *plagiarism* . . . , I may just mention, that the incident of the confinement in a madhouse of one of my characters was designed before I saw the fragment of 'The Wrongs of Woman,' by a Writer whose talents I greatly honoured, and whose untimely death I deeply regret; from her I should not blush to borrow, and if I had done so I would have acknowledged it" (I, iv–v).

The passages in the two novels share a few similarities. Like Maria, who gets help from Jemima, a servant at the madhouse, Laura wins over a goodhearted servant to assist her. Smith's description of the setting, moreover, resembles Wollstonecraft's. Additionally, both women are victims of a legal system that allows those with money and power to victimize women. But Smith's story has no parallel for the love affair between Maria and Darnford. And the madhouse scenes in *The Young Philosopher* resemble those in Burney's *Cecilia* more than Wollstonecraft's *Maria*.

Yet Smith's mention of "the wrongs of woman" halfway through volume 4 is difficult to explain. *Maria* appeared on January 19, 1798, in Godwin's publication of Wollstonecraft's posthumous works.[40] *The Young Philosopher* must have been either finished or very nearly so by that time. In a letter to William Davies dated February 27, 1798, Smith asks him to "send . . . every sheet of the corrected letter press as fast as it is worked off" because a "literary Man of considerable reputation" (Huntington) is critiquing it for her. She refers specifically to the sheets for volume 4, so the novel was printed in letter press proofs only a few weeks after *Maria* was sold to the public.

Thus, the reference to the "wrongs of woman," in the middle of the fourth volume, suggests that Smith wrote the passage before *Maria* was published. And since some time would have necessarily elapsed between Godwin's submission of copy to the printer and its appearance in bookstores, we are left with the interesting possibility that Smith either saw the manuscript of *Maria* before the novel was printed or knew enough about it to refer to "the wrongs of woman." This possibility raises yet another: that Godwin is the "literary Man of considerable reputation" who critiqued *The Young Philosopher*.[41]

That Smith saw a copy of *Maria* in manuscript is a fascinating speculation that cannot be resolved with certainty. The homages to Wollstonecraft in *The Young Philosopher*, however, amount to a declaration of intellectual kinship that critics have not sufficiently noted. Janet Todd, for instance, writes, "Charlotte Smith coupled her overt political and social statements with almost farcical exaggeration of the elements of the traditional feminine novel which for financial reasons she felt she had to write" and goes on to compare Smith with Burney and Radcliffe as women who established a sort of moral authority in fiction, achieving a "conjunction of genre and gender" in the novel "and setting it in critical perspective"[42]

Indeed, Smith's novels do superficially resemble those of Radcliffe and Burney. Like Burney, she focuses on love relationships frustrated by parental authority. And in the Preface of *The Young Philosopher,* Smith admits that, like Radcliffe, she used the "giants, and necromancers, and ogers [sic] of ancient romance" to attract and hold readers. But unlike Radcliffe, she presents them in the form of "people of that sort whom I *have seen*" (I, vii)—those who corrupt the British system of law and government for selfish purposes and who create the sort of mental subordination of women she describes in her novels. The portrayal of social injustice in Smith's fiction has no parallel in the works of Radcliffe or Burney. And textual evidence in Smith's political novels reveals a close ideological relationship between her thoughts on the plight of women and those of Wollstonecraft and others who wrote on gender issues in her day. For Smith, writing fiction was of necessity a "literary business." At the risk of losing her reading audience, however, she continued to embed social and political ideas in her novels and attempted to educate her readers regarding the wrongs of woman.

# Chapter Seven

# *Letters of a Solitary Wanderer*
# and Books for Children

In a delightfully gossipy letter to Sarah Rose dated July 30, 1804, Smith writes:

> I began a novel . . . , three years ago & did a great deal of it, but cares encreasing and comforts decreasing, in a blessed proportion & being sick both in spirit & in body, I threw it by & said—"it is time to have done— write lullabies for thy grandchildren but don't twaddle about love with spectacles on thy nose." . . . However now that my lullabies are done—I took out again my old Novel, & really I don't think it *very foolish,* & it is as little boring as may be—so if I could divest myself of the fear of grow- ing as foolish in my old age, as some certain good Ladies of *more eminent fame,* I should even finish it, in the hope of getting £400 by my imagi- nary hero to help any living stories—Tell me honestly my dear Madam if you think I ought to do this—or go on making Childrens [sic] stories— as Mr. Johnson seems to recommend.

Rose's answer has not survived, and neither has the fragment of a novel to which the letter refers.

## *Letters of a Solitary Wanderer*

By the turn of the century, Smith's career as a novelist was almost fin- ished. Her only work of fiction published after 1799 is *Letters of a Solitary Wanderer.* As early as 1789, Smith had conceived the idea for a book comprised of short tales. On September 28 of that year, she writes to a publisher, "Having now completed my last engagement with Mr. Cadell—& *finding much of scruple and hesitation abt. him which is irksome to me;* I wish to know whether I may consider you as being willing to *treat* with me for a work I purpose [sic] immediately to begin, of tales, in the way of Marmontel.[1] I am told there is no such book well done in Eng- lish—I thot three small volumes wd. probably be successful" (Princeton). Apparently Davies did not encourage the idea, as it was 11 years before she applied it in *Letters,* a series of four tales linked by a framing device: a romantic wanderer who meets individuals with stories to tell, which the Wanderer relates to a correspondent.

William Low published the first two volumes of *Letters* in 1800. He had contracted for three more, but he died before they were published. At an auction of Low's copyrights, manuscripts, and contracts with authors, Crosby and Letterman bought the final two volumes of *Letters,* which, according to the Preface for volume 4, were published in 1802.[2] Smith had a sixth volume in mind that would round off the work. But Low's demise led the book, as she writes in the Preface to volume 4, "to appear under very aukward [sic] circumstances; and prevented my concluding it, at least at present, according to my original agreement" (iv). Therefore, she had to forgo telling the story of the Wanderer in a sixth volume.

By 1800 governmental repression had effectively ended the discussion of reform, and *Letters* has no systematically developed political theme. All but the last volume are set outside England. But comments in the two prefaces (in volumes 1 and 4) and incidents in the tales reflect the hatred of tyranny expressed in all of Smith's later novels. Volume 1, however, "The Story of Edouarda," is a gothic thriller replete with monkish superstition, sublime settings, and suggestions of the supernatural in the style that Ann Radcliffe had made popular by this time. One of the many ironies of Smith's life is that at the beginning of her career, she created the conventional sentimental/gothic that Ann Radcliffe adapted to achieve fame, and at the end of it Smith imitated the heightened gothic style that Radcliffe had made popular. But volume 2 is "The Story of Henrietta," with its condemnation of slavery. Volume 3, "The Story of Corisande," set in 16th-century France, is a history lesson culminating in a paean to the French king Henry IV, whom British republicans and French Girondists saw as the model for monarchs.

Volumes 4 and 5, titled "The Hungarian," begin in Hungary, part of the Austrian empire in 1800. While Austria was allied with Great Britain in the wars against France, British republicans viewed the Hapsburg empire as the epitome of tyrannies. Thus, Smith's hero, Leopold Somerfeldt, is an English liberal in Hungarian clothing. The youngest son of an elderly count, he reads works by Sidney and Milton, books, he writes, "such as taught me to idolize political liberty" (IV, 41). His eldest brother ingratiates himself with the Hapsburg court; loses his Hungarian identity; and, when he discovers that his father is setting aside money to give Leopold an independence so that he can marry Gertude, an English girl, gets an order from the emperor to imprison the old count and take his property.

The scene later shifts to England and Ireland, where Smith introduces Leonora Wardenell, Gertrude's sister and another autobiographical character, who tells her story in a digression.[3] Even in an English setting, Smith reintroduces the theme of the romantic individual oppressed by forces of tyranny. Leopold meets one of his brothers who, like the eldest, has lost his Hungarian identity and won a place in the Austrian Court. When the two quarrel, the brother uses his political influence as an Austrian to have Leopold expelled from England under the Alien Act. The story ends happily when the Wanderer, who is enormously wealthy, provides for Leopold and Gertrude.

Smith had long since lost favor with the reviewers. Reviews of *Desmond,* a novel that might have inspired sedition charges a few years after it was published, were uniformly positive in 1792. Yet one reviewer's comments on *The Old Manor House,* published just one year later, reflect the change in political climate: "From the name of Mrs. Charlotte Smith we certainly were led to expect something above the common love cant of novels."[4] The writer then criticizes the work on moral grounds. Reviews of later novels are rarely so negative as this one, but neither are they as long (a sign of respect for the author) nor as flattering as reviews of Smith's early work. Even worse for her "literary business," fewer magazines bothered to review her novels at all.

In the February 7, 1804, letter cited above, Smith comforts Sarah Rose on a personal loss and mentions that in her fifty-fourth year—near the end of what she calls "my long & weary pilgrimage"—she is "tremblingly alive . . . and bleeding at every pore," wounded by those who express sympathy that is "commonplace cant" (Huntington). Throughout her career, she was also "tremblingly alive" to all forms of criticism. In the preface of volume 4 to *Letters of a Solitary Wanderer,* Smith suggests that the change in tone of the reviews was politically motivated. She rails at reviewers who had criticized the intrusion of her personal problems in her works. "The consequence of this abuse of the design of reviewers," she writes, "is, that these monthly oracles are, for the most part, considered as the mere vehicles of political animosity, written by the humblest retainers of party," many of whom have natural talents that are at best "adequate to the task of correcting the advertisements of a country newspaper" (IV, viii).

In the last few years of her life, Smith received little encouragement from publishers. Even Joseph Johnson showed less interest in her work.

In a letter to Sarah Rose (December 26, 1805, Huntington), she writes that she is a prisoner in her room because of her illness and is "the more in despair about it, because he [Johnson] does not seem to think any thing I can now do, worth purchasing & has never published the last book he purchased of me."[5]

## "My Coming Book Is for the Governesses"

During the last five years of her life, Smith devoted her time to writing children's books and to preparing what she hoped would be the third volume in a three-volume edition of *Elegiac Sonnets*.[6] Thus, on August 12, 1804, she tells Joseph Cooper Walker in a letter, "My coming book is for the governesses" (Huntington). She had begun writing such books 10 years earlier. On July 22, 1794, she writes to Davies that she has been thinking of producing a schoolbook over the rest of the summer because "I can only do poetry occasionally." She planned a book "intended to form their [children's] taste for poetry and natural history" (Beinecke). Then on October 2, 1794, she proposes what would become *Rural Walks* (published in 1795), modeled on Mrs. Barbauld's *Evening at Home*. "The idea of writing such a book," she tells Davies, "occurred to me from the extreme difficulty of finding such books as were fit for my youngest daughter, a child of twelve years old" (Beinecke). *Rambles Farther* followed in 1796 and *Minor Morals* in 1798. In the years following the turn of the century, she devoted most of her writing time to books "for the governesses," completing the highly regarded *Conversations, Introducing Poetry* (1804), *History of England* (1806), and *The Natural History of Birds* (1807).[7]

These books seem a far cry from the sentimental/gothic style and the political themes of her novels from the 1790s and the heightened romanticism of her mature poems. Yet Smith's children's books parallel the didacticism of her fiction, though dedicated to younger readers. As the audience for her novels was, for the most part, young women, her children's books seem primarily dedicated to girls. *History of England,* for instance, is subtitled *from the earliest records, to the peace of Amiens; in a series of letters to a young lady at school.* And *Rural Walks* begins with a Charlotte Smith–like woman, Mrs. Woodfield, taking charge of her brother's teenage daughter, Caroline Cecil, whose mother had recently passed away and who has been spoiled by the dissipated lifestyle of London. Mrs. Woodfield, who lives in a small village, has two daughters of her own, and she changes the proud Caroline's values to sympathy for the unfortunate and an appreciation of nature. Similarly, in *Minor Morals* a father places his four daughters, ranging in age from seven to 12, under the care of Mrs. Belmour, an aunt, who forms their values and teaches them lessons in natural science. Sophy, the eldest, has been spoiled by the fashionable lifestyle of her family, and Mrs. Belmour must teach her to feel for nature and other people. Throughout her writing career, Smith sought to instruct her readers. Her earliest novels teach lessons on conduct for young women, and her later novels expand the lessons to politics, botany, geology, and history. Like other women writers influenced by the revolutionary thought of the day, she recognized the need for women's education. Because boys from middle-class families would be likely to receive formal schooling, Smith wrote her children's books for girls, just as she had used her novels to bring knowledge to young women.

# Chapter Eight
# Charlotte Smith's Achievement

Until the past few years, when Charlotte Smith was remembered at all by literary historians the commentary might resemble that of Miss Stanley in "Catherine or the Bower," one of Jane Austen's juvenile works. Austen's Miss Stanley, a gushy young lady with "accomplishments" but little education, refers to Smith's novels as the "sweetest things in the world" and finds Emmeline "*so much* better than any of the others."[1] In the nearly two hundred years following Smith's death, most literary historians have written of her works in similar fashion. Samuel Chew finds that although in *Desmond* and *The Young Philosopher* she is "close to the doctrinaire novelists," nonetheless "in general she is closer to Ann Radcliffe."[2] Ironically, Smith has often been remembered for precisely the sort of fiction that she deplored. Only recently has she been rediscovered as a major literary talent.

Smith was a woman of her times, caught between the class assumptions of the country gentry that she inherited from her family and the revolutionary ethos that swept Europe in the 1790s. Her lifetime was a period of change, and Smith's works demonstrate a psychic split between the old class-structured society and the egalitarian thought of the day. In both her fiction and her poetry, she attacks British governmental policies and defends republican positions on political and social issues. Yet she clung to her own identity as a member of the ruling class, remaining "Charlotte Smith of Bignor Park." Even though her heroes espouse republican ideology, they express contempt for the very class from which that ideology sprang.[3] None of her heroes can bear working in business. Marchmont speaks for all of them, and no doubt for the author, when he says, "Whoever has had, as a distressed man, much to do with the money-getting and money-saving part of the British nation, will not talk in a very elevated strain of its liberal minds and noble spirits" (IV, 70). And although Smith speaks out against the mental subordination of women, she assumes, as does Wollstonecraft, that the proper role for womankind is motherhood.

Perhaps more than any writer of her time, Charlotte Smith expanded the horizons of the novel. She accepted the conventional character types and plots of the sentimental novel as written by Samuel Richardson and his imitators. But Smith was a bellwether of innovation. She enhanced the novel of sensibility with the romantic description of nature that her readers admired. She also brought the language of the Burkean sublime to fiction, and she used the sublime and the picturesque as part of the sentimental-gothic style that she first developed and Ann Radcliffe later imitated and made popular. It was in Smith's work, however, that we first see the beautiful, vulnerable heroine of the sentimental novel against the backdrop of the sublimely ruined castle. The testimony of contemporary reviews demonstrates that Smith charmed the readers of her day with *Emmeline* and *Ethelinde.* And in her best work, her fiction rises above convention. She created memorable characters in *The Old Manor House* and *Desmond,* and when she had leisure in which to plan her work, she wrote carefully plotted and coherent fiction.

But if Smith had written nothing more than the early novels of didactic sensibility and the first six editions of *Elegiac Sonnets,* she might justly be remembered as the innovator of an amusing but trivial sub-genre of fiction and a poet with a judicious eye for popular taste. Her later novels, however, are on the cutting edge of change at a critical moment in history. In *Desmond,* she dramatizes the current of ideas that swirled through this period of dynamic transformation, a time when democratic revolutions rocked the world. Because of the necessity of supporting her family through her "literary business," Smith was tied to the conventions of the sentimental novel. Many of her novels are flawed by the weeping sentiment and digressive structure of that genre of fiction, and by the haste in which she often wrote. But readers interested in the liberal thought that led to the fall of the monarchy in France, a challenge to the aristocratic establishment in Great Britain, and a reform movement that would change Great Britain over the next hundred years—as well as to the beginnings of the feminist critique and the antislavery movement—will find Smith's novels a gold mine of information.

Smith thought that her claim to be remembered by later generations would come from her poetry. A year before her death, she wrote to William Davies, "It is on the poetry I have written that I trust for the little reputation I may hereafter have. I know that it is not the least likely among the works of modern poets to reach another period and any judgment can be formed from the success it has had in this" (August 18, 1805, Beinecke). Ironically, literary history has almost ignored her poems, and such recognition as she has had—up to the past few years, at least—has come from her novels. As does her fiction, Smith's poetry reflects the climate of change in her time, spanning the shift in taste from the preromanticism of the 1780s to a fully articulated romanticism in her later works.

In her best poems, Smith deserves to be read not simply as a writer whose work demonstrates changes in taste, but as one of the premier lyric voices of her time and a worthy contemporary of the male romantic poets. The moving "St. Monica," for instance, written near the end of her life, is not only a manifesto of the romantic sensibility, a fully realized perception of what Smith elsewhere calls the "Divine Omnipotence that pervades all nature,"[4] but one of the finest poems of that era. Smith had grown enormously in the mastery of her art by the time *Beachy Head with Other Poems* was published. Curran perceptively notes that "none of the canonical male Romantic poets who lived long enough to grow old got better,"[5] while Smith did her finest work at the end of her career and in rapidly failing health.

It is heartening to see anthologies including Smith's poetry and journals publishing articles on her work. As recognition spreads of Smith's novels and poems, perhaps the final lines from "To My Lyre" will at last accurately reflect her place in literary history:

> And as the time ere long must come
> When I lie silent in the tomb,
>     Thou wilt preserve these mournful pages;
> For gentle minds will love my verse,
> And pity shall my strains rehearse,
>     And tell my name to distant ages.

# Notes and References

*Chapter One*

    1.  Charles Dickens, *A Tale of Two Cities* (New York and London: Oxford University Press, 1987), 1.

    2.  Dickens, 1.

    3.  Jean-Jacques Rousseau, *Julie, ou La Nouvelle Héloïse,* trans. Judith H. McDowell (University Park, Pa.: Penn State University Press, 1968), 238–39.

    4.  Smith's sister, Catherine Anne Dorset, wrote an essay that Sir Walter Scott included in *The Lives of the Novelists* (London and New York: Dent and Sons, n.d.). Also, *British Public Characters, 1800–1801* (London: Richard Phillips, 1798) includes a brief description of the author's life, apparently based on an interview given a few years before her death. Another biographical essay appears in Sir Edgerton Brydges's *Censuria Literaria,* published in 1815. The best biography, however, is by Florence M.A. Hilbish, *Charlotte Smith: Poet and Novelist* (Philadelphia: University of Pennsylvania Press, 1941).

    5.  *British Public Characters of 1800–1801,* III, 39. The discrepancy between the title and the date of publication (1798) is one of the vagaries of 18th-century publishing.

    6.  Hilbish, 36.

    7.  Charlotte Smith, "To My Lyre," in *The Poems of Charlotte Smith,* ed. Stuart Curran (New York and Oxford: Oxford University Press, 1993), 311. Unless otherwise indicated, all citations of Smith's poetry will be taken from this edition and will appear in the text. The terms in this quote are the jargon of Benjamin Smith's business. All appear in the *Oxford English Dictionary.* A "tret" is a duty paid on goods going out of country. "Drawbacks," on the other hand, are duties returned on excise or import duties previously paid. The word "tare" has an obscure meaning but in mercantile context probably meant both waste and deterioration of goods and the weight of wrapping or containers deducted from the gross weight of the product. "Bottomry" was a sort of specialized mortgage that enabled the owner of a ship to pay for the expenses of the voyage.

    8.  Dorset, "Charlotte Smith," in Scott, 307. Scott presents Dorset's biographical essay first and follows with his critical assessment.

    9.  Hilbish, 39.

    10.  Dorset, 312.

    11.  Dorset, 312.

    12.  Dorset, 313.

    13.  Hilbish includes the will as an appendix, 565–580.

    14.  Dorset, 313.

15.  Hilbish, 85.

16.  Dorset, 315.

17.  Libraries that hold Smith's letters are identified by name in the text or in Notes and References.

18.  Dorset relates the incident, which she says her sister described in a letter (316).

19.  Hilbish, 118. Manon is the passionate but rather dissolute heroine of the work, and Werther (modern translations usually include an "h," but the letter is omitted in English translations of Smith's time) is the hero of *The Sorrows of Werther,* who kills himself because of his love for Lotte, a married woman. Werther became a sort of cult hero among those who admired sensibility. Despite Steevens' squeamishness, *Manon Lescaut* became quite popular in conservative Britain. In a letter to William Davies on July 22, 1795, Smith relays an order from a circulating library owner for 21 books, which are the "light reading as are most in request" (Beinecke) and includes Prévost's novel as one. The only book she includes from her own works is *Ethelinde, or the Recluse of the Lake.*

20.  Hilbish, 321.

21.  By the terms of her father's will, Smith would receive another £2,000 on her stepmother's death.

22.  June 4, 1804. William Davies was the managing partner in Thomas Cadell's publishing firm, which published several of Smith's books. When Cadell retired in 1793, he left his interest to his son, Thomas, and the firm was renamed Cadell and Davies. Smith's letters to Davies are extraordinarily confessional, and one wonders what this businessman must have thought of her four to five close-packed pages of details about her personal life.

23.  Hilbish, 321.

24.  Charlotte Smith, *The Banished Man* (Dublin: Wogan et al., 1794), II, 200 (hereafter cited in the text). The Dublin edition is the second.

25.  Two other works have been attributed to her. *D'Arcy,* a novel, was published in Dublin in 1793 with the name C. Smith on the title page. Hilbish argues convincingly that Charles Smith, another writer of the period, may have written the book (189–90). At any rate, Smith denies authorship of the work in her letters. She writes to Davies, "Mr. [Joseph Cooper] Walker promis'd to send me a Novel call'd . . . Darcy, published *in my name at Dublin* with a dedication to the Duke of York. The Manouvre [sic] was even more impudent than the usual impudent attempts of Irish bookmakers and booksellers, & I had rather a curiosity to see what the worthy Author said to his RH [Royal Highness] in my name" (September 3, 1795, Beinecke).

In her anthology *Modern Theatre* (London: Hurst et al., 1811), Elizabeth Inchbald attributed the play *What Is She,* a comedy of manners, to Charlotte Smith. Smith never mentioned the play by title in her letters, but that she had tried her hand at comedy is quite certain. In a letter, she writes: "You have little reason to fear that if the comedy should be matured you will be deprived of your darling privilege—of curtailing, altering—hinting—so far from it, had I not been encouraged to believe you would condescend to take such trouble, I had never ventured to think of an undertaking to which I still fear my talents are unequal. . . . The scenes I have written I will not trouble you with till they are more worthy of being attended to . . . a comedy of three acts is no light undertaking" (Beinecke, dated February 10, probably 1788; no addressee listed, but probably to William Hayley, an early mentor).

   The play's light and lively style is unlike most of Smith's work, but internal evidence suggests she may have written it. The Epilogue refers to the author as a woman, and the plot hinges on a disastrous marriage not unlike Smith's It also has a good deal of satire of the law, a staple in Smith's works, and a sneering allusion to a sham sentimentalist, who "sighs over the distresses of a novel" but "avoids sickness and poverty as though she herself were not human." This condemnation of false sensibility is exactly like Smith's rejection of sentiment for its own sake in favor of a radical sensibility in her later poems and novels (Inchbald, I, 260). That Smith wrote the play seems likely, but attribution must remain uncertain.

   26.   Beinecke. Smith often places the pound sign after the number in her letters.

   27.   She occasionally uses this expression in her letters. See, for instance, letter to an unidentified correspondent dated August 23, 1797 (Huntington).

   28.   April 16, 1797, Beinecke. Smith had written *Marchmont* in 1796, which earned £200 for its four volumes, and completed her subscription publication of the Seventh Edition of *Elegiac Sonnets* in 1797.

   29.   Judith Stanton, "Charlotte Smith's Literary Business: Income, Patronage, and Indigence," *The Age of Johnson: A Scholarly Annual* 6 (1987): 375–401.

   30.   See John Brunet, *A History of the Cost of Living* (Harmondsworth, England: Penguin Books, 1969).

   31.   October 25, 1802, to William Davies (Beinecke). Egremont apparently tired of Smith's unending troubles. She describes in a letter to Sarah Rose (July 30, 1804) her attempt, through her daughter Charlotte Mary, to get some part of the interest or principal of the estate from him; he rather haughtily refused to assist. "I shall leave it among my Aphorisms to my Grandchildren," she writes, "never to put their trust in a Lord" (Huntington).

   32.   Sir Edgerton Brydges, *Biographia Literaria* 3 (London, 1815): 250.

   33.   A letter to Sarah Rose written on April 26, 1806 (Huntington), suggests that Smith suffered from ovarian cancer.

   34.   Charlotte Smith, *Marchmont, a Novel* (Delmar, N.Y.: Scholars' Facsimiles and Reprints, 1989), v. This reprint of a four-volume novel in one volume places four pages of the original on one page. Further references will be to page numbers, and will appear in the text.

   35.   Brydges, 258.

36.   Rufus Paul Turner, "Charlotte Smith (1749–1806): New Light on Her Life and Literary Career" (Ph.D. diss., University of Southern California, 1966), 63.

*Chapter Two*

1.   The letter carries no date, but its place in the collection suggests it was written in 1798 (Beinecke).

2.   Wordsworth appended this remark as a note to "Stanzas Suggested in a Steam-Boat off Saint Bees' Heads." He precedes this assessment by noting: "The form and stanza in this Poem, and something in the style of versification, are adapted from the St. Monica, a poem [by Charlotte Smith] of much beauty upon a monastic subject." *The Poetical Works of William Wordsworth,* ed. William Knight (London: Macmillan, 1896), VII, 351.

3.   *The Poetical Works of Samuel Taylor Coleridge,* ed. James Dykes Campbell (New York and London: Macmillan, 1898), 543. Bowles's first book of sonnets appeared in 1789, when *Elegiac Sonnets* was in its fifth edition.

4.   Curran, xix.

5.   Stuart Curran, "The I Altered," in *Romanticism and Feminism,* ed. Anne K. Mellor (Bloomington: Indiana University Press, 1988), 200.

6.   A. O. Lovejoy, "On the Discrimination of Romanticisms," *PMLA* (*Publication of the Modern Language Association*) 39 (1924): 236–53.

7.   J. R. Foster, "Charlotte Smith, Pre-Romantic Novelist," *PMLA* 43 (1928): 463–476. See also chapter 8, "The Pre-Romantic or Post-Augustan Mode," in Bertrand Harris Bronson, *Facets of the Enlightenment* (Berkeley: University of California Press, 1968).

8.   Preface to the second edition of *Lyrical Ballads, Wordsworth's Literary Criticism,* ed. W. J. B. Owen (London: Routledge and Kegan Paul, 1974), II, 71.

9.   *The Critical Review* 67 (June 1784): 472.

10.   See Janet Todd, *Sensibility: An Introduction* (London and New York: Methuen, 1986), for an overview of this complicated phenomenon. G. J. Barker-Benfield traces beliefs about sensibility in the period to the works of Newton, Locke, Cheyne, and others who describe a psychoperceptual system based on a neuropsychology of feeling, and defines a "cult of sensibility" whose tastes in literature and art dominate the thought of the late 18th century. See especially chapter 1 in *The Culture of Sensibility: Sex and Society in Eighteenth-Century Britain: 1760–1800* (Chicago and London: University of Chicago Press, 1992).

11.   *The Complete Poems of Thomas Gray,* ed. J. R. Hendrickson and H. W. Starr (Oxford: Clarenden Press, 1966), 43.

12.   Each of the subsequent editions of *Elegiac Sonnets* includes the prefaces of all previous editions. Harvard University holds a copy of the First Edition (from which this quote from Smith's preface is taken), and a notation in

the cataloging indicates that this copy has the author's corrections. The handwriting does appear to be Charlotte Smith's. In this copy, which I have quoted, she strikes "lines" and inserts "little poems," perhaps to avoid the repetition of "lines" a few words later ([London: Dodsley, 1984], vii). The revision, which appears in the Preface to the First Edition reprinted in all subsequent editions, is the one Curran uses. But Smith made few changes in her earlier poems as new editions were published.

13.   See Hilbish, 239, for a sample of comments.

14.   Conventions of capitalization for titles had not developed in the late 18th century, and Curran follows Smith's usage.

15.   A comment from the Preface to the third edition shows that Smith had thought about the sonnet form: "A few of those last [sonnets] written, I have attempted in the Italian model; with what success I know not; but I am persuaded that, to the generality of readers, those which are less regular will be more pleasing" (3–4). See, for instance, sonnets 29, 31, and 34 (the numbers are the same in the original third edition and Curran's). In her later editions, Smith occasionally experiments with the sonnet form and mixes the Italian and English style. But the majority of her sonnets as collected in the ninth edition follow the English model.

16.   *The Critical Review,* ICV (June 1788), 531.

17.   See Alex Preminger, ed., *The New Encyclopedia of Poetry and Poetics* (Princeton, N.J.: Princeton University Press, 1993), 713–729, for a definition of the term "lyric." Poets of the late 18th century seem to have known what they meant by it, as evidenced by Wordsworth's and Coleridge's use of the word in titling *Lyrical Ballads.*

18.   Todd, 53.

19.   "On leaving a part of Sussex," 42. Similar allusions to nature recur in "Beachy Head" at line 346, where the author refers to herself as an "early worshiper at Nature's shrine" and in "St. Monica," quoted on the final page of this chapter.

20.   Curran identifies the "Countess of A———" as Mary, Lady Abergavenny, the daughter of John Robinson, who was the poet's brother-in-law by marriage. In letters dated a few years later, Smith vilified Robinson as one of the trustees who refused to release her children's estate. William Hayley was the poet and patron of poets who launched Smith's career by agreeing to a dedication for her first edition of *Elegiac Sonnets,* and Lord Egremont was the nobleman who for many years assisted her in settling the disputed will. "Mrs. G." remains unidentified.

21.   See, for instance, "Written in Farm Wood, South Downs, in May 1784" and "To the naiad of the Arun" (34–35).

22.   Hilbish refers to a total of 817 subscribers (105), but the list published with the edition includes only 765 names. The list reads like a *Who's Who* of the day. Many subscribers bought multiple copies, bringing total sales by subscription to 1,130.

23.  The sixth edition has 12 additional sonnets and three longer poems. Four of these 12 poems had first appeared in *Emmeline,* published in 1788. In addition, the fifth and following editions include "The Origin of Flattery" and "Song from the French of Cardinal Bernis," which had been published in the first and second editions but were dropped in the next two. The sixth edition has 15 new poems: 11 sonnets, 5 of which are labeled "From the Novel of Celestina," and 4 longer poems. Inclusion of poems from *Celestina* is puzzling, since the sixth edition is dated 1790 and *Celestina* was published in 1791. Apparently Smith had begun work on the novel and had written the poems for it by the time the edition appeared.

24.  The final line alludes to Collins's "Ode to Fear."

25.  The purchase of multiple copies by subscribers, as many as 20 in four cases, certainly suggests a desire to assist the author.

26.  See Samuel Holt Monk, *The Sublime* (Ann Arbor: University of Michigan Press, 1960), or Walter John Hipple, *The Beautiful, the Sublime, and the Picturesque* (Carbondale: University of Southern Illinois Press, 1957), for complete discussions of the gradual development of theories on the sublime.

27.  In an undated letter apparently written in 1793 to James Dodsley proposing "a poem in blank verse" that would be about 1,200 lines (no doubt *The Emigrants,* which in published form is 849 lines in length), Smith felt it necessary to assure the publisher that "it is not on politics [but] on a very popular and interesting subject" (Princeton).

28.  Smith's letters to William Davies and others express her embarrassment at the delay in publication of the second volume. Many subscribers had paid for their books in 1795, when the subscription began. In addition to tragedies in her personal life, Smith attributes part of the delay to problems in getting engravings of the quality she desired, such as a portrait of the author. Also, in a series of letters to Davies, she protests amusingly about an engraving of a nymph, complaining that "the figure of the nymph is too fat—It takes off all the pensive look which becomes such an ideal being and looks more like the plump damsel of the Dairy than a Naiad" (March 5, 1797, Princeton).

29.  Curran omits "Ode to the Poppy, Written by a deceased Friend" and "Verses Written by the same Lady on seeing her two Sons at play," both by Henrietta O'Neill, Smith's friend who died in 1793. The former poem also appears in *The Banished Man* and prompted speculation that Smith might have been addicted to laudanum, a mix of alcohol and opium commonly used as a painkiller in her time. Also, Curran omits "Fragment, Descriptive of the Miseries of War," which had appeared as part of *The Emigrants* (lines 253–281 and 292–312).

30.  Four sonnets from *Celestina* were published in the sixth edition, a year before the novel. Similarly, the publication date of sonnets 85, 86, and 87, all of which also appear in *The Young Philosopher,* precedes the 1798 publication of that work. Since the sonnets have no specific reference to characters, Smith

must have written the poems for *Elegiac Sonnets,* then used them in the novel later.

31.   See also "Snowdrops" (67), "To the Sun" (76), and "Reflections on some drawings of plants" (77) for references to Augusta's death. "To Dr. Parry at Bath" (57) expresses gratitude to the physician who treated Augusta, apparently without demanding payment.

32.   Hilbish, 227.

33.   Letters suggest that some of Smith's antiwar sentiment sprang from fear for the safety of her sons Charles and Lionel.

34.   See "To a querulous acquaintance" (63) for a similar criticism of false sensibility.

35.   "Nothing is more singular," Rousseau writes in *Rêveries,* "than the ravishment, the ecstasy which I felt at each observation I had made upon the structure and the vegetable organization, and upon the play of the sexual parts in the fructification, of which the system was then altogether new to me" (trans. John Gould Fletcher [New York: Bert Franklin, 1927], 108). Here, Rousseau brings the language of sensibility to the study of botany

36.   In a letter to William Davies, dated August 20, 1799, Smith mentions "looking over my favorite book, The Botanic Garden of Darwin" (Beinecke).

37.   An interest in botany had overtones of radicalism in the 1790s. In his article "'Jacobin Plants': Botany as Social Theory in the 1790's," Alan Bewell describes Gallery's painting *New Morality* (1798) and a satirical poem in *The Anti-Jacobin,* a reactionary journal of the period. The painting portrays the goddess Flora (Smith's poem "Flora" appears in *Beachy Head*) and a cornucopia with all sorts of radicalism emerging, from copies of *The Rights of Man* to revolutionary red hats on sticks. The poem is a commentary on the painting. Bewell cites Erasmus Darwin's descriptions of plant reproduction in terms of human sexuality, the connection in many minds between botany and Rousseau, and the interest British radicals such as William Godwin and Mary Wollstonecraft had shown in the green world as alarm bells to conservatives. See *Wordsworth Circle* 20 (1989): 132–139.

38.   William Wordsworth, "Lines Composed a Few Miles above Tintern Abbey," in *Wordsworth's Poetical Works,* ed. William Knight (Edinburgh: William Paterson, 1933), I, 267.

39.   Smith probably refers to Martin Lister, author of a number of books in the 17th century on what might today be called zoology, including *Historiae Animalium Angliae* (London: Martin Regiae Societis Typographum, 1678).

40.   See also "The gossamer," "The glow worm," and "Snowdrops."

41.   Wordsworth, Preface to the Second Edition of *Lyrical Ballads,* 77–8.

42.   The theme of madness caused by disappointed love recurs often in Smith's novels, and Lydia is like Phoebe in *Marchmont* (1796).

43.  In the letter, the number 7 is smudged and written over, suggesting some uncertainty as to the poem's length at this time.

44.  In this long, chatty letter to Johnson, who had published some of her books for children, Smith tells him that she wants to omit "all the adulatory lines" from the new edition, "particularly as the only means by which I can express my regard for having written them." Both the letter to Johnson and the rather defiant tone to Davies show the change that financial independence had wrought in the author.

45.  "Beachy Head," line 368 in Curran's edition. Further references are cited internally by line number.

46.  According to Alan Bewell, French geologists posited a geological past based on violent and sudden change, a position that paralleled revolutionary social theory. British scientists, however, maintained their belief in either slow, evolutionary changes (as in the works of Hutton) or the scriptural account of the Creation and the Deluge, both theories reflecting the conservatism of the nation. See Bewell, *Wordsworth and the Enlightenment* (New Haven, Conn.: Yale University Press, 1989).

47.  Smith quotes Gilbert White's *History of Selbourne* as a source in an endnote (the full title is *The Natural History and Antiquities of Selbourne: with engravings, and an appendix, published by T. Bensley of London in 1789*). But in a letter to Davies dated July 26, 1805 (Beinecke), she ordered John Horsley's *Britannia Romana* (full title *Britannia Romana: or the Roman antiquities of Britain*, published in London in 1732); Michael Drayton's *Polyolbion* (sometimes spelled *Poly-Olbion* and first published in 1613); Hay's *History of Chichester* (presumably Alexander Hay's *The Chichester Guide: Containing an account of the ancient and present state of the city of Chichester and its neighborhood*, published by C. Jacques in Chichester, 1783); and Pennant's *Zoology* (probably Thomas Pennant's *The British Zoology*, first published anonymously in 1777, no publisher or city listed). Just why Smith should have asked her publisher for books that were probably long out of print is not clear. *Poly-Olbion*, for instance, had last been printed in a complete works of Drayton in 1753. For a recent discussion of the evolution of geological science, see Frank Darwin Adams, *Birth and Development of Geological Science* (New York: Dover, 1990).

48.  A letter to William Davies identifies the misanthrope as the true story of Parson Darby, "a man who disgusted with the world, has many years as tradition tells [lived] in a cave of the cliff by Beachy Head; and was lost in attempting to save some shipwrecked seamen" (July 12, 1806, Beinecke). Smith also identifies Darby in an endnote.

49.  See note 2 above.

*Chapter Three*

1.  Samuel Pratt, *Emma Corbett* (London, 1789), I, 130.
2.  Pratt, III, 81.

3. J. M. S. Tompkins, *The Popular Novel in England: 1770–1800* (Westport, Conn.: Greenwood Press, 1976).

4. Robert Heilman, *America in English Fiction: 1760–1800* (New York: Octagon Books, 1968), 43.

5. Tompkins, 9.

6. Janet Todd, *Sensibility: An Introduction* (London and New York: Methuen, 1986), 91–2.

7. Henry Mackenzie, *The Man of Feeling* (New York and London: Oxford University Press, 1970), 70.

8. Abbé Prévost des Exiles, *Manon Lescaut and Carmen* (London: Everyman Library, 1929), 56.

9. Rousseau, *La Nouvelle Héloïse*, 233.

10. *Ela, or the Delusions of the Heart* (London: G. G. J. and John Robinson, 1787), 77. The novel was published anonymously.

11. Charlotte Smith, *Ethelinde, or the Recluse of the Lake* (London: Cadell, 1788), II, 168. Further references will appear in the text. Sir Walter Scott uses a similar expression in an essay on "Maturin's Fatal Revenge," when he refers to novels as "[t]hose light and airy articles which a young lady might read while her hair was papering" (*Miscellaneous Prose Works*, 18 [London, 1835], 158–159). In *Mary, a Fiction* (1788) Mary Wollstonecraft comments that she hopes to make her book so interesting "that the fair peruser should beg the hairdresser to settle the curls himself, and not interrupt her" (*Mary and Maria, with Mary Shelley's Matilda*, ed. Janet Todd [New York: NYU Press, 1962], 6). The connection of novel reading and hair dressing was probably a commonplace, but it offers an instructive insight into the critical reputation of the novel at this time and the gender identification of readers.

12. Many of her allusions presuppose that the reader understands the significance of the reference. She sets a scene in *Emmeline*, for instance, with Fitz-Edward reading *Cecilia*. The knowledgeable reader would recall that like Cecilia, Adelina, the woman whom Fitz-Edward wants to win, has gone mad for love. Also, Mortimer in Burney's novel cannot find the distracted Cecilia, just as Fitz-Edward seeks futilely for Adelina. When the hero in *Marchmont* reads Mackenzie's *Julia de Roubigné* aloud to his family, his father weeps. The author does not bother to mention that, like the de Roubignés, the Marchmonts have fallen from wealth to poverty. These and other casual allusions to novels in Smith's works offer an interesting insight into the writer/reader relationship in this period.

13. *The Critical Review* 65 (June 1788): 530. Fanny Burney's *Cecilia* was the benchmark for quality to reviewers. Mary Wollstonecraft offered a dissenting opinion on *Emmeline* in her review, finding the novel worthy of notice but possessed of "the same tendency as the generality [of novels], whose preposterous sentiments our young females imbibe with such avidity," creating "false expectations" that "tend to debauch the mind." Reprinted in Janet Todd, ed., *A Wollstonecraft Anthology* (Bloomington: Indiana University Press, 1977), 217.

14.  *The Monthly Review* 6 (October 1789): 162.

15.  Basil Willey, *The Eighteenth-Century Background: Studies on the Idea of Nature in the Thought of the Period* (Boston: Beacon Press, 1961), 207.

16.  Willey, 206.

17.  Smith routinely describes her sentimental female characters as "interesting," and the adjective is ubiquitous in novels of the period. For the most part it denotes a melancholy demeanor or even a sickly appearance somehow attractive to other sentimentalists. In *The Pupil of Pleasure,* Samuel Jackson Pratt gives the latter quality a special twist when the unscrupulous Sedley, a disciple of Lord Chesterfield, lusts for the apparently consumptive Fanny Mortimer because "like certain fruits, she is delicious in decay" ([London, 1777], I, 68). But the word can probably best be summed up as a synonym for "evocative" and is usually applied to women.

18.  Charlotte Smith, *Emmeline, or the Orphan of the Castle* (London: Oxford University Press, 1971), 2. Further citations will appear in the text.

19.  Jane Austen may have had these characteristics of heroines in mind for her tongue-in-cheek description of Catherine Morland, in *Northanger Abbey,* as an unlikely candidate for a heroine because she "never could learn or understand anything before she was taught." *The Novels of Jane Austen* (London: Oxford University Press, 1923), V, 14.

20.  Smith takes note of the possible stain on Emmeline's honor. Delamere had seen her with Adelina's child and assumed it was Emmeline's. The young man flies into a rage and cancels his engagement. Godolphin then considers approaching Delamere to explain, since, as he says, he "would by no means suffer your [Emmeline's] generous and exalted friendship for my sister to stain the lovely purity of a character which only the malice of fiends could delight in blasting" (388).

21.  Frances Brooke, *The History of Emily Montague* (Ottawa, Canada: Graphics Publishers, 1931), 31.

22.  Reviewers took enthusiastic note of Smith's descriptive passages in *Ethelinde.* The writer for *The Monthly Review,* for instance, comments, "We are so much pleased, however, with the *ruralities,* with the pages descriptive of the more beautiful scenes of nature, that we cannot but wish that the fair authoress had more frequently indulged her talent in the same way" (2 [May 1790]: 165).

23.  In an amusing aside in his *Guide through the District of the Lakes,* Wordsworth warns his reader that "Grasmere Abbey [has] no existence but in the pages of Romance, though the wreck of a sheep-fold has been more than once archly pointed out as its last remains by a peasant in answer to questions eagerly put to him by Votaries whose heads were full of Sir Ed Newenden & the Recluse of the Lake." See *The Prose Works of William Wordsworth,* ed. W. J. B. Owen and Jane Worthington Smyser (Oxford: Clarendon Press, 1974), II, 308.

24.  Smith makes no distinction between the possessive case for "it" and the contraction for "it is" in her early novels. Apparently that rule had not yet been established.

25.   Edmund Burke, "On Taste," 5–6, appended to the edition of the *Enquiry* cited earlier.

26.   Bellozane's lines appear in French, and Smith gives the reader a translation in a footnote.

27.   *The Novels of Jane Austen,* V, 161.

28.   Ann Radcliffe, *The Mysteries of Udolpho* (London and New York: Everyman: 1931), I, 230.

29.   Louis Bredvold, *The Natural History of Sensibility* (Detroit: Wayne State University Press, 1962), 88–89.

30.   Horace Walpole, *The Castle of Otranto* (London: Oxford University Press, 1964), 7.

31.   Clara Reeve, *The Progress of Romance* (New York: The Facsimile Text Society, 1930), 111.

32.   Sir Walter Scott, *Chivalry, Romance, and the Drama: The Miscellaneous Prose Works* (London, 1834), IV, 129. The antithesis of Smith's title for her translation of *Les Causes Célèbres—The Romance of Real Life*—suggests that she would have understood the distinction between the novel and the romance.

33.   She quotes a passage of the novel on page 49 of *The Old Manor House* (London: Oxford English Novels, 1969). Further references will appear in the text.

34.   Montague Summers uses this term to distinguish between the mild thrills of the Radcliffian gothic, the more potent terrors of the *schaeurromane,* and the "historical gothic." See *The Gothic Quest* (New York: Russell and Russell, 1964), 28–29.

35.   John Mullan, *Sentiment and Sociability: The Language of Feeling in the Eighteenth Century* (Oxford: Clarendon Press, 1988), 112.

36.   Many novelists before Smith had used the reason/passion dichotomy to point out a lesson, characteristically through repetition of the words themselves or cognates. Sarah Fielding, for instance, quotes the *concordia discors* passage from Mandeville's "Fable of the Bees" at the end of *David Simple.* And in Fanny Burney's *Evelina,* the heroine says of Sir Clement's forged letter, "To what alternate *meanness* and *rashness* do the passions lead when reason and self-denial do not oppose them" (New York: Everyman, 1958), 370. In the same author's *Cecilia,* when the heroine begins to fall in love with Delville, she believes that "her passions were under controul [sic] of her reason" ([New York: Oxford University Press, 1988], 251). The author's description of Mrs. Delville, the hero's mother, strikes even closer to the moral norm: "Her feelings were extremely acute, and to curb them by reason and principle had been the chief and hard study of her life" (461).

37.   Scott, *Lives of the Novelists,* 329.

38.   The title of Goethe's novel does come up once during *Celestina,* when Cathcart, a man of feeling, falls in love with Jessy, Celestina's friend, but cannot marry her because of his poverty and the necessity of supporting Mrs. Elphinstone, his sister. When he finds that Jessy has *The Sorrows of Werther* but

has not read it, he tells her, "It is my book . . . , and it is the story of a poor young man who was as unfortunate as I am: but he had the resolution to end his calamities; he indeed was not enchained to life as I must be" (I, 101).

39.   The issue of dueling comes up repeatedly in sentimental fiction, beginning with Sir Charles Grandison's lecture to Polexfin on the subject in Richardson's novel. Almost every Smith novel has duels and rumors of duels. Her young men are strutting game cocks, always at flash point and ready to fight. One suspects that Smith and others introduce the subject so frequently because (apart from the fact that a duel is an exciting plot incident) women saw the practice as a threat to the home. See Donna T. Andrew's excellent article "The Code of Honour and Its Critics: the Opposition to Duelling in England, 1700–1850," *Social History* 5 (1980): 409–434, and V.G. Kiernan, *The Duel in European History* (Oxford: Oxford University Press, 1988).

*Chapter Four*

1.   *The Prelude,* XI, 108–9, in Knight, 352.

2.   A lettre de cachet could bring imprisonment without trial for the person against whom it was issued. Smith, by the way, does not criticize that instrument when Lord Montreville places his erring daughter, Frances Croft, in a French convent via the same device in *Emmeline,* published three years earlier.

3.   *The Prelude,* IX, 247–48, in Knight, 315.

4.   Allene Gregory, in *The French Revolution and the English Novel* (Port Washington, N.Y.: Kennekat Press, 1965), refers to only one British novel that was actually set in France during this time, *The Bastile, or The Adventures of Charles Townley* (1789), and Tompkins cites only *Lindor and Adelaide* (1792), which she describes as a conservative reaction.

5.   *Critical Review* 2 (September 1792): 100.

6.   Charlotte Smith, *Desmond, a Novel* (New York and London: Garland, 1974), I, i. Further references will be cited in the text.

7.   Neither Smith's early biographers nor her letters mention a visit to France at this time. But in a letter to Joel Barlow dated November 18, 1792, she asks him to deliver a note to a friend in Paris and to make an enquiry there for she is "trying to go over in March or April—an enquiry which is so important in this plan on which my *rebellious* heart is set" (Huntington). This and other letters suggest that Smith hoped to leave England.

8.   From *Poetical Works,* 4th ed., H. S. Milford (London, Oxford University Press, 1967), V, 388–392.

9.   Alfred Cobban, ed., *The Debate on the French Revolution: 1789–1800,* 2d ed. (London: Adam and Charles Black, 1960), 55.

10.   Conservative journals, such as *The Anti-Jacobin,* express a level of paranoia in discussing these groups reminiscent of McCarthyism in the United States in the 1950s. Surviving papers suggest that most members were moderate in their reform agenda. But some radical elements had connections with

French officials. According to Mary Thrale, "The French were aware of the LCS [London Corresponding Society] and planned that a conquered Britain should have Thomas Hardy as Minister of Police and another prominent LCS member, John Thelwall, as one of the five members of an English *Directoire.*" See *Selections from the Papers of the London Corresponding Society, 1792–1799* (London: Cambridge University Press, 1983), xv.

11. Cobban, 64.

12. Paine, an Englishman, had traveled to America in time to help persuade the colonists to establish a new nation with works such as *The American Crisis* and *Common Sense.*

13. Samuel Edwards, *Rebel: A Biography of Tom Paine* (New York: Praeger, 1974), 121.

14. Dorset, 322. Clifford Musgrave notes that the Duc d'Orléans (who later took the name Phillipe Égalité) was in Brighton in 1790, temporarily exiled by Louis XVI because of his republican sentiments. Brighton seems to have been a resort for Anglophile French for several years before the revolution, many of whom, no doubt, brought the radical thought of the continent to the city. See *Life in Brighton from the Earliest Times to the Present* (London: 1970), 105–106.

15. That Smith was acquainted with Williams can be demonstrated by one of Wordsworth's letters. He mentions stopping to see Smith in Brighton before leaving England for France in 1791. He reports that Smith treated him cordially and gave him a letter of introduction to Williams. See Ernest de Selincourt, *The Early Letters of William and Dorothy Wordsworth (1787–1805)* (Oxford: Oxford University Press, 1935), I, 66–67.

16. Helen Maria Williams, *Letters from France* (Delmar, N.Y.: Scholars' Facsimiles and Reprints, 1955), II, 52. This edition condenses eight volumes to two.

17. See Simon Schama, *Citizens: A Chronicle of the French Revolution* (New York: Vintage Books, 1989) for a fascinating and brief discussion of the flamboyant Mirabeau. Smith's and Williams's admiration for the man probably stems from his relative conservatism. He spoke in favor of a constitutional monarchy, but Schama (532–534) and other historians note that Mirabeau was in the pay of the king.

18. *The Analytical Review* 13 (August 1792), 428.

19. Williams, Smith, and others refer to Henry IV repeatedly as a model king, and they apparently got this perception from French reformers in the early stages of the Revolution, when many assumed that a constitutional monarchy might be the best model. Peter Burke reports that Good King Henry's name came up often in the *Cahiers* (letters from the provinces solicited by the Estates-General) as the sort of ruler the nation needed. See *Popular Culture in Early Modern Europe* (New York: NYU Press, 1978), 151.

20. James Boswell, *Life of Samuel Johnson* (New York: Heritage Press, 1963), I, Aetat 54: 317.

21.   Jean-Jacques Rousseau, *The Social Contract and Discourses,* trans. G.
D. H. Cole (New York: Everyman's Library, 1950), 311.

22.   Cited in Goodwin, 539.

23.   Jerome D. Wilson and William F. Ricketson, *Thomas Paine* (Boston:
Twayne, 1989), 82.

24.   Doyle, *The Oxford History of the French Revolution,* 130. The
metaphor of the liberty tree manured with blood was probably a popular
expression of the day. Thomas Jefferson's statement from a letter to W. S.
Smith written in 1787, "The tree of liberty must be refreshed from time to time
with the blood of patriots and tyrants. It is its natural manure," is another vari-
ation, although the earlier date is puzzling. See J. P. Foley, ed., *The Jefferson
Cyclopedia* (New York: Russell and Russell, 1900), I, 499. Smith uses the
metaphor again in *Marchmont,* when Althea comments on the death of a
friend's husband who had gone "in search of a higher fortune . . . to those cli-
mates where the soil, manured with blood, seems to produce only disease and
death" (III, 58). And a long footnote in *The Young Philosopher* details the sins of
European kings, noting that "England . . . has seen its best blood manure its
fields" in wars begun by tyrannical rulers (I, 88).

25.   The asterisks are present in the text and result from a printer's error
in this edition.

26.   Allusions to the paintings of Salvator Rosa became *de rigueur* in
gothic fiction.

27.   In a curious letter at the end of the novel, Montfleuri declares his
passion for Fanny in a letter to Desmond, which makes the sexuality of his
response quite apparent, as opposed to Desmond's disinterested love for Geraldine. Montfleuri jokingly refers to Mrs. Waverley's concerns about his financial
prospects and the danger to Fanny's soul in marrying a Catholic. He then
affirms that her soul is not the object of his desire: "I shall not lead [her] out of
the path that has been followed by the *souls of her ancestors,* or divert, from any
other, it may like better to follow—*My* ambition lying quite in *another line.*"
Later in the letter he writes, "My Fanni is a little angel, and I must have her—
There is a good many chances of being reasonably happy with her, at least, for
three or four years, and that is as much as any body has a right to expect" (III,
237–240). Perhaps Smith intended to contrast Montfleuri's carnal passion and
clear-eyed realism about sexual attraction to Desmond's purer love, or perhaps
she indulges in cultural stereotypes. But this "man talk" about women was
unique in British sentimental fiction of the time, where sexual references were
disguised by the language of sensibility.

28.   Schama, 153.

29.   Lefebvre, I, 241–242.

30.   In a letter to Joseph Cooper Walker dated December 16, 1792, to
an unnamed correspondent, Smith mentions "a Poem in two Books—which I
am writing—about 1000 verses I think—& which will be sold here in quarto at

4. and then printed in a small edition to make a second volume to the Sonnets and other poems already published" (Huntington).

31.   Curran, 133–134. Since the poem is organized into two books, citations are to volume and line number in Curran's edition.

32.   See Schama, 49 ff, for a discussion of the inequities of income between high officials of the church and lower clergy.

33.   Smith's comment about the excesses of the masses in France is probably another republican commonplace. Mary Wollstonecraft suggests that the excesses of the mob in Paris stems from centuries of repression in her *Historical and Moral View of the Origin and Progress of the French Revolution* (1794).

34.   In a letter to Joseph Cooper Walker dated January 20, 1794, she mentions having finished the first volume of "the Novel called 'The Exile'" (Huntington). Apparently she later changed the title to *The Banished Man.*

35.   Reviewers had begun to note the number of errors in Smith's texts. She scolded William Davies in letters for sloppy work by his compositors, who, she writes, had "suffer'd many words to pass, which are not in English or any other language" in *The Banished Man* (August 29, 1794, Beinecke).

36.   Du Fosse was the friend with whom Helen Maria Williams stayed in France. There seems no connection between him and Smith's turncoat aristocrat other than the fictional character's rejection of the ancien régime.

37.   See R. R. Palmer, *The Age of the Democratic Revolution,* vol. 1 (New Brunswick, N.J.: Princeton University Press: 1959), 411–435, for a discussion of Polish Jacobinism.

38.   *The British Critic* 4 (December 1794): 623. The early approval of *Desmond* soon changed, as evidenced by a letter from William Cowper to William Hayley written in 1793: "There goes a rumour likewise which I have with equal confidence gainsaid, that Mrs. Smith wrote her *Desmond* bribed to it by the democratic party, by whom they say she is now actually supported." Cowper also reports rumors that Hayley actually wrote *Desmond.* See *The Correspondence of William Cowper,* ed. Thomas Wright (New York: Haskell House, 1969), IV, 407–408.

*Chapter Five*

1.   See Roger Wells, *Insurrection: The British Experience, 1795–1803* (London: Alan Sutton, 1983).

2.   Cited in Carl Cone, *The English Jacobins* (New York: Scribner's, 1968), iii. In fact, those labeled "Jacobin" would be better described as Girondists, the more moderate reformers in France.

3.   Scott, *Lives of the Novelists,* 330.

4.   Walter Allen, *The English Novel* (New York: Dutton, 1954), 98. The Oxford English Novel edition was published in 1969.

5.   *The Letters and Prose Writings of William Cowper,* ed. James King and Charles Ryskamp (Oxford: Clarenden Press, 1984), IV, 249.

6. The name is an allusion to the heroine of *The Orphan* by Thomas Otway. The characters share nothing beyond lack of parents.

7. Cookson observes that the peace movement consisted of a large number of people from quite diverse backgrounds, ranging from Quakers to the reform societies. Thus, "no peace society existed and . . . formal organisation was carried no further than a few temporary local committees." See *The Friends of Peace* (Cambridge: Cambridge University Press, 1982), 1.

8. Pratt, *Emma Courtney* (I, 194). When Raymond visits General Washington and tells him Emma's sad story, "The soldier's cheek was not without the graceful dignity of a tear. He wept" (I, 66).

9. "Rotten boroughs" were parliamentary districts with few inhabitants who met the property qualification for voting; according to republican views, those votes could be easily bought. Republicans believed that London and other cities had insufficient representation in Parliament and fought for redistricting.

10. The letter is one of a series in which Smith describes attempts to legitimize her daughter Augusta's marriage to the Chevalier de Faville by French law and to gain Madame de Faville's approbation for her son's marriage as well as financial support.

11. Doyle, 212.

12. Quartering is a list of alliances with noble families.

13. Tompkins's comment about Burney's *Cecilia* suggests how unusual this type of heroine really is: "One realizes how daring it was of Miss Burney to let Cecilia discover Henrietta Belfield washing up; but Henrietta, of course, is not the heroine, and Cecilia, who is, never touches a dishclout" (104).

14. Charlotte Smith, *The Wanderings of Warwick* (London: J. Bell, 1794). Further references will appear in the text.

15. Charles James Fox, the most articulate spokesperson for republican views in Parliament in the 1790s, had long favored abolition of the Trade, as it was called, and was prime minister in 1806 when the House of Commons passed the act that ended slavery. Religious leaders in the abolition movement would have deplored Fox's disorderly lifestyle, however. The fact that Edmund Burke had also long sought abolition shows the broad spectrum of support for ending the slave trade.

16. See Reginald Coupland, *The British Anti-Slavery Movement* (London: Frank Cass: 1968), for an overview of this topic.

17. The word "Maroon" is a corruption of the French *marron,* meaning "chestnut" or "mahogany-colored." At one time or another, there were wars against the Maroons on most of the islands of the West Indies. In a letter to Joseph Cooper Walker dated April 14, 1800, Smith mentions that her son Lionel had escorted 600 Maroons to Sierra Leone, where they were resettled after a rebellion (Huntington). She probably got a good deal of her information about the Maroon wars from Lionel, who served in the West Indies for many years.

18.   Charlotte Smith, *Letters of a Solitary Wander, Containing Narratives of Various Descriptions* (London: Sampson Low, 1800), II, 176. Hereafter cited in the text.

19.   *The British Critic* 4 (December 1794): 623.

20.   *The Critical Review* (March 1797) 19: 236.

21.   The name comes from the poem by the Cavalier poet Richard Lovelace "To Althea, from Prison," an appropriate allusion as a result of the long prison sequence in the novel. Lovelace's poem contains the oft-quoted lines "Stone walls do not a prison make,/Nor iron bars a cage."

22.   The Marchmonts' relatives deplore this expedient as beneath the dignity of gentlewomen, but through Althea's comments, Smith defends the girls' enterprise. She no doubt has her own "literary business" in mind and the disapproval of her relatives who express disgust that she works to earn money but refuse to give her support.

23.   Cone, 218.

24.   The mutiny at Spithead in 1797, which is the backdrop for Melville's *Billy Budd,* was only one of many insurrections. See Wells, chapter 5.

25.   In other *Candide* allusions, Althea wonders "why the best of all possible laws are often abused to the worst of all possible purposes" (II, 224–225); and she is happy that "Marchmont was no long liable to suffer from their [Vampyre and his cohorts'] abuse of the laws of the best governed of all possible communities" (III, 29). Anti-Jacobins would have been especially sensitive to allusions to Voltaire.

26.   Several cities, including Toulon, rebelled against the revolutionary government. Toulon then surrendered to British forces, which occupied the city. Eventually French troops surrounded it, and after a siege of three and a half months, forced the British to evacuate, taking 7,000 refugees with them. French forces executed nearly 1,100 citizens, most without trial. At Lyons, 1,880 were executed (Doyle, 254–5).

27.   Doyle notes that two-thirds of the third-estate deputies elected to the Estates-General in 1788 had "some form or other of legal qualifications" (101).

28.   Rousseau, *Julie,* 38.

29.   Lionel Stevenson, *The English Novel: A Panorama* (Boston: Houghton-Mifflin, 1960), 173.

30.   That reactionary forces understood the dangers of a radical sensibility can be seen from a poem in the July 9, 1798, edition of *The Anti-Jacobin* entitled "The New Morality." The writer refers to sensibility as the "Sweet child of sickly Fancy!—her of yore/From her lov'd France Rousseau to exile bore." The writer condemns votaries of the cult of sensibility for wasting tears on "cureless pangs, and woes that mock relief," and last of all "for parents, friends, and king and country's fall." According to the author, radical sensibility ignores "Foul crimes, but sicklied o'er with Freedom's name." Wylie Sypher includes the poem in *Enlightened England* (New York: Norton, 1962), 1287.

31.  Those opposed to the revolution expressed dark suspicions of a plot by the Illuminé or Illuminati, a secret society (sometimes thought to be linked with Free Masons) that masterminded the overthrow of the ancien régime.

32.  The sentence restates a line from part 1 of *The Age of Reason,* published in 1793: "I believe that religious duties consist in doing justice, loving mercy, and endeavoring to make our fellow-creatures happy." *The Life and Works of Thomas Paine,* ed. William M. Van der Weyde (New Rochelle, N.Y.: Thomas Paine Historical Association, 1925), VIII, 4.

33.  The sentence appears to be an allusion to Thomas Paine's opening statement in *Common Sense,* in which he offers the American colonists "simple facts, plain arguments, and common sense" as arguments against reconciliation with England (*Works,* II, 122).

34.  Kelly, 12.

*Chapter Six*

1.  See Jane Rendall, *The Origins of Modern Feminism: Women in Britain, France and the United States, 1780–1860* (New York: Schocken Books, 1984), 42–54, for a discussion of feminism in France during the revolution.

2.  See Cone and Kelly.

3.  Mary Wollstonecraft, *A Vindication of the Rights of Woman* (Norton: New York, 1967), 261. Of the duties she describes elsewhere, the first is "to themselves as rational creatures" and "next in point of importance, as citizens, is that which includes so many, of a mother" (218).

4.  Among conservatives, *A Father's Legacy to His Daughters,* published in 1774, was a respected conduct book for young ladies.

5.  Wollstonecraft, *Vindication,* 250.

6.  Mary Hays, *Appeal to the Men of Great Britain on Behalf of Women* (New York and London: Garland, 1974), 40.

7.  Married and widowed at an early age, Robinson became an actress on the London stage. An extraordinarily beautiful woman, she attracted the attention of the Prince Regent, who offered her a lifetime annuity of £400 to become his mistress. Robinson acquiesced, but when the Regent quickly tired of her, the annuity was never paid. When word spread that the Regent had discarded her, she was hissed off the stage. She went on to write novels (*Walsingham* is the best known) but was living in poverty until the Regent was finally prevailed on to pay her an annuity of £200.

8.  Mary Robinson, *Thoughts on the Condition of Women and on the Injustice of Mental Subordination* (Longman and Rees: London, 1799), 2.

9.  Robinson, 92.

10.  *The Critical Review* 2, Second Series 6 (September 1792): 100. Very soon, as the reaction against events in France set in, *Desmond* would no longer be considered a suitable work for "fine young ladies."

11.  See, for instance, Samuel Johnson's *Rambler,* No. 4.

12. Italics are mine.

13. Wollstonecraft, *Vindication,* 34.

14. Wollstonecraft, *Vindication,* 39.

15. Helen Maria Williams, *Julia* (New York: Garland Press, 1974), I, iii.

16. Quoting a wide variety of sources, Barker-Benfield, in *Culture of Sensibility,* demonstrates that men believed women excessively susceptible to feelings and deficient in reason. See especially chapter 1.

17. Quoted in Barker-Benfield, 26.

18. Wollstonecraft, *Vindication,* 52.

19. Wollstonecraft, *Vindication,* 206.

20. The language here echoes several similar passages in Wollstonecraft's *Vindication.* If women are beautiful and display *"outward* obedience and a scrupulous attention to a puerile kind of propriety," she writes, "everything else is needless, for, at least, twenty years of their lives" (49–50).

21. "Nothing so true as what you once let fall, / *Most Women have no characters at all.* / Matter too soft, a lasting mark to bear, / And best distinguish'd by black, brown, or fair."

22. She alludes to the anonymous poem "The Vicar of Bray" (1734), a satire of Church of England clergymen who change their politics as needed to secure preferment. The allusion reflects both Smith's republican dislike for politics in the established church and her criticism of a parent who would order a daughter to marry such a man.

23. Smith alludes to a line from one of Lord Chesterfield's letters to his son: "Women, then, are only children of a larger growth. . . ." *Lord Chesterfield's Letters* (Oxford and New York: Oxford University Press, 1992), 91.

24. Mme. Roland's home was a meeting place for Girondists, and she exercised a good deal of influence on their policies from 1792 until she was guillotined in November 1794, along with many other Girondists, after the Jacobins gained control of the Assembly. In a time of memorable final words, hers stand forth. According to bystanders, as she stood at the steps of the guillotine, she extended her arm toward the nearby statue of Liberty and said, "Oh Liberty, what crimes are committed in thy name" (Gita May, *Madame Roland and the Age of Revolution* [New York: Columbia University Press, 1970], 288). Roland wrote her "Appeal to Impartial Posterity" while in prison, and it was published in 1794. Smith quotes from the work in her footnote.

25. Mary Wollstonecraft, *Maria, or the Wrongs of Woman* (New York and London: Norton, 1975), 27.

26. Wollstonecraft, *Maria,* 103.

27. Wollstonecraft, *Maria,* 107.

28. Charlotte Smith, *Montalbert, a Novel* (New York: Scholars' Facsimiles, 1989), I, 222. This facsimile edition condenses four volumes to one and

places four pages of the original on each page. Further references will be to page and volume number in the text.

29. In yet another cultural stereotype, Smith describes Montalbert's mother as "the most violent and vindictive of Italian women" (II, 204). Indeed, Montalbert's behavior reflects the cliché of the passionate and jealous Mediterranean temperament.

30. Rosalie takes lodgings at Beachy Head.

31. See Preface to Scholars' Facsimiles edition of *Marchmont*, 7–10.

32. Robinson, 80.

33. See Wollstonecraft, *Vindication*, 201–206, for a discussion of patriarchal attitudes to women's reputation.

34. New York: Garland Publishing, 1974, 17–18. Either Pohlwele did not read Smith's political novels or he failed to see her criticism of British society.

35. Pohlwele, 6.

36. A dagger appears at this point leading to a footnote defining nature as "the grand basis of all laws human and divine." And, Pohlwele continues, any woman who fails to follow nature "will soon 'walk after the flesh, in the lust of uncleanness, and despise government.'"

37. Pohlwele, 35.

38. Smith's name comes up occasionally in Godwin's journal. For instance, Godwin reports that Smith was "full of applause" for his novel *St. Leon* and that she visited his second wife on June 3, 1806. See Peter H. Marshall, *William Godwin* (New Haven, Conn., and London: Yale University Press, 1984), 209, 243.

39. Smith's preface is dated June 6, 1798.

40. Marshall, 193.

41. Although Smith never identified the person who read the proof sheets of *The Young Philosopher*, circumstantial evidence suggests Godwin as a possibility. The philosophy that Smith articulates through her character Armitage certainly resembles Godwin's, and Smith's prologue to his play *Antonio* proves their professional relationship.

42. Janet Todd, *The Sign of Angellica: Women, Writing and Fiction, 1660–1800* (New York: Columbia University Press, 1989), 228.

*Chapter Seven*

1. Jean-François Marmontel (1723–1799), a French novelist, playwright, and academician.

2. The publishing history of *Letters* is quite confusing. Apparently, Low brought out the first three volumes in 1799, with a preface in volume 1. Crosby and Letterman then bought the copyright to the first three volumes, and Longman and Rees published the final two, for which Smith had been paid. She wrote a second preface for volume 4. This information comes from the two

prefaces of *Letters* and a letter to an unnamed correspondent dated December 3, 1801 (Huntington).

3.   Mr. Wardenell, another feckless husband who resembles Benjamin Smith, has squandered the family's money collecting artworks in Italy, hoping to profit on their sale in England. In a letter to Sarah Rose (apparently written in 1804, although the year does not appear), Smith tells of her husband's begging the estate "for that money which he lays out, as I have recently learned in a collection of scarce books, a new hobby horse of his, though he cannot write even his own language" (Huntington). Fiction became reality.

4.   *The Critical Review* (May 1793), Second Series, 8: 52.

5.   Smith may refer to *History of England,* eventually published in 1806. She mentions writing "short history of England for the use of young Women, which I am very ill paid for & find extremely labourious" in a letter written in 1801 (Huntington). Johnson apparently held the manuscript back for several years.

6.   As noted in Chapter 2, Johnson published the third volume of this proposed work as *Beachy Head* after Smith's death.

7.   New editions of *Conversations* appeared well into the 19th century, the last in 1863. Hilbish reports that Smith wrote only the first two volumes of *History* and that her daughter Charlotte Mary wrote the third after her mother's death (313–314).

*Chapter Eight*

1.   Jane Austen, *Catherine and Other Writings,* ed. Margaret Anne Doody and Douglas Murray (Oxford: Oxford University Press, 1993), 192.

2.   Samuel Chew, *The Nineteenth Century and After (1780–1939),* vol. 5 of *Literary History of England,* A. C. Baugh (ed.) (New York: Appleton-Century Crafts, 1948).

3.   In "The Meaning of Revolution in Britain," George Woodcock states that with the exception of the small group of young aristocrats and gentry who composed the "radical Whigs," the bulk of the reform movement came from dissenters, merchants, and artisans. See *The French Revolution and British Culture,* ed. Ceri Croisley and Ian Small (Oxford: Oxford University Press, 1989), 7–14.

4.   "The Story of Henrietta" in *Letters of a Solitary Wanderer,* II, 291–292.

5.   Curran, xxviii.

# Selected Bibliography

## PRIMARY SOURCES

Curran, Stuart, ed. *The Poems of Charlotte Smith.* New York and Oxford: Oxford University Press, 1993. Contains nearly all the original poems published in the nine editions of *Elegiac Sonnets* during Smith's lifetime, as well as *The Emigrants, Beachy Head,* some of the children's poems, and the prologue to William Godwin's play *Antonio.* Also has an excellent introductory discussion of Smith's poems.

Smith, Charlotte. *The Banished Man.* 2d ed. 2 vols. London: Cadell, 1795. Cadell published the first edition in 1794.

———. *Beachy Head, with Other Poems.* London: Johnson, 1807.

———. *Beachy Head, with Other Poems.* New York: Scholars' Facsimiles and Reprints, 1993. Introduction by Terrence Hoagwood.

———. *Celestina, a Novel.* 3 vols. Dublin: Cadell, 1791.

———. *Conversations, Introducing Poetry; Chiefly on Subjects of Natural History for the Use of Children and Young Persons.* 2 vols. London: Johnson, 1804.

———. *Desmond, a Novel.* 3 vols. London: J. Robinson, 1792.

———. *Desmond, a Novel.* 3 vols. New York and London: Garland, 1974. Introduction by Gina Luria.

———. *Elegiac Sonnets.* London: Dodsley, 1784. Eight more editions would appear in Smith's lifetime.

———. *Emmeline, or The Orphan of the Castle.* Cadell: London, 1788.

———. *Emmeline, or The Orphan of the Castle.* London: Oxford English Novels, 1971. Introduction by Ann Ehrenpreis.

———. *Ethelinde, or The Recluse of the Lake.* 5 vols. London: Cadell, 1789.

———. *History of England, from the Earliest Records to the Peace of Amiens: In a Series of Letters to a Young Lady at School.* London: 1806. 3 vols. Vol. 1 and 2 by Smith; vol. 3 by Charlotte Mary Smith.

———. *Letters of a Solitary Wanderer, Containing Narratives of Various Descriptions.* 5 vols. London: Sampson Low, 1800.

———. *Marchmont, a Novel.* 4 vols. London: Low, 1796.

———. *Marchmont, a Novel.* 4 vols. in one. New York: Scholars' Facsimiles, 1989. Introduction by Mary Anne Schofield.

———. *Minor Morals, interspersed with sketches of natural history, historical anecdotes, and original stories.*

———. *Montalbert, a Novel.* 3 vols. London: Lowe, 1796.

———. *Montalbert, a Novel.* 3 vols. in one. New York: Scholars' Facsimiles, 1989. Introduction by Mary Ann Schofield.

————. *A Narrative of the Loss of the Catherine, Venus and Piedmont Transports, and the Thomas, Golden Grove and Aeolus Merchant Ships Near Weymouth.* London: Sampson Low, 1795.

————. *The Natural History of Birds, Intended Chiefly for Young Persons.* London: Johnson, 1807.

————. *The Old Manor House, a Novel.* London: J. Bell, 1793.

————. *The Old Manor House, a Novel.* Edited by Anne Henry Ehrenpreis. London: Oxford English Novels, 1969. Ehrenpreis includes an introduction.

————. *Rambles Farther: A Continuation of Rural Walks: In Dialogues Intended for the Use of Young Persons.* 2 vols. London: Cadell and Davies, 1796.

————. *The Romance of Real Life.* 2 vols. Dublin: 1787. A translation of *Les Causes Célèbres.*

————. *Rural Walks: In Dialogues Intended for the Use of Young Persons.* 2 vols. London: Cadell and Davies, 1795.

————. *The Wanderings of Warwick.* London: J. Bell, 1794.

————. *What Is She.* In *Modern Theatre.* Edited by Elizabeth Inchbald. 10 vols. London: Hurst Rees, Orme, and Brown, 1811. Attribution is uncertain.

————. *The Young Philosopher, A Novel.* London: Cadell and Davies, 1798.

————. *The Young Philosopher, a Novel.* 4 vols. New York: Garland, 1974. Introduction by Gina Luria.

## LETTERS

Beinecke Library, Yale University. New Haven, Conn. Charlotte Smith's Letters.

Harvard Library. Cambridge, Mass. Charlotte Smith's Letters.

Huntington Library. San Merino, Calif. Charlotte Smith's Letters.

Princeton University Library. Princeton, N.J. Charlotte Smith's Letters.

## SECONDARY SOURCES

Barbauld, Anna Laetitia. Introduction to *The Old Manor House.* London: F. C. and J. Rivington, 1820. Vol. 36 and 37 in Barbauld's British Novelists series.

Bowstead, Diana. "Charlotte Smith's *Desmond:* The Epistolary Novel as Ideological Argument." In *Fetter'd or Free? British Women Novelists, 1670–1815,* edited by Mary Anne Schofield and Cecilia Macheski. Athens: Ohio University Press, 1986. Bowstead finds that Smith used narrative voice in order to present a number of distinctive political positions. Brief mention of Smith's works appears in other essays of the collection.

Bray, Matthew. "Removing the Anglo-Saxon Yoke: The Francocentric Vision of Charlotte Smith's Later Work." *Wordsworth Circle* 43 (1993): 155–158. Bray argues that Smith's later works, including her children's

books, demonstrate "a vision that went against the patriotic Anglo-Sax-
onism" current in England during the war with France.

Brydges, Samuel Egerton. *Censura Literaria.* Vol. 7. London, 1815. Brydges, a
poet himself, was acquainted with Smith and defends her against those
who disliked her political views.

Curran, Stuart. "The I Altered." In *Romanticism and Feminism,* edited by Anne
K. Mellor. Bloomington: Indiana University Press, 1988. Curran places
Smith in the context of other women poets of the late 18th century and
the development of romanticism.

Dorset, Catherine Ann. "Charlotte Smith." In Sir Walter Scott. *The Lives of the
Novelists.* London and New York: Everyman Library, n.d. Dorset, Smith's
sister, wrote this biographical essay, which Scott included preceding his
evaluation of the author's novels.

Foster, James R. "Charlotte Smith, Pre-Romantic Novelist." *PMLA* 43 (1928):
463–475.

————. *History of the Pre-Romantic Novel in England.* New York: *PMLA,* 1949.

Fry, Carrol L. *Charlotte Smith: Popular Novelist.* New York: Arno, 1980.

Hilbish, Florence M. A. *Charlotte Smith: Poet and Novelist.* Philadelphia: University of Pennsylvania Press, 1941. An excellent biography with copious
references to letters and other historical documents.

Kavanagh, Julia. "Charlotte Smith." In *English Women of Letters: Biographical
Sketches,* Vol. 1. London: Hurst and Blackett, 1863.

Phillips, Richard. *British Public Characters of 1800–1801.* Vol. 3. London, 1798.
The discussion is apparently based on an interview with Smith.

Rogers, Katherine M. "Inhibitions on Eighteenth-Century Women Novelists:
Elizabeth Inchbald and Charlotte Smith." *Eighteenth-Century Studies* 11
(1988): 63–79.

————. *Feminism in Eighteenth-Century England.* Urbana: University of Illinois
Press, 1982. A fine study of the work of women writers in this period,
with insightful commentary on Smith's works.

Scott, Sir Walter. "Charlotte Smith." In *The Lives of the Novelists.* London and
New York: Dent, n.d. Scott's discussion offers interesting insights into a
more or less contemporary perspective on Smith's work.

Stanton, Judith. "Charlotte Smith's Literary Business: Income, Patronage, and
Indigence." *The Age of Johnson: A Scholarly Annual* 6 (1987): 375–401.
Stanton's study of Smith's correspondence offers interesting insights into
the career of letters in the 1790s, as well as the author's life.

Tompkins, J. M. S. *The Popular Novel in England 1770–1800.* Lincoln: University of Nebraska Press, 1961. A thorough study of the British novel from
1770 to the early 1800s.

Zimmerman, Sarah. "Charlotte Smith's Letters and the Practice of Self-Presen-
tation." *Princeton University Library Chronicle* 53 (1991): 50–77. Zimmerman uses Smith's letters to show the author's establishment of a public
image.

# Index

# About the Author

Dr. Carrol L. Fry is a professor in the English Department of Northwest Missouri State University. He lives in Maryville, Missouri, with his wife and two daughters. Dr. Fry is a confessed generalist. His dissertation (*Charlotte Smith: Popular Novelist*) was included in the Arno Gothic Series, and he has written on Victorian literature. He has a strong interest in film, which has resulted in a number of articles in academic journals, a regular spot on his university's public radio station as reviewer, and a column in the local newspaper. He has also published articles on science fiction and fantasy literature in journals such as *Extrapolations* and *Journal of Popular Culture*. In addition to his literary interests, Dr. Fry is an independent producer of documentaries distributed to public stations via National Public Radio. Two programs from his most recent series (on communal societies) have won prizes in the NPR News Directors' competition, including a first place for "Children of Krishna" in 1994. He has numerous hobbies, ranging from gardening to wine making.